NEW ESSAYS ON CANADIAN THEATRE
VOLUME FIVE

DANIEL MACIVOR

ALSO IN THIS SERIES:

ASIAN CANADIAN THEATRE
EDITED BY NINA LEE AQUINO AND RIC KNOWLES

NEW CANADIAN REALISMS
EDITED BY ROBERTA BARKER AND KIM SOLGA

LATINA/O CANADIAN THEATRE AND PERFORMANCE
EDITED BY NATALIE ALVAREZ

THEATRES OF AFFECT
EDITED BY ERIN HURLEY

NEW ESSAYS ON CANADIAN THEATRE
VOLUME FIVE

DANIEL MACIVOR
EDITED BY RICHIE WILCOX

PLAYWRIGHTS CANADA PRESS
TORONTO

Unpublished letter to Mitch Douglas from Tennessee Williams Papers, 1920–1983; unpublished letters to Milton Goodman from Tennessee Williams Papers, 1979–1981; unpublished letters to Mitch Douglas from Tennessee Williams Papers, 1980–1981; letter of recommendation for Verne Powers from Tennessee Williams Papers, January 1983; letter to *Prism International* from Tennessee Williams Papers, 1963–1983; and unpublished essay titled "Twenty Years of It" from Tennessee Williams Papers, 1960 Copyright © 2014 the University of the South. Reprinted by permission of Georges Borchardt, Inc. for the Estate of Tennessee Williams.

First edition: May 2015
Printed and bound in Canada by Marquis Book Printing, Montreal

**PLAYWRIGHTS
CANADA PRESS**

Playwrights Canada Press
202-269 Richmond Street West, Toronto, ON M5V 1X1
416.703.0013 :: info@playwrightscanada.com :: playwrightscanada.com

Cover photo of Daniel MacIvor © Guntar Kravis
Cover design by Leon Aureus
Photos on pages 44, 49, and 83 © Guntar Kravis
Photos on pages 168, 171, and 175 © Jeremy Mimnagh

LIBRARY AND ARCHIVES CANADA CATALOGUING IN PUBLICATION
Daniel MacIvor / edited by Richie Wilcox.

(New essays on Canadian theatre; volume 5)
Includes bibliographical references and index.
ISBN 978-1-77091-349-3 (pbk.)

    1. MacIvor, Daniel, 1962- --Criticism and interpretation.
I. Wilcox, Richie, editor II. Series: New essays on Canadian
theatre ; v. 5

PS8575.I86Z63 2015   C812'.54   C2014-908403-X

We acknowledge the financial support of the Canada Council for the Arts, the Ontario Arts Council (OAC), the Ontario Media Development Corporation, and the Government of Canada through the Canada Book Fund for our publishing activities.

Canada Council
for the Arts

Conseil des arts
du Canada

ONTARIO ARTS COUNCIL
CONSEIL DES ARTS DE L'ONTARIO
an Ontario government agency
un organisme du gouvernement de l'Ontario

Canadä

Ontario
Ontario Media Development
Corporation

Dedicated to David Overton, who led the way.

CONTENTS

GENERAL EDITOR'S PREFACE
by Ric Knowles   V

ACKNOWLEDGEMENTS   IX

"I SEE DEAD PEOPLE": AN INTRODUCTION TO DANIEL MACIVOR
AND HIS WILDER WAYS
by Richie Wilcox   1

THE AUTHENTIC ARTIFICIAL
by Daniel MacIvor   15

TOGETHER GROWING: AN INTERVIEW WITH DANIEL BROOKS
by Richie Wilcox   28

SELLING SOLO: *CUL-DE-SAC* AND *THIS IS WHAT HAPPENS NEXT*
by Susan Bennett   42

THREE WOMEN AND IDENTITY IN *MARION BRIDGE* AND *WAS SPRING*
by Ann Wilson   53

REWRITING SELF AND MEMORY IN *THE SOLDIER DREAMS*
by Wes D. Pearce   68

"HERE'S TO SHUTTING UP": LESSONS OF THE MU-KOAN
IN *A BEAUTIFUL VIEW*
by Jenn Stephenson   89

SEARCHING FOR THE MUSE: CHANGING INSPIRATION
  by Caroline Gillis   109

DANCE PLAYS ON THE CANADIAN IMAGINATION
  by Ray Miller   118

2 MacIvors: GAY/QUEER REPRESENTATION AND RADICAL INTIMACY
  by Thom Bryce McQuinn   135

DANIEL MACIVOR'S *ARIGATO, TOKYO*: CULTURAL PALIMPSESTS
IN PERFORMANCE
  by Peter Kuling   162

SOMEWHERE I HAVE NEVER TRAVELLED: DANIEL MACIVOR'S GAY
HOMETOWN PLAY
  by Christopher Grignard   179

TENNESSEE WILLIAMS, DANIEL MACIVOR, AND BIODRAMA IN CANADA
  by John S. Bak   205

WORKS CITED   231
NOTES ON CONTRIBUTORS   245
INDEX   251

GENERAL EDITOR'S PREFACE
RIC KNOWLES

New Essays on Canadian Theatre (NECT) is a book series designed to complement and replace the series Critical Perspectives on Canadian Theatre in English (CPCTE), which published its last three of twenty-one volumes in 2011. CPCTE was primarily a reprint series, with each volume designed to represent the critical history since the 1970s of a particular topic within the broader field of Canadian theatre studies. Most volumes, however, also included essays specially commissioned to fill gaps in the coverage of their respective topics and to bring the books up to the moment. These new essays, some of them scholarly prize winners, were often among the volumes' most powerful, approaching the field and the discipline from important new perspectives, regularly from those of minoritized and other under-represented communities.

NECT consists entirely of newly commissioned essays, and the volumes themselves are designed to fill what I perceive to be gaps in the critical record, often, once again, taking new approaches, often, again, from minoritized and under-represented perspectives, and always introducing topics that have never before received book-length coverage. NECT volume topics may range as broadly as did those of CPCTE, from the work of an individual playwright, as in this volume, to that of a whole community, however defined, and they are designed at once to follow, lead, and instantiate new and emerging developments in the field. Volume editors and their contributors are scholars, artists, and artist-scholars who are doing some of the most exciting and innovative work in Canadian theatre and Canadian theatre studies.

Like those published in CPCTE but more systematically, NECT volumes complement the catalogues of Canada's major drama publishers: each volume serves as a companion piece either to an already existing anthology or to one published contemporaneously with it, often by the editors of the NECT volumes themselves. As a package, NECT and their companion volumes serve as ideal introductions to a field, or indeed as ready-made reading lists for Canadian theatre courses in these topic areas.

But generating new materials and entirely new fields of study takes time, and while CPCTE published at the heady pace of three volumes per year, the production of NECT is more leisurely with, initially at least, only one volume launched each spring, beginning in 2011. The first of these was *Asian Canadian Theatre*, edited by Nina Lee Aquino and myself and designed to ride the tide of a flurry of activity in the first decade of the twenty-first century among Asian Canadian theatre artists. It complements Nina Lee Aquino's two-volume anthology *Love + Relasianships*, published by Playwrights Canada Press in 2009. The second, *New Canadian Realisms*, edited by Roberta Barker and Kim Solga, dealt with a wholesale revisioning of realism in Canada, and was published alongside the companion anthology *New Canadian Realisms: Eight Plays*, also edited by Barker and Solga. The third, *Latina/o Canadian Theatre and Performance*, together with its companion anthology *Fronteras Vivientes: Eight Latina/o Canadian Plays*, both edited by Natalie Alvarez, launched an exciting and vibrant new sub-field within the disciplines of Canadian Theatre Studies and Latina/o Studies more broadly. And the fourth, *Theatres of Affect*, with its companion six-play anthology *Once More, With Feeling*, both edited by Erin Hurley, introduced to Canadian theatre scholarship and teaching the rich approach to theatre that is involved in taking feeling seriously. It is enormously satisfying that each of these volumes has been recognized by awards for their editors, contributors, or both, a sign, I believe, of the tremendous health of a field of study that is still young.

The current volume, edited by Richie Wilcox, aims to correct the egregious neglect within scholarship of the much anthologized and widely produced work of Daniel MacIvor. The final volume in the series under my general editorship, before it passes into the capable hands of Roberta Barker, will be a new collection on Indigenous theatre edited by Yvette Nolan and myself featuring an all-Indigenous table of contents that will accompany Playwrights Canada's two-volume anthology *Staging Coyote's Dream*.

It has been exciting for me to see the development of Canadian theatre criticism since its inception as an academic discipline in the mid-1970s, when the first academic courses on the subject were offered and the first journals founded, together with the then Association for Canadian Theatre History (now the Canadian Association for Theatre Research)—the first and only scholarly association to specialize in Canadian theatre. It was also very satisfying to serve as founder and general editor for the CPCTE series that tracked that development and made some of its key writings widely available and key critical histories and genealogies visible. I am equally excited by the contributions already made by the NECT series, and by the opportunities it affords to continue to contribute to the further development of the field.

ACKNOWLEDGEMENTS

This book has been a labour of tough love. I am in debt to many leaders and mentors. I thank general editor Ric Knowles for his guidance and keen eye as well as his patience. I am also very grateful for Annie Gibson as well as Blake Sproule at Playwrights Canada Press, who also assisted me in this large endeavour and kindly led me through the process. My sincerest thanks to all of the contributors for believing in this project and offering up their time and efforts. This volume, quite simply, would not exist without all of these people.

It is necessary to thank Daniel MacIvor for his ongoing support of my research and this book. MacIvor answered questions, provided scripts, found old photos, and offered an article to the collection himself. I am very thankful for his numerous contributions to the project and, ultimately, thankful for his art.

I must also thank Marlis Schweitzer for being a very, very patient mentor and someone who, whether she realized or not, was there at important moments in the process to be a sounding board.

Lastly, but certainly not least, I have to give my thanks and love to my husband, Aaron Collier. Thank you for listening to my ramblings, my fears, my joys, and my dreams. You truly are an inspiration that keeps me going. This book certainly would not have been realized without your love.

"I SEE DEAD PEOPLE": AN INTRODUCTION TO DANIEL MACIVOR AND HIS WILDER WAYS

RICHIE WILCOX

Daniel MacIvor is a theatre artist.

Daniel MacIvor is a Cape Bretoner.

Daniel MacIvor is queer.

I jokingly tell people I am researching myself all the time because I, myself, am a theatre artist who is from Cape Breton Island and identify as queer. Of course, more people than just MacIvor and I hold these identity markers in common, but my choice to study and write on MacIvor is certainly influenced by my connection to this trio of labels. To be clear, this connection should not be read as a comparison (a grandiose delusion this is not). Highlighting these three distinct and overlapping roles in MacIvor's life, whose interplay is fruitful and integral to his career, serves as a great summation and foundation for a condensed look into the work.

Daniel MacIvor is a theatre artist. MacIvor is one of Canada's most celebrated theatre practitioners who, starting in the late 1980s, succeeded as an actor, playwright, and director across the country and beyond. The sheer quantity of MacIvor's work being produced, published, and awarded year to year makes this theatre celebrity practically impossible to miss. His extensive biography includes writing nearly thirty plays and an ever-growing list of accolades too long to mention in this brief introduction.[1] For ten years, he was part of da da kamera, an international touring theatre company that brought his work to Australia, Israel, Europe, the UK, and throughout Canada and

---

1   For a thorough biography of the artist and his work please refer to Craig Walker's entry in *The Canadian Encyclopedia* online.

the US. A Siminovitch Prize recipient, MacIvor was first celebrated for his tour-de-force one-man shows such as *House, Here Lies Henry*, and *Monster*. These shows, created with Daniel Brooks, are known for their theatrical yet minimal stagings and the quick-witted, sardonic characters at their centre. The past decade has seen MacIvor reunite with Brooks and return to the solo-show format (*This Is What Happens Next* and *Who Killed Spalding Gray?*). MacIvor is also a Governor General's Literary Award–winning playwright who is author to numerous popular two and three-hander plays, such as *Marion Bridge, In On It, A Beautiful View, Never Swim Alone*, and *The Best Brothers*, which have played at theatres ranging from the Victoria Playhouse on Prince Edward Island to the SoHo Playhouse off-Broadway to the Stratford Festival in Ontario.

Daniel MacIvor is a Cape Bretoner. MacIvor hasn't lived in his birthplace for decades but the East Coast Canadian still labels himself a Cape Bretoner. MacIvor credits his chosen profession to the folklore ways of his home, for "we're all storytellers in Cape Breton" ("*Bingo!*"). The humour in MacIvor's scripts is rooted in Cape Breton as the biting sarcasm requires a "balance of cynicism and sentimentality" that is "part of our DNA in Cape Breton" ("*Bingo!*"). Touches of the rhythmic lilt of the Cape Breton accent combined with the island's crass and dark humour can be found in virtually all of MacIvor's solo shows, along with more obvious culprits such as the Mulgrave Road Theatre–commissioned *Marion Bridge* and the recently produced *Bingo!* MacIvor's Cape Breton roots also permeate his work through themes and autobiographical content, as his childhood upbringing in Sydney, Cape Breton, weighs heavily in his work through tropes of the alcoholic father, the surroundings and characteristics of a conservative small town, and direct references to MacIvor's Cape Breton hangouts.

Daniel MacIvor is queer. MacIvor has been out as a homosexual male for close to three decades now and it is an element of his life that has influenced his work in major ways. MacIvor can credit a large portion of his early success to his relationship with Buddies in Bad Times Theatre, Canada's leading queer theatre, located in Toronto. In the 1980s MacIvor was a regularly featured artist in the now-legendary annual Rhubarb Festival hosted by Buddies.

MacIvor honed much of his acting and writing skills amidst the wide array of experimental pieces in Rhubarb and networked with many queer artists, such as Hillar Liitoja and Ken McDougall, who would serve as highly influential figures in his work. Several of MacIvor's major works showcase queer sexualities. *2-2-Tango*, *In On It*, and *This Is What Happens Next* revolve around homosexual male couples. *Marion Bridge*, *A Beautiful View*, and *Bingo!* question and break down sexuality, in particular the lesbian label. New works such as *I, Animal* dissect the label of queer itself, and *Arigato, Tokyo* gives a glimpse into polysexuality. Indeed, MacIvor's scripts feature a cluster of sexualities that, in sometimes subtle ways, challenge the heteronormative world. The work may not constantly be defined as "queer theatre" but this is theatre that contains the queer.

A LASTING IMPRESSION

The first play that Daniel MacIvor was ever in was Thornton Wilder's classic Pulitzer Prize–winning *Our Town*. MacIvor was a late bloomer, as this debut did not come until his university years in Halifax. Prior to this, the young Cape Bretoner did not want to give the high-school jocks at Sydney Academy any reason to suspect his queer sexuality for fear of bullying and violence, so MacIvor veered away from any school drama groups. But the safety of being in a university in a city that was a five-hour drive away from home allowed MacIvor the courage to let go of his fears. The Wilder production was presented by King's Theatre Society at the University of King's College in 1980 and featured MacIvor in the lead role of the Stage Manager. This experience had a lasting effect on MacIvor's career; he admitted in 2012 that "[his] entire methodology is based on that of Thornton Wilder's *Our Town*" ("Daniel MacIvor Speech").

A quick analysis of MacIvor's repertoire proves this to be true. The Stage Manager in *Our Town* controls everyone, describes everyone, cues everyone, and largely performs direct address for the entire show. The Stage Manager also plays a variety of characters (switching genders and roles in the span of a few lines). Many of MacIvor's solo shows, and some of his two-handers and beyond, utilize these same presentational techniques. One of MacIvor's first major hits, *House*, is performed completely in direct address and includes moments of the character commanding the technical crew to perform certain cues. Solo shows such as *Monster*, *Cul-de-Sac*, and *This Is What Happens Next* boast MacIvor's tour-de-force skill of performing a host of different characters in quick succession using minimal production values.[2]

MacIvor's aesthetic is definitely indebted to Wilder's metatheatrical stylings, but the major influence from *Our Town* is a content-driven thematic one. The overarching theme that can be drawn from MacIvor's decades-long career is one of mortality. This concentration on death can be traced to a variety of factors, but I'll begin by highlighting how the mortality in *Our Town* can be understood to be directly inspirational for a number of MacIvor's plays.

The first convention appropriated from the Wilder system is the inclusion of characters who have died and are given the opportunity to speak from the afterlife. In the third act of *Our Town* we see Emily join the dead and we are introduced to characters such as "A Woman From Among the Dead" and "A Man Among the Dead" and, at points, the gender specificity is lost and we simply hear "The Dead" speak to Emily. Interestingly, the character list for *Our Town* does not feature the dead characters. The choice of omitting their presence from the character list could be purposeful as to not reveal spoilers to the reader/audience. Wilder does not want to give away the afterlife convention from the start nor bluntly state that death is on its way. He lets the Stage Manager hint at the idea of death throughout the play and then outrightly confronts it towards the end.

This concept of the character from the afterlife is repeated again and again throughout MacIvor's body of work. In the early, critically panned *Somewhere I Have Never Travelled*, we meet the dead father. The solo shows *Here Lies Henry* and *Cul-de-Sac* are narrated by Henry and Leonard, respectively, who

---

2   *In On It* features the actor transforming into Brenda by simply "cross(ing) one arm over his chest and hold(ing) his other hand to his throat" (167). *Cul-de-Sac* showcases MacIvor playing eight different characters at a Christmas party in what is routinely referred to as the "tour-de-force" moment of the show (Hoile).

are both dead. In his companion pieces *In On It* and *A Beautiful View*, we are introduced to Brad, who was killed in a car crash, and L and M, who were mauled by a bear while camping. In *The Soldier Dreams* we meet two versions of the character David—one who is dying of AIDS and one who is dead. The MacIvor twist, which is somewhat reminiscent of Wilder's anti-spoiler character list, is revealing the characters are dead before the play even begins. In the same way that M. Night Shyamalan shocked moviegoers by revealing that Bruce Willis's character was actually dead in the 1999 supernatural film *The Sixth Sense*, MacIvor artfully reveals his characters' true afterlife existence, usually in the latter parts of the play.

The previously deceased character, what I refer to as "the afterlife conduit," serves many purposes but always fulfills two important tasks within MacIvor's pieces: 1) the afterlife conduit describes what happens when you die, and 2) the afterlife conduit tries to teach something such as a value, a tip, or a philosophy to the living. Again, this combination of situations occurs in *Our Town*. After Emily dies, the Stage Manager states, "You watch it, you see the thing that they—down there—never know. You see the future. You know what's going to happen afterwards" (99). Just as Wilder's Stage Manager knows what happens when you die, MacIvor's characters are also privy to this information, and choose to relay it to each other and/or the audience. In *A Beautiful View*, Mitch asks Liz what happens after death and Liz states that:

> We go to a place where we're standing on the edge of a cliff . . . and
> we turn and see someone, and we look into their eyes and we see all
> of our history. Something about ourselves, something good about
> ourselves. Our best self. (235)

Near the end of *Here Lies Henry*, Henry echoes *Our Town*'s Stage Manager when he asks the audience to imagine that they've died and then states, "I know that's a scary thing but only because you don't know what happens, so I'm going to tell you" (86).

The act of passing on a lesson—from the dead to the living—is the second task that is charged to MacIvor's afterlife conduits. Returning to *Our Town*, we can discover this impulse within Emily when she says, "Do any human beings ever realize life while they live it?—every, every minute?" (108). In Wilder's text the Stage Manager responds with a heavy "No," but MacIvor's characters try to fix this problem by attempting to talk sense into people or show them how we should be grateful for every single moment. The two campers in *A Beautiful View* give their life lessons within the play. Mitch tells the audience to make sure to give guitars as gifts to kids so they learn how to play music (229) and Liz wants her battle against labels, especially sexuality labels, to continue on through others: "I'd say, if I had to say something, and since I can, I'd have to say stop naming things . . . Those are just names so other people can feel comfortable. It's not about other people" (241). Brian, in *In On It*, replays his last moments with his lover Brad, which are filled with quite banal everyday domestic requests regarding show tickets, prescriptions, and "toilet paper for the how many-eth time" (196). Before Brad leaves to get into a car that will lead him to his death, Brian says, "You've helped me to see the beauty in people and you've been a really good friend" (198). This is a moment of "could have, should have." It is a line in the dialogue that Brian wishes he had said to his living lover when he had the chance. It is Brian trying to live out the lesson Emily offers to us in *Our Town*. Brian is showing his gratitude. But this is a replay and Brad is able to point out to Brian and the audience "that's not how it went" (198). We learn through Brian's regret about things never said that we should be saying things now, before it's too late.

One last MacIvor convention that *Our Town* shares with his work is this notion of the dead reliving their days. Wilder's Stage Manger orchestrates Emily's visit to her past against the wishes of Mr. and Mrs. Gibbs. Before she is transported back to her twelfth birthday, the Stage Manager warns her that "you not only live it; but you watch yourself living it" (99). Emily then achingly relives her birthday and all of the nonchalant attitudes of the day-to-day. She watches every missed opportunity for love and connection until saying loudly to the Stage Manager, "I can't. I can't go on," and begs to be taken back to the dead (108). This Scrooge-like excursion is repeated in the already discussed *A Beautiful View* and *In On It*. MacIvor may not be as blunt as Wilder in playing out the scenario but we are let in on the secret that the afterlife conduits are reliving their days. The solo show *Cul-de-Sac* features the afterlife conduit of Leonard reliving his death at the hands of a male prostitute. Indeed, reviewer Christopher Hoile refers to Leonard as "our tour guide through this miniature *Our Town*" ("Reviews 2003"). Many of these characters are given second chances but not in order to change their ending. All of the characters who start off dead will remain dead. This is not a supernatural world such as Scrooge's where you make good when you get back and continue living. This is a supernatural world where the afterlife conduits try to make good their second time around in order to show us, the audience, what we can be doing when we are living. The theatrical concept of utilizing the afterlife conduit to teach an audience is summarized quite nicely in MacIvor's early hit *Here Lies Henry*, in his explanation of what happens after you die:

> And then they tell you you must enter a room filled
> with people and you must tell these people
> something that they don't already know . . .
> and you try to tell these people something that they
> don't already know.
> And then you realize that that is quite impossible. (53)

Henry may find it a challenge but MacIvor chooses again and again to attempt the impossible.

As previously stated, MacIvor's fascination with death is one that cannot solely be attributed to his being cast in *Our Town*. MacIvor's death gaze is also influenced by his sexuality. As Gregory Woods purports in *History of Gay Literature*, being gay "has been acquainted with death for a long time" (359). Of course this linkage instantly conjures thoughts of the AIDS crisis when discussing death and gay sexuality, but "AIDS was by no means the first instance that homosexuality and death were consigned to the same association" (Woods 359). In a large amount of mainstream literature and film, even to this day, the person who is non-heterosexual is the person who dies. James Rawson wrote a cutting article in 2013 for *The Guardian* that lists movies such as *Black Swan, Brokeback Mountain, Milk, A Single*

Man, *Monster*, and others as examples of the gay character being killed
whether by knife, gun, hand, execution, or any other cause (Rawson). The
killer does not have to be AIDS but there does indeed have to be a killer.
The connection between death and being gay is not always so literal as to
be the actual death of a human, for there is also the symbolized "death of
innocence, death of heterosexual identity, death of parental/adult authority,
death of the natural order" (Levidow 187).

Another major influence on MacIvor's psyche is the land that he grew up
on—Cape Breton Island. Many people feel strongly about their homelands,
but East Coast Canadians definitely plant firm roots within their families with
the land. For example, Cape Breton is an island that is part of Nova Scotia,
but you rarely hear of anyone from Cape Breton saying they are from Nova
Scotia. Whereas other Canadians might answer that they are from Toronto,
Ontario, or Calgary, Alberta, a person from Sydney would say they are from
Sydney, Cape Breton. In their own subtle way Cape Bretoners are separatists
at heart. The Canso Causeway, built in the 1950s to connect the mainland
to the island, still allows Cape Breton to stay a true island as the causeway is
separated by a canal, which cars travel over via a small swing bridge. MacIvor
may have moved off to live in places like Toronto and Halifax and tour the
world with his productions but he still stays true to his Cape Breton roots: "I
think of myself as a Cape Bretoner. . . . I am an Islander" (qtd. in Coleman).
The experience of growing up on a relatively large island, one that is approximately 175 kilometres long and 130 kilometres at its widest (Muise), can still
be claustrophobic. MacIvor credits the independent land mass as instilling
his psyche with existential views early on:

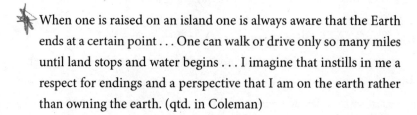
When one is raised on an island one is always aware that the Earth
ends at a certain point . . . One can walk or drive only so many miles
until land stops and water begins . . . I imagine that instills in me a
respect for endings and a perspective that I am on the earth rather
than owning the earth. (qtd. in Coleman)

In addition to the "endings" of the land, Cape Breton is also known for being a dying economic region. There is much depression and finality that comes along with the decline and eventual closure of industries such as steel-making, mining, and fishing. The loss of these industries has led to high unemployment rates that have either forced people to move away or driven them to alcohol and drug abuse, gambling and poverty. The endings MacIvor speaks of in Cape Breton are actually endless.

MacIvor, to this day, is an artist who is obsessed with death. His most recent solo show offers conspiracy theories on how MacIvor himself helped kill famous monologist Spalding Gray. Through the multiple ruminations on death offered in his oeuvre we, the audience, are slowly and gently led to an acceptance and understanding of the end.

THE VOLUME

Surprisingly, the world of academia has largely ignored MacIvor's work. This book aims to fill a major gap in Canadian theatre scholarship while offering new insight into a leading figure in theatre. This is just a beginning. It is a challenging task to cover all of the bases in this first volume on an artist as prolific and successful as MacIvor. Since this is a series dedicated to Canadian theatre I have chosen to strictly abide by this mandate and forego essays focused on MacIvor's abundant film and television work. There is also further work to be done on MacIvor's solo shows and the general aesthetic of his plays, and critical feminist and race theories have yet to be applied to their full potential. It is my hope that this volume will encourage further academic inquiries and generate a new scholarly interest in MacIvor's works within the fields of performance studies, film studies, media studies, queer studies, and beyond.

This collection of essays opens with a piece penned by Daniel MacIvor himself. The prolific playwright who has published many fictional writings embarks on new territory with theoretical writing, proposing a system that posits a Theatre of Observation and Appreciation against a Theatre of

Communion and Transformation.[3] MacIvor pays tribute to the communal experience of theatre in an attempt to define truth and expound on our continuous search for it within the art form.

The next contribution features a conversation between myself and Canadian theatre director Daniel Brooks. Brooks has had a working relationship with MacIvor since the 1980s and makes up part of the trio behind MacIvor's now defunct theatre company da da kamera. Director of MacIvor's critically acclaimed solo shows *House, Here Lies Henry, Monster, Cul-de-Sac*, and *This Is What Happens Next*, Brooks offers up an insightful glimpse into the working process behind these shows and touches on some of the goals and influences inherent in the work.

The majority of scholarship on MacIvor outside of this volume has focused on his solo shows in which he is both playwright and performer. Robert Wallace's "Technologies of the Monstrous: Notes on the Daniels's *Monster* Trilogy" connects *House, Here Lies Henry*, and *Monster* with an analysis of the minimalist stage aesthetic and the connecting theme of the abject. Ann Wilson examines the concept of deceit in her article "Lying and Dying: Theatricality in *Here Lies Henry*." Johanne Bénard focuses on *House* and the solo-show format in Jenn Stephenson's Critical Perspectives volume on solo performance. In the current volume performance studies scholar Susan Bennett builds upon this previous scholarship with her incisive essay on MacIvor's solo shows *Cul-de-Sac* and *This Is What Happens Next*. Bennett teases out reasons behind the success of MacIvor and these shows by focusing on marketing and the MacIvor brand, pinpointing "affinity" as a quality shared by each solo show. Ultimately Bennett credits the production values of a MacIvor show just as much as the performance by the artist himself as integral elements in creating the intimate audience interaction—the affinity—that MacIvor's reputation is built upon.

MacIvor has written several plays which feature only female characters—*See Bob Run, Marion Bridge, Was Spring, Communion, A Beautiful View, Small Things*—and has been praised by professionals for his craftsmanship in

---

3   For an earlier theoretical exploration of performance by MacIvor see "This Is An Article."

penning, in particular, female voices.[4] The majority of this work has yet to be interrogated with a critical eye, especially a feminist one. Ann Wilson initiates the conversation by offering an analysis of two female-character driven texts of MacIvor's—*Marion Bridge* and *Was Spring*. In her study of the formation of individual identity Wilson utilizes Freud's theory of the Oedipus complex to highlight the common themes of abandonment and separation in the duo and argues the importance of the concepts of lack and absence within these particular scripts (and MacIvor's work in general).

Wes D. Pearce is another scholar in this volume who considers the construction or, more precisely, the deconstruction of identity within MacIvor's work. In his essay Pearce explores the act of autobiographical rewriting within MacIvor's AIDS play *The Soldier Dreams*. Pearce analyzes the trope of confession from characters within earlier works, such as the murderous hitchhiking runaway in *See Bob Run* and the ever-deceitful narrator in *Here Lies Henry*, as a foundation for his analysis. Pearce attempts to illustrate how MacIvor problematizes autobiography by largely focusing the analysis on the characters in *The Soldier Dreams* who are grieving the inevitable death of David and, even as it is called a memory play, demonstrating the falsehood that is inherent in the act of remembering.

Jenn Stephenson, author of *Performing Autobiography: Contemporary Canadian Drama*, began her research on MacIvor with a chapter in that book on his male two-hander, *In On It*. Within her analysis Stephenson examines the characters of *In On It* grounded by autobiographical theories, particularly by concepts of autothanatography. For this volume of essays Stephenson delves into the companion piece to *In On It*, the female two-hander *A Beautiful View*. Canadian theatre audiences have seen many iterations of the script toured across the country,[5] and Stephenson utilizes one of the more recent

---

4   Many newspaper interviews and articles compliment MacIvor on what Linda Moore refers to as his "fine ear for the female voice" (Foreword x).

5   The original da da kamera production, starring Caroline Gillis and Tracy Wright, was presented in Toronto at Buddies in Bad Times Theatre and Tarragon Theatre. It had also been workshopped in Montreal at Usine C; Kazan Co-Op presented it at Neptune Theatre in Halifax; Ruby Slippers Theatre toured a production to Montreal and Vancouver;

productions, from Volcano Theatre and BeMe Theatre, to interrogate identity within MacIvor's script. Stephenson connects *A Beautiful View* to Buddhist principles in order to emphasize the wish for a state of nothingness that is articulated by the characters. In contradistinction to the studies of Pearce and Wilson, Stephenson focuses not on how identity is constructed but on how MacIvor's characters strive to eliminate identity altogether.

Actress Caroline Gillis, a good friend and collaborator of MacIvor's, details her professional relationship with him in her contribution to this volume and, in doing so, speaks to a variety of practical and theoretical issues within MacIvor's work. Gillis outlines the early history of her and MacIvor's career through personal anecdotes revolving around MacIvor's first major success, *See Bob Run*.[6] Through her reminiscing Gillis pinpoints several figures who influenced MacIvor, including theatre maker and dancer Ken McDougall and Canadian actress Tracy Wright. The humorous memories shared in this piece not only feature first-hand experiences in the rehearsal room for productions such as *Never Swim Alone*, *Jump*, *Communion*, *Was Spring*, and *A Beautiful View*, but expand on MacIvor's fascination with death and how what she calls his gentle existentialism has evolved over the years.

American dance scholar Ray Miller offers a unique study of MacIvor's repertoire by analyzing his use of dance and movement. Miller's essay considers numerous scripts, particularly ones from what might be considered a more experimental stage in MacIvor's career. The physically demanding, stylized plays *2-2-Tango* and *Never Swim Alone* serve as perfect fodder for Miller's study, along with shows such as *The Solider Dreams* and *In On It* that emphasize the act of dancing.

MacIvor, who has ties to numerous theatre companies across Canada ranging from the provocatively queer Buddies in Bad Times Theatre to the classical powerhouse that is the Stratford Festival, and from Winnipeg's

---

and Volcano/BeMe toured their production to Munich, Germany, and to Toronto and Kingston, Ontario.

6   Kate Taylor, writing for *The Globe and Mail*, interviewed Caroline Gillis about her relationship with MacIvor and also highlights the origin of their collaborations. See Taylor.

Prairie Theatre Exchange to Nova Scotia's Mulgrave Road Theatre, has rarely shied away from including diverse sexual representations in his theatre creations. In an essay that spans MacIvor's career to date, Thom Bryce McQuinn investigates MacIvor's repertoire under a queer theoretical lens in order to illuminate two very distinct aspects of his work: one that speaks to gay writings and another that speaks to queer writings. Bryce McQuinn illuminates MacIvor's ability in some scripts to challenge heteronormativity with themes and images of same-sex desire, drag, polysexuality, and more, while at the same time employing homophobic stereotypes and encouraging heterosexual desires in others. Bryce McQuinn's analysis of scripts such as *Never Swim Alone*, *Bingo!*, *Arigato, Tokyo*, the rarity that is *Theatre Omaha's Production of The Sound of Music*, and the brand new *I, Animal* continues conversations around MacIvor and queer theatre originally taken up by scholars such as Robert Wallace, Dirk Gindt, and Sky Gilbert.[7]

Peter Kuling's essay tackles one of MacIvor's more contemporary scripts, *Arigato, Tokyo*, which premiered in 2013. This show marked a return to Buddies in Bad Times Theatre for MacIvor and, because of this reunion of Canada's leading queer theatre with one of Canada's "greatest living playwrights" (Brendan Healy, qtd. in Maga), it was marketed with much hoopla. The lacklustre response from Toronto audiences and the majority of critics towards the production is challenged through Kuling's interpretation of the cultural identities at play in the script. The text, which features a Canadian writer travelling to Japan, contains numerous layers of cultural performance revolving around race and sexuality that are all interrogated within Kuling's comprehensive analysis.

A third essay that centres around sexuality is Christopher Grignard's examination of an earlier unpublished play of MacIvor's titled *Somewhere I Have Never Travelled*.[8] This piece launched the 1988 season at Tarragon Theatre in

---

7   See Wallace's introduction to *Making, Out*, Gindt's "Queer Embodied Absence," and Gilbert's *Ejaculations from the Charm Factory*.

8   The script of *Somewhere I Have Never Travelled* is available to read at the L.W. Conolly Theatre Archives, McLaughlin Library, University of Guelph.

Toronto and has gone on record as MacIvor's largest critical flop. The auto-biographical script, set in Cape Breton, features a son returning to his small hometown and serves as a strong foundation for Grignard's research into the hometowns of Canadian gay male playwrights. Grignard exposes MacIvor's developmental years in Sydney, Cape Breton, and how this industrial town on a rural island influences MacIvor and his work to this day. Grignard illuminates the characteristics of *Somewhere* that could be deemed as gay and reclaims this script of MacIvor's that was tossed aside by the critics by framing Sydney as a gay hometown.

To close out the volume, John S. Bak, a Tennessee Williams historian, examines MacIvor's script *His Greatness*. MacIvor may not mention the famous playwright by name but there is no doubt the events that play out in the script are based on Williams's visit to Vancouver in the 1980s. Bak's dissection of *His Greatness* fleshes out the artistic and scholarly discussions surrounding this Vancouver trip that have previously been provided by Sky Gilbert's playscript *My Night With Tennessee*, Dirk Gindt's article "Sky Gilbert, Daniel MacIvor, and the Man in the Vancouver Hotel Room: Queer Gossip, Community Narrative and Theatre History," and J. Paul Halferty's review "Defying Tragedy: Hope in *His Greatness*."

Each essay in this volume contains traces and investigations, large and small, of the trio of labels attributed to MacIvor I articulated at the outset of this introduction. MacIvor, as a queer theatre artist who hails from Cape Breton, has a unique voice in Canadian theatre that owes much to this transformative triad. It is a voice that continues to contribute to the Canadian theatre landscape and is one certainly deserving of this focused inquiry.

THE AUTHENTIC ARTIFICIAL
DANIEL MacIVOR

The following speech was delivered as a keynote address by Daniel MacIvor at the Alberta Playwrights' Network PlayWorks Ink conference in November of 2011.

THE THING IN THE BODY

The first dead body I saw was my grandmother when I was eleven years old. I had been close with my grandmother. My mother was a mostly frigid and brittle woman in love with my father and my father was the victim of his own complicated demons—which meant my parents were self-centred in the way only an addict and someone addicted to an addict can be. So it was my grandmother who was the one warm, loving, and seemingly "together" adult in my world. She was the only adult I remember as a child who touched me in a comforting, loving way. So this was a real relationship—mine with my grandmother. When I saw her there across from Wentworth Park in T.W. Curry's funeral home, in full makeup and looking better than she had in years—and I remember the moment in that kind of crystalline way, the feel of the clothes on my body, the temperature of the room, the smell of the carpet—I was not disturbed or afraid as I thought I might be. I was more confounded. Confronted with a mystery. This was not my grandmother. This was a body. My grandmother was not in the room. What remained there was something that represented my grandmother in the most banal way—a shell—something artificial. My grandmother, the woman, the human, the energy of my grandmother was gone—the thing in the body, the authentic thing was absent. And in recognizing its absence I was comforted because its absence proved its existence.

As a child I felt outside, always: in my family, socially, even in nature. I remember sitting in a park in downtown Sydney as a young boy and staring across the pond to a stand of birch trees waving in a breeze and willing myself to connect to this image, to feel its beauty, its "realness," but all I could muster was a sense of observation. Not a part of but apart from. I swear that if at twelve years old an alien had appeared at my bedside, waking me and telling me, "It's time to take you back to your home planet," I would not have been in the least surprised. More, I would have been relieved. And as an adult I have heard enough stories from enough people to realize that I'm not the only alien in the room.

It wasn't until I went to Dalhousie University to study journalism and somehow slipped and fell into the theatre department that I had another experience like the one I had at T.W. Curry's funeral home with the body of my grandmother. We had been rehearsing for some weeks, or it may have been months, and it all seemed relatively familiar, nothing really startling or new—pretend with a bunch of people and then go out and drink beer. That's pretty much how I'd been living my life. But the first night with an audience I walked out on stage and something shifted for me. Again, I remember it in that crystalline way—what I was wearing, the heat of the lights upon my body. Something woke up. Partly I suppose it was just this intense focused attention upon me, but in that attention was an expectation—these people were looking for something—and armed with the tools of the theatre I had what they were looking for. But this thing I had was not something I knew, it was not something I was or had accomplished, it was for me, once again, proof in myself and in every person in that room of the thing in the body.

WHAT WE DO

We work in the most artificial of environments, spending weeks in rooms repeating passages of texts and physical actions in an effort to perfect a portrayal
of an imagined event. That imagined event is then presented on a platform before rows or banks of audiences in dark and silent rooms. And all this artifice
is to result in something authentic occurring. This falseness creates something
genuine. We understand what the falseness is—a poster is made, a ticket is
bought, a light is hung, a chair is placed here, a doorway there, we pretend
there's a wall where there is no wall. Even in the direct address solo work I've
done—which happens here, tonight, for you, on an acknowledged stage—well
that same thing happened last night, and will happen tomorrow night, and
I'm going to say and do pretty much exactly the same thing—the spontaneity
is manufactured, pretended, false. We suspend our disbelief but our disbelief is only a cellphone ringing, or a noisy bar upstairs, or a dropped line or
a fumbled prop away. The false is clear. So what is the authentic? It's harder
to explain but we know it as an audience when we see it and when we feel it.

Recently I saw a production of Larry Kramer's *The Normal Heart* in
Toronto directed by Joel Greenberg. This is a difficult play, a true story written
by a ridiculously intelligent, possibly unstable narcissist about a ridiculously
intelligent, possibly unstable narcissist and his experiences at the beginning
of the AIDS crisis in New York City in the early '80s. There were two senses
of the authentic at work for me here. One was an extended moment when, in
a long breakdown monologue, the actor Ryan Kelly articulated his frustration
with both the Larry Kramer character and his own fears about his culpability
in possibly spreading the virus. Kelly so embodied this frustration and fear
that the lines between the actor and the character, the text and the actor's intention, the acting and being, crossed, collided, and disappeared. Something
was actually happening that transformed time and space. And I want to come
back to that "time and space" idea because that's a key to what we do. But in
this moment, these few minutes of the play, there was another sense of the
authentic, and that was the genuine belief in the importance of the story that
was embodied by the production and the full company of artists. It was felt

in the room even during the scene changes. It was this belief in the need to tell this story now that eased out the ego of the production. And ego is the death of the authentic. More than that, in a soil of ego the authentic will never root. Because the ego will never allow true communion. The ego must stand alone and will not allow itself to be absorbed into the collective. This collective experience is what creates communion, which is at the heart of theatre.

And things get difficult here. In this work we do the ego is essential. It is the trick of the theatre that we think on some level that by practising our art we are healing some wound, gaining some needed approval, proving our worth, blah blah blah. It is ego that seems to get us to the laptop or into the rehearsal room or up on the stage—and wounds are healed and approval is gained and by practising this art we can become more worthwhile feeling and become better humans. But that's the trick the theatre plays on us. You see, theatre is so much bigger than we are and it will exist as long as there are humans on earth. It is necessary to our being. We are not the theatre; we are disciples of it or workers for it or adherents to it. It serves the same purpose as religion does—and in fact I think theatre is far more successful than religion is in doing the job—it creates a context for being and in that context allows reflection, communion, and ultimately transformation. Our ego wants to believe that we are serving ourselves, serving the ego itself, but in reality we are serving the very energy of theatre that creates context, reflection, communion, and transformation. And we can let our ego believe that we are serving it because it is useful as a fuel—an excellent fuel but a shitty engine.

There is of course theatre that is created by ego—and this theatre is what I call the theatre of Observation and Appreciation. This is where the audience is called only to observe and appreciate the ideas and the intelligence and the commentary of the practitioners. This theatre of Observation and Appreciation needs distance and detachment in order to exist. This ego-based theatre of Observation and Appreciation only regards the notion of context from the outside—it is smarter than context, it already has this information, it distains reflection as sentimental, sees communion as detrimental to the uniqueness of the individual and its overvalued ideas, and thus will never result in transformation. So what is this theatre of Observation and

Appreciation? Where does it occur? Shall I name names? It's not about that. I have seen this occur at every level—at universities, in dirty theatres, in houses, in parks. I'm not for example talking about the Stratford Festival—in fact, quite the opposite. Of course there are the twenty or thirty percent of people who go to Stratford to see the five-thousand-dollar floor-length cape made from real rose petals that Yanna McIntosh will wear for five minutes in one scene, but most of the people are there to see Yanna McIntosh and the kind of communion and transformation she can generate and conjure. If you've ever sat in the audience at the eighteen-hundred seat Festival Theatre you know how intimate a space it is: it is a temple to intimacy. A marvel of theatrical architecture. To stand on that stage—which I've only done in an empty house—is to hold that whole room just here. Wander around Stratford mid-season and you've never seen people so crazy hungry for theatre. Like New York, there are the crowds who want to see Julia Roberts or James Gandolfini in a real live play, but the bulk of those audiences are sweatpants-wearing, bag-lunch-carrying people lining up for any small taste of communion and transformation.

So where does this theatre of Observation and Appreciation come from? I think in part it comes from practitioners feeling they must have all the answers. Practitioners afraid of asking the most important questions like "why bother?" and "who cares?" and who are afraid to acknowledge their psychic wounds and need for approval. It comes from practitioners who can't comprehend the most profound answer to any question in a rehearsal hall: "I don't know." I'm speaking of those who get caught up in the personalities of the theatre rather than the principles of the theatre. And in large part I think it comes from an idea that the theatre is in some way "sophisticated." There has been a lot of talk these days in Toronto about the notion of sophistication. In certain circles, or in a certain circle, there is a notion that there is work being produced that is in some way sophisticated and that audiences in Toronto don't like it and so the audience in Toronto is being blamed as not being sophisticated enough. So what is this "sophistication"? The free online dictionary defines sophistication as "to make less natural." Aha. Interesting. So this would mean to remove something from its nature. And in this removal is a distance—a space between what is happening and our observation of that thing happening—the space where we are expected to appreciate what we are observing. And it is that very space—let's call it six centimetres—and it is in this six centimetres in which communion is meant to occur. Without communion, without that space for communion we as practitioners and audiences leave the theatre unchanged and thus unsatisfied. I don't know what sophistication is—I know that I'm probably not it—but whatever it is it sounds very, very closèd. And the theatre cannot be closed. This removal of a thing from its nature, this notion of a sophisticated theatre could very well be our undoing. And when I talk about "nature" I'm not talking about naturalism.

Let's for a moment—as I love to do whenever I get the chance—talk about the One Yellow Rabbits. Now I don't know that I've ever met a less sophisticated bunch of yahoos in my life—and as a Cape Bretoner I mean that as the most sincere compliment. And yet there could very well be something in their work, their process, that could be viewed by some as sophisticated. It's not simple, it stems from a deeply developed, almost private lexicon. It does not set out to answer questions and it lifts things out of their "natural" state of being. But the thing that brings the communion and possibility of transformation to the work is the overarching theme of the communion between the participants of the work. *Thunderstruck* may seem to have little to do with *Permission* and less to do with *Doing Leonard Cohen*, but what we are witnessing in the work of the Rabbits is a full-on life commitment to the idea of theatre and its possibilities. You don't have to see all the work to feel the effect of all the work in each piece. It's unconscious. It is an energy. In it there is truth.

WHAT IS THE TRUTH?

And what is truth? Well, I have a feeling that the nature of truth is such that if I could tell you what it was, in words, it would make it immediately untrue. I believe that human language, like Burroughs said, is a kind of virus (Burroughs 47). It arbitrates and mitigates our impulses and feelings. It is not so much the voice of the thing in the body as it is a distortion of and filtering for that voice. I had said that what I wanted to talk about tonight was truth-telling in the theatre. So what does that mean? Let's look at a play. Now for the sake of simplicity let's talk about the process of play-making as it is traditionally defined. There is an idea and from that idea comes text, then that text through the guidance of direction ignites performance that is illuminated and contained by design and then presented to the public through marketing. So what of that is the truth? None of it. The text is just made up; the performances are pretended; and the direction, design, and marketing are based on those other inventions. It is all artificial. What *is* true and what *is* authentic is why we do theatre. Now for many of us, if we were to ask that question of ourselves and feel safe enough to be honest about that answer, our ego would have us shame ourselves with answers along the lines of "I want to be liked," "I want you to think I'm smart," "I want to find a boyfriend," "I need to be around people who drink as much as I do so I'll feel like less of an alcoholic." Or the more evolved might honestly say, "I want to make a difference" or "I want to communicate with people." And what does that really mean? "Communication" is not "communion." I mean, if what you're really interested in is communication then get into advertising or social work or stay on Facebook full time. The truth of why we do theatre is because each of us understands (and when I say "understand" I don't mean understand with your head, but each of us understands with the thing in our body), each of us knows that the truth is that time and space are relative ("Time" and "Space" being the two main tools of theatre—the only two real requirements for making theatre along with silence and darkness, but silence is just a treatment of time and darkness is just an element of space). But "Time" and "Space," which together are the essence of theatre, are engaged with directly by the theatre like no other art form. A novel? The space of the object of the book or the space of the room or the park that you read it, the time it takes to read it, are up to you. Visual art and film? Their basic essence is nostalgic—the viewing of something that once occurred. None are actually "human-experience occurring" like theatre is. Human experience occurring in time and space. And the theatre knows, and we know, the thing in our body knows, that the truth is that time and space—the basis of all human measurement and the focus of our physical being—are relative to our experience of them; they do not exist outside of our perception of them. When time falls unobserved in the forest of space it makes no sound. That's just physics—and outside of fairy tales and nature that's the closest we're going to get to God.

THE BOTTOM LINE

Now there are two bottom lines I would like to address here. The first is simply to say that the philosophy of theatre is bigger than we are and we are called to its practice due to an energetic, metaphysical need that human society has for communion and transformation. The second is the bottom line of the red or black variety—the kind that the general managers in the room understand all too well. So let us embrace that first notion and for the sake of argument let us call it "true." How does that help us when we are trying to deal with programming and budgets and box office and plain old bums in seats? First and foremost we have to look at our approach and intention. The ego-based theatre of Observation and Appreciation is always going to let us down in the end. Audiences are amused but not stirred. Audiences are impressed but not affected. And let me be clear, this has very little to do with programming—it is an expansive pasture this area of the theatre of Communion and Transformation—there is room in this field for Norm Foster and Judith Thompson. It is not a question of high art versus low art. It is the same conversation whether dealing with a dinner theatre or a secret theatre. The point of our work is to create something authentic in an artificial environment, or from another point of view, to make something perfect with imperfect tools (something that is for all intents and purposes impossible). I once lived with my niece who works in the corporate world at Home Depot, and one day I came home from rehearsal and she asked me how my work had gone that day and I said, "It was very, very difficult," and she said, "Oh I'm sorry." And I realized that in her mind the idea of difficult work was somehow unpleasant and apart from the point—why would one choose a life of difficult work? I then tried to explain to her that it is supposed to be difficult, that it is actually impossible, so of course it is difficult. This quickly led to a silence and then a conversation about the weather. We are led to believe—or there is something in our learned nature that tells us—that we are supposed to be answering questions with our work; checking boxes; moving from the in box to the out box; definitively solving and eradicating problems. As a writer I often have to fight the impulse to explain the play in the play, to answer the questions raised by the play in *that* monologue. You know the one: the one in the penultimate scene that is delivered by the character who has seemingly undergone the most change that makes one cringe a bit to listen to because it's grasping and desperate and obvious and manipulative but we do it as writers and we allow it as directors and actors and we accept it as audiences because it seems to answer the question. But the point is the question. And the "answer," for lack of a better word, is the production and the audience in communion. If I answer the question in the play, that can be the only answer, and that answer is observed and appreciated by the audience— agreed with or disagreed with—left in the room as a statement of subjective fact. The production and all its elements are questions not answers; the only answer we can know is the "truth" of the first bottom line—that the practice of theatre is inarguably essential. And that must inform our intention and our approach from the stage, to upstairs in the office, to out front in the box office. We are all creators of this theatre of Communion and Transformation. The audience's experience of the play begins with the press release and continues through their engagement with the energy on the other end of the line when they call for a ticket. We are all creators. And if each of those creators understands unquestionably the importance of this work, we are truly working together. We believe in this truth, we trust our instincts, we check our ego, we get comfortable with the phrase "I don't know," we embrace the notion that enough is never enough and together we will discover the right questions.

Now, around all this talk there is a buzzing—even as I work on this address in my little room at my little laptop there is a buzzing—like an angry, annoyed, entitled mosquito. And that buzzing is "money money money money money"—the real bottom line! My favourite explanation of the superstition around "The Scottish Play" has nothing to do with witches or seamen. The explanation is that whenever a theatre posts that the next production is "The Scottish Play"—a real crowd-pleaser—it means that the theatre is in financial trouble and everyone's job is in jeopardy. It's not a new problem. And on one level I just want to say, "If you build it they will come"—which is probably just flat out annoying to most people who have to deal with the money. Although the fact that it's annoying doesn't mean I believe it any less. We must be giving audiences something they can't get anywhere else—otherwise they'll go somewhere else—but we are already. It's a given that the experience of theatre cannot be duplicated in any other venue. Perhaps it can be duplicated in a church, and perhaps many people get their communion and transformation there—at least they think they do. It is my humble opinion that true transformation cannot occur in an atmosphere of judgment, and it has been my unfortunate experience that churches build their coffers on that very fear. Judgment is not part of what we do when we practice this philosophy. A real question, a profound question, raises the idea of judgment but it is only an answer that carries judgment. It is we, as practitioners, who must be rigorous with our approach and intent, fearless in our questioning, and unwavering— beyond our egos and our careers and the red and black bottom line—in our belief in the act of communion and the possibility of transformation that this work offers. And yet, after saying all that, I'm not proposing that we tell them—the audience—that this is what we're doing. Imagine! "Come for communion and be transformed." Cue tumbleweeds in the aisles. We don't have to state what we're doing—it's simply what we do. We still sell things like people sell things, "It's funny, it's sexy, you'll laugh, you'll cry," whatever. The surface doesn't have to adjust, it's the underpinnings that we need to oil. And we do that with recommitting with our intent and our approach to the things we know to be true. If we didn't know this stuff we wouldn't be here, we wouldn't bother with this difficult work. All we need to do is to remember, just remember what we already know. Why we're here.

THINGS TO REMEMBER

To finish off I'd like to run through a few practical ideas that have been helpful to me to remember in my continuing journey through the artificial to the distant destination of the authentic.

Avoid Boosterism. Keep the bar high. There is a city that I know and love and have worked in that shall remain nameless where the closest thing they have to booing is not giving a standing ovation—so certainly not Toronto. Now granted, the standing ovation is partly just handy because one can get their coat on quicker. But there is a sense that the audience feels it's simply good manners to stand. In that same city there is very little critical voice in the press, everything is on the nice side, kind, fair, appreciative. Now my ego loves this of course, but this polite back-slappery is artificial and does not help the community develop authentically. Everything is pretty much good enough simply because it got done. We will never get better at what we do if we don't know that what we do is not working. We have to push one another to work with more rigour. We need to be able to be critical with one another and not feel that we're offending some sense of the importance of theatre. The theatre is important and sturdy, it needs us pushing and pulling at it and one another. And we need in our criticism to trust our instinct, not our taste. If you don't like something because it's sentimental that's just because you don't like things that are sentimental. If the sentimentality of something interferes with that work achieving communion and offering the possibility of transformation—that's a problem. This is understood instinctually. And in your criticism, understand the difference between criticism and judgment, which is grace.

The Show Does Not Have To Go On. There comes a point in most rehearsal processes—certainly in most of mine—that occurs somewhere around week three and the previews where something is just not working. Something central and important. It is at this critical juncture where we go in one of two directions. Either we try to fix the problem or we figure out a way to distract from the problem. And usually it is the latter that ends up being the solution because the problem is often a problem with the central question, the approach or the intent. That's a lot to fix. The thing that has been most helpful to me in actually addressing the real problem is to have realized that the idea that "the show must go on" is not true. No it doesn't. Yes there are tickets sold and yes there are posters. But we can stop; we can walk away; we can suck it up and call it a lesson learned. And when we do hit that problem, that juncture, and we truly entertain the possibility that this does not have to "go on," we will then ask ourselves the difficult and most important question, the scary question, "What's the point?" And, more often than not, just asking will remind us of the real solution.

Enough Is Not Enough. Daniel Brooks and I were working on one of the solo shows—I think it may have been *Cul-de-Sac* in Montreal in its first production (and for a real nightmare tale of the search for the authentic read Daniel Brooks's preface to the published version of *Cul-de-Sac*)—and after a run-through of something that was supposed to resemble a show—we were really struggling with what it was and what it was for and why it was and all the nasty stuff—Daniel said to me, "It's not half bad," and I agreed. And for a moment we were both content with that, but when that moment passed we both realized that "not half bad" left at least a third to be truly bad. The thing we all know, and the thing that keeps us here—until it doesn't keep us here anymore—is that enough is not enough. And in fact nothing will probably ever be enough. In this search for the authentic in the artificial we are really seeking transcendence. We are seeking something that can only be sought because when reached it will obliterate us. But this search in our rehearsal halls and in our theatres is a perfect mirror of the search of all humans. Our struggle is a microcosm of the eternal human struggle. And that makes one understand why a life in corporate Home Depot might be a bit of an easier go. But we are blessed with the difficulty of not being able to hide behind the myth of enough.

The Audience Is Enough. However, to contradict myself on the "enough" front, once the house is closed and we've gone to black and there are only twenty-two people in a two-hundred-seat theatre, we need to remember that for the next twenty or seventy or ninety or one-hundred and twenty minutes, they are the most important twenty-two people in the world.

If You Make Money Your God It Will Happily Take That Position. Nothing more to be said on that one.

The Problem Is The Gift. And the gift leads us to the question. And the question is the key that opens all the doors. The answer does one thing only: closes the door. And if the door is closed there is nowhere to go and the only thing to see, as nice a door as it may be, is a door.

We Love What We Do. As difficult and impossible as it may be, as much as we may feel it is killing us, as frustrating and as annoying as it can get, we do love this thing we do. When we see the authentic, fleetingly, in the light in an actor's eye as she steps to her mark and inhales before speaking, here in this patently artificial world, we remember that we are alive. We remember the thing in the body. We remember that the thing in the body is love.

TOGETHER GROWING: AN INTERVIEW WITH DANIEL BROOKS

RICHIE WILCOX

The following is an interview with Daniel Brooks conducted over Skype on 18 September 2014.

Daniel Brooks is a Siminovitch Prize–winning Canadian theatre director/writer/creator. He has had an expansive career in Canadian theatre with many notable works, but I will highlight his long-standing working history with Daniel MacIvor in this brief introduction. Brooks, along with Daniel MacIvor and producer Sherrie Johnson, made up da da kamera, an award-winning international touring company that lasted from 1986 to 2006. Brooks directed MacIvor in almost all of his solo shows, including *House*, *Here Lies Henry*, *Monster*, *Cul-de-Sac*, *This Is What Happens Next*, and *Who Killed Spalding Gray?* Brooks also helped create and direct *The Soldier Dreams* and *The Lorca Play* with MacIvor. In the professional Canadian theatre scene the two prolific artists are simply referred to as "the Daniels."

WILCOX: I guess we should start at the beginning with this infamous meeting that both of you have discussed in many speeches or interviews. Daniel and his cohort Caroline Gillis went to a show in the Toronto Fringe Festival that was put on by your then theatre company, the Augusta Company. Daniel believes the show contained a parody of his show, *Somewhere I Have Never*

Travelled. This has been a source of constant debate between you and Daniel, so let's set the record straight.[1]

BROOKS: Well, I would be the expert on that. Given it was my show. So, there's his opinion, which is his opinion, I don't question it. But then there is my experience, which is, you know, questionable in terms of "is my memory lying or am I lying?" I can tell you that neither is the case.

It actually began with a script that both Don McKellar and I saw at the Tarragon Theatre but it was *not* Daniel MacIvor's script. It was a different play. It was a kind of David French knock-off. It conveyed a particular structure of what we, for our amusement, called Canadian Naturalism. Don and I were both interested in the aping of a form. It was only after that we saw Daniel's play (*Somewhere I Have Never Travelled*). In fact he was really bucking at the Tarragon dramaturgy at the time.

WILCOX: *Somewhere I Have Never Travelled* was exceptionally criticized.[2] But when I read it and I read the reviews, I see the beginnings of Daniel's aesthetic and his techniques.

BROOKS: I saw the play and I read the reviews. I've always felt, I could be wrong about this but I think I'm not, that I have been able to discern between writing and direction. Most critics are not able to. And that's all I will say.

It was very clear to me that there was talent in the writing and the direction was simply not helping it. You want to encourage young writers of talent and the public beating that they can take can have a really deleterious affect on their work. I had intended to talk to MacIvor about it but I never got around to it.

---

1 For MacIvor's telling of this introductory meeting, see his acceptance speech for the 2008 Siminovitch Prize, which is published on the prize website.

2 While most reviews panned the Tarragon season opener, Ray Conlogue for *The Globe and Mail* and Robert Crew for *The Toronto Star* ("Not a Family") were two critics who outrightly attacked MacIvor and his script.

WILCOX: Right. Well, it all worked out in the end. Before you met Daniel, had you known of his work before that and what had you seen?

BROOKS: I had a pal named Chris Gerard Pinker who produced Daniel in *Wild Abandon* at the Passe Muraille Backspace which I saw and I met him there briefly. That would have been the first time I met him and I can't remember if that was before or after *Somewhere I Have Never Travelled*.

WILCOX: I know you met again after your Augusta Company show in the Toronto Fringe. They were quite taken with you guys and your art. How did the working relationship come about?

BROOKS: Daniel asked me if I wanted to work on *House*. *House* existed as a series of a few stories. I can't remember how many pages of text, but what we began with—although some of that material did make it into the show—it couldn't have been more than a quarter of the text we ended up with. We had no idea what the form of the piece would be. We stumbled through many attempts and iterations of things.

WILCOX: You've talked about that in your previous writings and in your interviews or forewords. To sum it up: It's two guys making it up as they go along.

BROOKS: Two guys with some vision and desire. In terms of performance and what I was seeking in performance and what performance could do for an audience through Daniel's spirit . . . I think I had some vague idea of that fairly early on and was only able to express it as we moved through the process. I think Daniel too had a sort of unspoken inclination or intuition about how he was self-mythologizing. And what that might do for an audience. I was really trying to tap into a very authentic way of being in the world that wasn't mediated by an idea of theatre.

WILCOX: This sounds similar to your writings on "Explosion of Self."[3]

BROOKS: That was an idea I had. A sort of mantra for me.

WILCOX: An uncensored person to their full potential.

BROOKS: Absolutely. Orson Welles once said that a work of art was successful insofar as it expressed its creator fully—the degree to which it expressed its creator. Now that of course is arguable but I think there is something to be taken from that.

WILCOX: You also proffered a theory of the "veil of fiction" when you wrote about *Here Lies Henry* ("Some Thoughts"). In essence, the veil of fiction gives MacIvor permission to use real stories and facts from his real life but present them in a theatrical manner to cover up their autobiographical nature. Have your theories of the explosion of self along with the veil of fiction continued and progressed throughout the solo shows?

BROOKS: I think that after *Cul-de-Sac* I became more interested in "Daniel." The simplest way to put it is that I became increasingly interested in Daniel the person as opposed to Daniel the writer. As he started to write more plays I was less interested in that aspect of him in my work with him. I was interested in trying to see what we could do with a less fictionalized presence on stage. We started to explore that in *This Is What Happens Next*. And clearly head-on, with some guidance, in *Who Killed Spalding Gray?* Because that's clearly what that piece demands and there is an obvious equivalence between the personal stories that Spalding Gray told and what Daniel is doing in that show.

WILCOX: Is there a change in the process with this new focus?

---

3   Brooks theorized the explosion of self in his article "Some Thoughts About Directing *Here Lies Henry*" for *Canadian Theatre Review* in 1997. In it, he discusses activating MacIvor to his full potential.

BROOKS: Yes, process changes all the time. Partially it is me trying to wrench the process away from Daniel writing, which is tricky because he is a writer; he's become increasingly a writer. However, he is aware of the difference between words that are created with a pen and words that are created through speech. We are kind of experimenting with the line between them. He still does write. And that was always the case from the beginning. In *House*, for instance, I would say something like, "I think we need to know more about the wife . . . you need to write a little something about the wife when he's looking at her at a party," and MacIvor would go away and write a paragraph. Now some of the editing that happens . . . I'm trying to bring back to the stage as opposed to the page. With *Who Killed Spalding Gray?* we're trying to create a less writerly text.

WILCOX: Daniel has talked about the conflict he had with *House* textually and how it was a struggle to write that down as text and publish it. He didn't necessarily want to freeze it.

BROOKS: That was a really interesting time. We had done this show a number of times and then it was published. We were doing a remount of the show at Theatre Passe Muraille and he had the published text in his hand and it was really tricky. It so contradicted the spirit of what we had tried to create in a very visceral present, lively relationship with language and the audience.

And then there was this book all of a sudden, which was dead, and he was learning the lines and that wasn't really the idea.

WILCOX: Was that true for all of the solo shows? Was it that free?

BROOKS: We are working towards refinement all the time. It's almost an unstated goal. We are trying to define every fraction of a second. And if we can carve those up into milliseconds and we haven't defined the milliseconds—*that's* where he has playtime.

Here's a phrase that we like to use: Absolute preparation. Absolute freedom.

WILCOX: You two have a history of going to the east coast of Canada, specifically Antigonish, to workshop solo shows. Had you been there before this work with MacIvor and how did the workshopping of the shows affect the production?

BROOKS: Daniel was my introduction to Nova Scotia. However, my grandma Bess is from Glace Bay, Nova Scotia. My great grandparents had a general store in Glace Bay and I'm sure they were amongst a very small handful of Jews living there. I have an affinity for the east coast. I have a lot of friends from the east coast. I am very comfortable with their sensibility.

Cut to Antigonish: there's a whole lot of layers of impact on the creation process.[4] When we were in Antigonish doing *Here Lies Henry* we stayed at the house of the mother of Daniel's then boyfriend? Were they on? Were they off? I can't remember. John Alcorn. His romanticism, the eros of that relationship, was a part of that show. The disappointments, the hunger, the doubts, the fire of that relationship with John was part of what that show was, and there we were living in Diane Alcorn's basement. That had some impact.

And the lack of technical resources meant the performance was everything. There was a real, very concentrated period of time where text was everything. Text and performance.

Although there's always performance anxiety, I think it's a little less out there.

WILCOX: A more forgiving audience?

BROOKS: Feels that way. More grateful that we made the trip. And I think also more generous in terms of seeing what is there as opposed to seeing what is not there. In Toronto, especially now, it becomes increasingly difficult for Daniel and I to meet some audiences here without them looking for what's

---

4   MacIvor and Brooks workshopped *Here Lies Henry* and *Monster* at Festival Antigonish Summer Theatre. Artistic Director and founder Addy Doucette programmed these workshop presentations as part of the theatre's Late Night Series.

wrong . . . as opposed to what we're offering. That's for any mature artist who has some success—they have to confront that problem at some point.

WILCOX: Yes, you have the problem of prior successes and the aesthetic that the two of you created. People can come to your show with certain expectations. It's hard to change.

BROOKS: It's both hard to change and also one can easily be met with, "Oh, this again." Daniel and I both in our own different ways now struggle with "How do you meet an audience?" "How do we cultivate our Toronto audience?" "Are we overexposed?" "Who are we in dialogue with?" "What are we offering?" These are ongoing questions.

WILCOX: You've also workshopped many shows in Montreal.[5] How does the Montreal culture affect the show?

BROOKS: I don't know that it does that much other than perhaps gives us a little confidence. Neither of us really fits into any of the structures in Toronto, although there were the structures that existed that were developed by the Theatre Centre or Buddies that were more suited to our needs. But we weren't Tarragon playwrights. Not that we espoused a European model but I would suspect that our work had more affinity with some of the work that was being done in Montreal than in Toronto at the time. Which was to our benefit because we could be more original here in Toronto. Being in Montreal they are not at all afraid of formal experimentation there and, in fact, in the venues that we work in there is a prejudice *for* experimentation with form. Oh, if it's just a play they'll throw tomatoes. They get really impatient with a kind of linear narrative. Express true dialogue between real people. There is a comfort and encouragement there. *Cul-de-Sac* is a perfect example of really being encouraged to follow through and fail. It's not important. The effort is

---

5   MacIvor and Brooks have a history of going to Usine C to workshop and develop solo shows such as *Cul-de-Sac* and *This Is What Happens Next*.

important. The measure of success and failure is different there. And I think because some of their finest artists toured and developed shows and they came back and went and came back and went that there is an understanding that they are in dialogue with their audience. The shows are still alive. They are not movies. They are not objects to be judged as dead things. They are alive and I think that has always been a problem in Toronto.

WILCOX: With da da kamera[6] you toured many of these solo shows internationally. In the spirit of keeping them alive and in dialogue, did these productions change as you travelled to different countries and cities?

BROOKS: Yeah. But then sometimes the refinement would get so fine that it was time for me to leave the show as director. I'm really cutting nits here. I'm slicing nits in half now. There's no point. Sometimes the touring with Daniel would be about fitting the design into a space and then adapting a strategy to different kinds of audiences. Daniel has gotten better and better at doing that himself. He does still need a director. Very much so. But he is very good at adapting to different situations. He's gotten much better at it. He's an extremely skilful performer. Very, very special.

WILCOX: Adapting to spaces and utilizing different theatre spaces is a huge part of being a touring artist. MacIvor always says that you need two things for theatre: silence and darkness. Do you agree with those elements?

BROOKS: I think it's important for artists to have prejudices. We're a good team partially because he has big opinions and I don't.

WILCOX: You've talked about how you felt ownership of *House* and that it was a very collaborative performance. All of these solo shows have now been

---

6   For a good history of what da da kamera accomplished, read MacIvor's preface ("The End Is the Beginning") to his Governor General Literary Award–winning collection of plays, *I Still Love You.*

published and people all over the world have been paying to perform these solo shows. Have you seen any of these shows not performed by Daniel?

BROOKS: I've seen two. Brendan Gall did *House* as his graduating high-school project. I used to go to the high school he went to and teach. He was very good. For a high-school student. He was charming and charismatic and he was much slower than Daniel and he managed to make that work.

The other one—I directed a French actor in French doing *Here Lies Henry*. Patrice Dubois. It was thrilling to do that in French. Unfortunately there was a spat between producers and that project died. That's it.

It's hard to see your work misinterpreted and it's very easy to . . . it requires a very particular kind of performance and these shows I don't think can withstand too much artifice. And it's very hard for actors who are always hungry to layer something on to something. The same thing would apply to Beckett. There are degrees of artifice that just don't work.

WILCOX: It goes back to your process for the show—if you're trying to act out an "explosion of self" of someone else's (MacIvor's) then the artifice is inherent.

BROOKS: I think the danger is always that actors have the impulse to act subtext. It's a terrible danger. And, as you say, the subtext is so profoundly implicit in our work that sometimes Daniel doesn't even really know what it is.

WILCOX: When Daniel was directing *Bingo!*[7] he was very upfront about not wanting to talk Stanislavskian.

BROOKS: Yes. At the same time an actor has to find a way to move through time and their performance and they have to have a way to do that. The question is what is the way and how do you define it. We developed a very, very precise road map for each of our shows.

---

7   I served as MacIvor's assistant director for the premiere production of *Bingo!* and was present in the room at all rehearsals.

WILCOX: Yes, the solo shows are a long journey for Daniel.

BROOKS: It is a long journey, and as I say, with that intense preparation has to come a profound freedom.

WILCOX: MacIvor was recently quoted on a program for *A Beautiful View* stating, "Some people say when you die you go to heaven, some people say you go to hell, I say when you die you go to the theatre" ("Overview" 2). This somewhat relates to Henry from *Here Lies Henry*. My question to you is why, philosophically, do we go to the theatre?

BROOKS: That is the core of my professional struggle these days. I don't really have an answer for it. I think it's really problematic when we are living in a time where the mediation of artists in public discourse is defective and it is questionable. I may be casting too large a net. Once you get people in a room together and there's a form of communion . . . something can happen that is restorative and beautiful. I would say, on one level, for me, intimacy is increasingly becoming the thing that can happen in theatre. I don't know if I'm right about that or exactly what that means but it's a sensation I have . . .

WILCOX: MacIvor has talked about his dream at one point being theatres like corner stores—each little neighbourhood having their own little corner-store theatre where they gather each week and watch a new play; a little space where thirty or so people come together and have that intimacy and community.

BROOKS: I've always been a huge fan of amateur theatre and I've always questioned professional theatre. Amateur theatre has a sort of natural stake that an audience brings to the event. Professional theatre is often about hoodwinking an audience and distracting them. I struggle with the theatre of consensus. I'm personally not interested in it. I often feel that plays end where they should begin. They end with thesis and they should *begin* with thesis. I do think that's part of what theatre is—expansion. Something in the soul, in the mind, or in the culture. Can it do that? Well, I don't know.

WILCOX: But we continue to do it.

BROOKS: Yeah.

WILCOX: Out of all of the solo shows that you've done with MacIvor, which one would you like to revisit if you had the chance?

BROOKS: *(thinks for a while)* Well, I had two thoughts: My first thought was *Here Lies Henry* because I think there was something . . . perhaps that was my favourite. My second thought was *This Is What Happens Next* because I'd like to do some editing. I think too much is said in that piece.

WILCOX: You talk a lot about the workshops where you go to Antigonish and you create something and the next workshop sometimes you're throwing half of that away or all of that away, and this might be hard to articulate, but how do you know what to discard?

BROOKS: I think there are a number of reasons. A very simple one—it just doesn't feel like it's interesting to us. Sometimes you have an idea very early on that is very powerful but it's just a little buried, or because it's such a na-ive spark, it's like a beautiful little infant, you don't really listen to it because it's just an infant, it's just you, growing, your unfettered imagination sort of speaking in its sleep. Sometimes you don't listen carefully enough to it and then you kind of discover its power down the road and it clarifies some things and it makes superfluous some of the work that you've been doing.

MacIvor is really good at that. He's very good at throwing out things that are not provoking the right root, shall we say.

WILCOX: Have you had to battle it out over what to discard sometimes?

BROOKS: Yeah, it always varies. It's so personal. *Here Lies Henry* was a re-ally interesting instance of it because I remember him . . . he so wanted this character to be dead.

WILCOX: Like all of his plays.[8]

BROOKS: I just didn't get it. It didn't mean anything to me. It seemed so artificial . . . I couldn't engage with the thinking. But in the meantime I had this other thought lurking in me that I wasn't acknowledging so we struggled over that. And then finally I said, "All right, he can be dead. But those people that he talks to in his dream . . . it has to be the audience. The audience has to be in his death sequence. They have to be the people that are talked about in death." And that framed the whole piece.[9]

It was an idea that was there. It only came out because I needed to respond to his death idea. It's a dialogue. Two people can be better than one because there's a, shall we say, dialectic of the imagination.

There's no formula at all. It's relational. When we're working together it's usually just the two of us. We're very much relaying what's going on in our relationship. It's more of course weighted towards his experience with the world and what I see in his experience. But sometimes it's about mine as well.

WILCOX: You mention that it was usually just the two of you. I was under the impression that the da da kamera process usually involved tech people throughout the rehearsals and that everyone was improvising together? Is that wrong?

BROOKS: We would work a considerable amount of time before that would happen. Then we would bring tech people in at a certain point. Often Richard Feren was with us the earliest. I remember when we did *Monster* an important part of the development was in Baltimore. I think Daniel and I were there for three weeks. The first week, week and a half it was he and I and I was playing

---

8 Plays such as *Monster, Somewhere I Have Never Travelled, A Beautiful View, In On It, Never Swim Alone, You Are Here,* and *Cul-de-Sac* feature speaking characters who are dead.

9 The moment Brooks speaks of here is where Henry explains what happens when you die and the culmination of this experience is the dead person entering a room, a theatre, where they have to explain something new to the crowd of strangers in front of them.

with lights. And then Andy Morrow arrived in Baltimore to help further what I had started. It varied but there was always a period where he and I were creating the foundation of the piece. And then sometimes Richard would slip in, particularly in the earlier days; Richard and Daniel had a lot of time to play. I mean, it would be really silly for hours on end.[10]

WILCOX: But something would come of it?

BROOKS: Yeah, often. Each technician and designer contributed to that language. But I think that language, I have to say, was really created by Daniel and I.

WILCOX: And it's sharing it with other people?

BROOKS: Bringing other people in to add to it, to finesse it, to "that's a good idea, but what if?" Usually because when we start we have no materials, we didn't work with materials, we worked with light. Light defines space. Light defines dramatic movement. Light was our furniture. Light was our walls. Light was space itself. From the beginning I was interested in light as an active theatrical metaphor. Or an animation of a spirit or something, some theatrically alive meaning that light had.

I would say perception is a huge theme for me and it is for Daniel in a slightly different way. But it's a central theme of interest I have. We perceive things, how an audience perceives what's before them, how that perception changes through the course of an hour and a half. How their eyes lie to them. I really enjoy playing with the phenomena of perception.

WILCOX: I sat in on Daniel's Playfinding workshop a few years back and a large part of the process is heavily influenced by his work with you on his solo shows. Are you able to pinpoint anything that Daniel has heavily influenced you on?

---

10   Richard Feren was the resident sound designer for da da kamera.

BROOKS: The music of language and the size that a verbal metaphor can have. My sense of acting developed with him in ways that I feel there is no boundary. I don't believe there is one. We developed together. I haven't really analyzed what that is. Certainly my sense of what an actor can do and how an actor can navigate time has developed *with* him . . . I would say that there is a "yes I've been influenced by him and he's been influenced by me," but I think in some ways that's a language that I wouldn't use. I would rather use the language that we have been together growing.

SELLING SOLO:
CUL-DE-SAC AND
THIS IS WHAT HAPPENS NEXT
SUSAN BENNETT

In a review of *Cul-de-Sac* for *Variety*, Richard Ouzounian began his enthusiastic report with the reputation of the performer: "Daniel MacIvor is one of Canada's most highly regarded performance artists" ("Review"). This pitch to a largely American readership is not surprising since, with a string of highly regarded one-man shows preceding *Cul-de-Sac* (among them *House*, *Here Lies Henry*, and *Monster*), MacIvor had become popular—and bookable—as a solo performer. Indeed, MacIvor's distinctive artistic signature was that of the monologist despite, as interviewer Martin Morrow notes, mainstream success with "the much-produced *Marion Bridge*, as well as acting in films like *The Five Senses* and the CBC-TV cult hit *Twitch City*" ("Writing").

Of course, solo performance had become, in the late twentieth century, an exponentially growing genre of theatrical production—one that, as Jenn Stephenson points out in her volume on the subject, was "persistently attributed to economic pressures and decreasing resources" (Introduction vii). She continues, "The economic advantages of the one-person show are obvious. With only one actor salary and significantly reduced costs for touring transport and accommodation, the one-person show offers the possibility of optimizing one's revenues against expenses" (Introduction viii). While selection of this genre represents an eminently sensible strategy for artists working with limited financial support—especially perhaps so in a geographically expansive country like Canada where travel costs can be exorbitant—there are other reasons, as the essays collected in Stephenson's volume ably illustrate, for the development and expansion of solo performance. In her introduction, Stephenson underscores the popularity of solo performances for contemporary audiences coming from stories that are intimate, activist, and, very often, autobiographical (the last of these a topic that she would later expand to a full-length monograph).

In this essay I examine two of MacIvor's solo performances, each of which I suggest speaks to the range of attributes that Stephenson suggested were definitional for the genre. What I hope to show is how plays like *Cul-de-Sac* (2002) and *This Is What Happens Next* (2010) function to produce and circulate the Daniel MacIvor "reputation" that Ouzounian promoted in his review. While, in fact, these two shows rely for their stage effects on a well-honed collaboration between the writer-actor and the director-dramaturg (Daniel Brooks), lighting designer (Kimberly Purtell), and sound designer (Richard Feren), I suggest that critical and popular reception of MacIvor as solo performer is particularly produced by a carefully crafted intimacy with his audience. This is, too, an intimacy that is not confined within a single performance but has been produced cumulatively across his solo works, encouraging fans, as it were, to see quite literally what happens next. This might be thought of as a marketing strategy that creates and relies on an experience of affinity.

Affinity, according to Martin Goldfarb and Howard Aster, "endows people with a sense of intimacy, a deep sharing, a proximity and attachment to a product. It is almost a moral category where people invest heavily in following, being attached to, being connected with" (63–64). For Goldfarb and Aster, addressing corporate clients, affinity is nothing short of charisma and, as such, takes a consumer product "beyond branding" (the subtitle of their 2010 book). This idea of affinity—the building of attachment and connection—translated into the relationship between artist and audience is, I think, a useful one for thinking about MacIvor's solo work. Historically, his monodramas dealt with difficult and often dark stories but nonetheless found remarkable success largely because of the compelling force of the performance itself: audiences were drawn to the experience of seeing MacIvor live on stage.

MacIvor in his compelling solo show *Here Lies Henry*. Photo provided courtesy of Guntar Kravis.

CUL-DE-SAC

This play was first performed at Montreal's Usine C in 2002, part of the programming for Théâtres du Monde[1] that year. With the writer-actor playing all eight roles, the drama explores life on a characterless street in a suburban anywhere. Its narrative composes a sombre illustration of how little we know of our neighbours in contemporary times—as Wes Folkerth concludes, *Cul-de-Sac* is "about isolation and the failure of communication" (124). MacIvor built the storyline retrospectively from the 2:05 a.m. murder of Leonard, a middle-aged gay man who has been killed by a hustler he picked up at a bar and brought home. The audience hears Leonard's account of events from beyond the grave, interspersed with recollections from the street's variety of neighbours, who range from a retired veterinarian who still likes to euthanize domestic animals to angst-ridden novel-writing emo-teenager Madison. Each reveals how they knew the deceased and what they thought of him, although

---

1   Théâtres du Monde alternated with Festival de Théâtre des Amériques from 1995–2005. The current format, the annual Festival TransAmériques, started in 2007.

what they have to say is ultimately more revealing of human frailty and individual anxieties generally than of their sometime neighbour. The play's title, then, refers to the dead end of Leonard's (quite literally) and his neighbour's lives. As *New York Times* reviewer Jason Zinoman described it, *Cul-de-Sac* is a "haunting suburban gothic" ("The Means").

Despite its grim subject matter, the play was critically well received over the several years it was on tour nationally and internationally—venues where *Cul-de-Sac* was performed included the Berkeley Street Theatre Downstairs (Toronto) in 2003, Calgary's High Performance Rodeo and New York's Performance Space 122 in 2004, and St. John's LSPU Hall in 2005. While text and performance are credited to MacIvor and Brooks, *Cul-de-Sac* also relied on the skills of their colleagues at da da kamera, the Toronto-based theatre company MacIvor founded in 1986: Purtell (lighting) and Feren (sound and music). Their importance to the success of the play was succinctly captured in Ouzounian's review, where he explains that *Cul-de-Sac* "transforms a potentially pedestrian story into an extraordinary final product, thanks to superb work from all connected with the show, right down the line" ("Review"). Arguably, then, the impact of *Cul-de-Sac* was generated by the onstage partnership between MacIvor as actor and the extraordinarily expressive soundscape and lighting design that so effectively shaped spectatorial engagement and response to what might otherwise be a predictable and somewhat tedious tale from a rather unlikeable character. But, while most reviews acknowledge the achievements of the creative team, emphases are invariably on MacIvor's tour-de-force performance. If MacIvor's acting is particularly compelling—and it is—this concentration in focus is something Stephenson expects of all solo dramatic work where attention is directed "to the basic building blocks of theatre and theatricality: the audience, the solo speaking voice, and now also the solo performing body. With no companions, the single staged body is an object of particular interest" (Introduction xi–xii).

Thus, as I have already suggested, the play was largely acclaimed as another MacIvor masterpiece. It is especially interesting, in this context, to look at the published edition of *Cul-de-Sac* (2005), which continues the impulse to concentrate on MacIvor as signature writer and solo performer. The opening stage direction in this published script—"*A storm builds. Lightning flashes. Rain subsides. Light up.*" (19)—hardly serves to suggest how dramatic and startling the suddenly immersive theatre environment was in performance, nor does it capture the affective power this sensory overload had on its audiences. Ouzounian's review had at least noted the thunderstorm as "artfully created" and described Purtell's "blinding lighting" as "surgically precise" ("Review"). My own memory of seeing *Cul-de-Sac* at the Vertigo Theatre in Calgary (as part of One Yellow Rabbit's High Performance Rodeo in 2004) rests on an almost melodramatic interplay between sound, light, and actor that gave the show its strength—credit I would be tempted to deliver primarily to director and dramaturg Brooks for orchestrating these elements into what was certainly an intense and arresting performance. Spectatorial experience might suggest, then, that *Cul-de-Sac* was more layered than simply a MacIvor solo performance, even if it has been generally characterized as such. Indeed, what I want to suggest here is that while MacIvor as exemplary solo artist has been the prevailing critical context for promotion of his work—for example, Johanne Bénard, writing about the 1991 *House*, puts his work alongside other notable monologists Antonin Artaud, Samuel Beckett, Yvon Deschamps, Clémence DesRochers, Robert Lepage, and Spalding Gray (29–34)[2]—this categorization has more to do with production of affinity than with the composition of the shows themselves.

This is ably illustrated by the extensive (ten-and-a-half page) foreword to the print version of *Cul-de-Sac*, written by Daniel Brooks. In this, Brooks gives an account of the creation of the play, every bit as dramatic as the performance text that follows. He starts: "*Cul-de-Sac* is the fourth one-man show I have created with Daniel MacIvor" (Foreword 5). An introduction, then, that takes collaboration as its beginning, but Brooks goes on to tell a story that is all about MacIvor's "feverish" (14) creation of the final script. He describes the

---

2   In 2014, MacIvor's new work, *Who Killed Spalding Gray?*, premiered at Magnetic North in Halifax (a festival where both *Cul-de-Sac* and *This Is What Happens Next* had been performed in earlier years). In a preview interview for the *Chronicle Herald*, MacIvor claims that he doesn't see the similarities between his work and Gray's, although he acknowledges others do. See Nemetz.

condition of its devising, that it was prompted by a booking at Usine C for a play that would be "an informal part of the Theatre du Monde Festival. We were to present our 'work in progress' [and the] show would be attended by a sophisticated audience, small in numbers, that would understand how to suspend judgment for a 'work in progress.' This was after all the land of Carbone 14 and Robert Lepage" (7–8). But, according to Brooks, things did not go well in the creative process although MacIvor was filling his customary black notebooks with questions and possibilities that both believed to be the core of an emerging script. They decided to take a break and go to dinner the night before Brooks was to leave for a weekend family visit in Toronto; MacIvor stayed past dinner to continue to drink. Brooks writes, "At ten the next morning I was riding my bike along Rue Ontario on my way to the theatre when I saw a strange looking gentleman on a bicycle, his eyes wide, pupils dilated, face pale. It was Daniel. He had stopped in front of me" (10). What Brooks discovered was that MacIvor's bag had been stolen in the bar the previous night and with it the *Cul-de-Sac* notebooks: "Daniel had fallen off the wagon and he was feeling guilty, ashamed, and hung over" (11). With only two weeks to go before the Usine C opening and in the face of the festival producer's insistence that the show would happen as planned, the Brooks-MacIvor collaboration was reduced to a state of panic. The night before opening, MacIvor wrote the play: "While I [Brooks] slept, and over the next ten hours, the voice of Leonard, the five-minute 'nooooo,' and the time structure of *Cul-de-Sac* were invented by a feverish and all too awake Daniel MacIvor" (14).

Clearly the process of making *Cul-de-Sac* was fraught, to say the least, but what interests me here is the representation of MacIvor as almost a latter-day Romantic poet in a heightened emotional condition of creation. Brooks's foreword is, in many ways, akin to a biographical essay. What readers are encouraged to take from his story is the charismatic performance, off stage as well as on, of the solo artist Daniel MacIvor. In this way, I read the foreword as a print-based strategy for promoting and encouraging what I have earlier claimed as affinity. For Goldfarb and Aster, affinity is always charisma-like; it is "what keeps the relationship [between product and consumer] tight, lasting and enduring" (63).

Notwithstanding my reading of *Cul-de-Sac* in performance and in print, MacIvor appeared to have ended that relationship with his audiences concurrent with the end of the play's tour. As Morrow describes,

> In the middle of the last decade, he [MacIvor] decided to call it quits. "I got concerned that I didn't have a real life," he says. "That my life was just about making crap up and pretending. So I thought I needed to go out into the real world and have a real life. And I did. I stepped away from the company. I got married and I bought a house and I moved to Nova Scotia." (qtd. in Morrow, "Writing")

da da kamera, the theatre company MacIvor had founded and run with Brooks and Sherrie Johnson since 1986, presented its last show in 2006, although Buddies in Bad Times hosted MacIvor and da da kamera in their 2006/07 season (a remount of three of the solo shows: *House*, *Here Lies Henry*, and *Monster*). At the end of this celebration of MacIvor's work, it seemed as if his career in the theatre was effectively complete.

In the years immediately following, MacIvor appeared on stage only once: as Ouzounian describes it, he gave an "unplugged" performance of *Cul-de-Sac* as part of a series of fundraising shows staged by Buddies in Bad Times in Toronto. Buddies was in the middle of a financial crisis brought about by a loss of a $20,000 grant and declining box-office numbers caused by the global recession that had impacted the entertainment sector across the developed world ("Buddies"). MacIvor was exactly the kind of buddy they needed—one who had a proven track record with the audience.

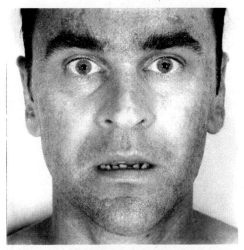

MacIvor in a promotional image for *Monster*.
Photo provided courtesy of Guntar Kravis.

THIS IS WHAT HAPPENS NEXT

But, only five years after he had publicly quit the theatre business, MacIvor was back for real: "his break didn't exactly go as planned, and after his attempt to 'go get a real life' ended in disaster, MacIvor contacted longtime collaborator Daniel Brooks and began work on a new solo show" (Priestly). This would be *This Is What Happens Next*, first produced by Necessary Angel Theatre Company and the Canadian Stage Company in April 2010 at the Berkeley Street Theatre Downstairs. The title, obviously a nod to the storytelling thematic of MacIvor's script, is also a reactivation of that once-cancelled, now-invigorated affinity with his audience. Indeed, *This Is What Happens Next* is palpably autobiographical. At the start of the play, the character listed as "Me" "*enters the theatre through the audience wearing street clothes (a pink shirt). He carries a book and a venti Starbucks coffee. He makes his way toward the stage. The house lights remain up*"—as the stage direction tells us (3). MacIvor's first lines, "I'm sorry I'm late, I'm sorry I'm late, I'm sorry I'm late, I'm sorry I'm late, I'm sorry I'm late. That's the first thing I say when I enter any room. I'm always late. Chronically late. Terminally late. And I'm really trying not to be late these days" (3), launch a nine-page (twenty-minute) monologue that sets the framework for the story that will follow. It also performs an intimacy with the audience—MacIvor speaking as himself, "Me." In the theatre—I saw the play at the Martha Cohen Theatre in February 2013 (part of the High Performance Rodeo program for that year)—audiences are encouraged even more earnestly to embrace the conceit that this is a "real" situation for the "real" actor as the performance started several minutes after the advertised curtain time. Thus the opening minutes of the performance complied with (and comically rendered) Sherrill Grace's observation that "the line between a life lived and the staging of a life is central to any auto/ biographical play, but it is not a sharp, clear line" (19).

If the first part of *This Is What Happens Next* appears as explicitly autobiographical, much of what follows seems to be from the same design as MacIvor's earlier shows: its production team was identical to *Cul-de-Sac*'s: MacIvor, Brooks, Purtell, and Feren; the format has MacIvor performing seven different characters; and lighting and sound play significant roles in shaping audience response. "Me" transforms, to the tune of "suspenseful music" (10), into alter ego Will (who has been reading a lot of Schopenhauer), who introduces the story of Kevin and its cast of characters—including his father Mike; his uncle Aaron (who used to be his auntie Erin); Warren, an angry gay man whose relationship has recently ended; and brittle divorce lawyer Susan—all of whom are, as usual, played by MacIvor alone. Richard Ouzounian's review for the *Toronto Star* points out how close the story is to recent events in MacIvor's own life and argues that although the play's format may seem familiar, "MacIvor is going into new and unchartered territory": "Just sitting in the showroom, the 2010 model MacIvor may look like all the others, but take it out for a test spin and you'll be dazzled by the heights it can climb and the treacherous curves it can take with ease" ("This").

The signal novelty of this MacIvor show was its happy ending, confirmed by both promotional materials ("Don't miss one of Canada's most celebrated playwrights and performers as he returns to the stage in this autobiographical fairy-tale fantasy with a happy ending," according to the One Yellow Rabbit website in advance of the 2013 performances in Calgary) and reviews alike. Indeed, at the end of *This Is What Happens Next*, Kevin metamorphoses back to Me, whose tasks it is to present the audience with a synopsis of the fates of all the different characters. This wrap-up speech starts "Nobody dies" (59)—unlike, then, Leonard in *Cul-de-Sac*—and describes how all move on to a decidedly human, more or less happy, and usually hopeful next phase in their lives. Like its predecessors, *This Is What Happens Next* was a well-travelled solo performance, although critical review was, with the exception of Ouzounian's four out of four stars in the *Star*, more measured than it had been for *Cul-de-Sac*. For my own part, I found the extended critique of the two women ordering ahead of "Me" in Starbucks and the presentation of the female divorce lawyer more misogynist than comic, and the breakneck speed of delivery exhausting as much as exhilarating, but there was no question MacIvor earned his enthusiastic applause for what Halifax reviewer Elissa Barnard called "a fascinating and soul-stirring piece of theatre ("MacIvor Dazzles"). Everything about *This Is What Happens Next* confirms the reputation that had been built on the twenty years of da da kamera and does not disappoint the expectations of performance.

Indeed, MacIvor's performance in *This Is What Happens Next* took up what Grace has defined as the purpose of autobiographical theatre: "to embody and perform a process of self-creation, recreation, and rediscovery" (21), a process to which his audience is generously welcomed. This is the skill of MacIvor's "affinity"-building. The "willingness of an audience to listen to that [autobiographical] story" (Stephenson, *Performing Autobiography* 19) seems never to be assumed by the performer; rather, he deploys intimacy and a sense of sharing to include them in the storytelling world. MacIvor's autobiographical project continues, too: in 2014, *Who Killed Spalding Gray?* premiered at the Magnetic North Festival in Halifax. Pre-performance publicity described the show as about "truth and lies and the four most important things in life"—a tag line that must have whetted the appetite of consumers of MacIvor's reinvigorated brand and its new positive messaging. Ryan Claycomb has drawn our attention to the "presentness made by autobiographical performance, the ways in which the body-as-text and the life-as-construction in tandem reveal the performativity of everyday identity, and the community-building functions of performed autobiographical narrative" (30). Ultimately, then, the marketing of MacIvor as tour-de-force performer invests in community-building between actor and audience, and if MacIvor is indeed a premium brand in Canada's performance scene, his is one that has earned the accolade of affinity.

THREE WOMEN AND IDENTITY IN
MARION BRIDGE AND
WAS SPRING
ANN WILSON

Many of Daniel MacIvor's plays explore the notion of identity and the intricate formations of individual identity. In *Marion Bridge* (published in 1999) and *Was Spring* (slated for publication in 2015) in particular, MacIvor tests the formation of identity through the shared memories of three female characters. Birth and death figure prominently, allowing MacIvor to introduce faith, an analogue for "belief" and key component of identity, which in these plays is less about whether an individual's memory of the past is factually accurate and more about what comes to be believed as true. Cohesive identity involves reconciling divergent narratives about one's past, in light of counter narratives.

In *Marion Bridge* only the three sisters appear on stage. The eldest of the three is Agnes, who has moved from the family's home to Toronto where she is pursuing her career as an actress, which she describes as "a very expensive, time consuming and demoralizing hobby" (46); the middle sister is Theresa, who is a nun "living in a farming order in New Brunswick" (7); and the youngest is Louise, who lives in the family home with her mother and is described by both her sisters as being "strange" (19). The play charts the changing dynamic between the three as they share the intimacy of attending to their mother as she dies. During this shared period they reminisce, addressing events in their life as a family. Their conversations reveal a family day trip they took as children with their parents to Marion Bridge, Nova Scotia. In an

My deep thanks to Richie Wilcox for arranging for me to have a copy of *Was Spring* and to Daniel MacIvor who generously provided the manuscript.

understated but remarkably deft moment of dramaturgical prowess, MacIvor shows the memory to have common elements, but in key ways each of the women contests the memory of her other sisters. The recollections converge around the shared memory that the trip featured sandwiches and that the geographic destination was Marion Bridge (located in MacIvor's birthplace of Cape Breton, Nova Scotia). They diverge around what might strike the audience as more critical details. Who was part of the trip? Who wasn't? What happened once the family arrived at Marion Bridge? Why does a memory of an apparently innocuous moment of familial history matter?

Was Spring is MacIvor's return to some of the same issues surrounding identity that he addressed in *Marion Bridge*. Like *Marion Bridge*, *Was Spring* features three female characters: Kit, a girl in her twenties; Kath, a mother in her fifties; and Kitty, a woman in her eighties (1), all variants of "Kathleen," suggesting that these women are the same person at different stages of her life (17). Indeed, this is the "twist" of the play—when the audience realizes that these women are one and the same: differently aged versions of the same woman. Each Kathleen has a distinct personality that relates to the other two, inferring that, metaphorically, the younger iterations of the self are siblings to the oldest self, Kitty.

In *Marion Bridge*, Theresa tells Agnes that the wish of their dying mother is for the sisters to visit their father, from whom the mother has divorced and from whom his daughters are estranged. The mother's hope, according to Theresa, is that they "all make amends" (41). The process of making amends is crucial to the formation of identity. In *Was Spring*, Kitty makes amends with her earlier selves. The MacKeigan sisters in *Marion Bridge* make amends with each other, even though they cannot make amends with their father, despite the gesture on their part.

The sisters honour their mother's wish by reluctantly agreeing to have dinner with their father, who has remarried a woman who is much younger than he. As Theresa says, "It's not so much him that I mind seeing as Lolita" (68). When they return home, Theresa is enraged by the new wife's neglect of their father. This "Lolita" seems largely oblivious to his being a frail old man:

Her acting the happy housewife. She didn't even know how to operate the stove! What does she feed him? You couldn't even eat the turkey, it was that tough. And I don't know who would have the nerve to call those grey things potatoes. And what was she wearing? . . . A little piece of nothing and some string. And prancing around like some kind of teenager. And that house! Who needs five bedrooms? And that awful little dog. "Baby"! What kind of a name is that for a dog? And Dad never liked dogs. And she's getting two more, did you hear her when she said she was getting two more? And a dishwasher! She can't use the stove what's she going to do with a dishwasher? Unless she's going to use it to wash the dogs. (72)

The audience cannot verify whether Theresa's rage is justified given that the dinner with the father and his new wife occurs in the gap between two scenes. The dinner is off stage and the audience is only privy to the sisters planning to go to the dinner, and their debriefing upon their return to the family home. Agnes is less upset by what she saw than her sister (71), which opens the possibility that Theresa is irritated because she and her sisters have been displaced from their father's life by his new wife who refers to her husband as "Daddy" (73). The sisters do agree that their father is incapacitated, seemingly by some form of dementia. They recall that at one point during dinner their father asked for the "binoculars" to be passed when he meant to ask for buns, and when the phone rang, their father instructed his wife to "get the tub" (74). These malapropisms have a degree of humour, save that they signal that their father is losing his capacity to use language accurately, manifest as his propensity to misname. Theresa reports that their father couldn't remember Louise's name, as if Louise were receding from his memory, suggesting that for him she is ceasing to exist (74). Their father is an absent figure through divorce, and the infirmities of advancing age suggest that there is little possibility of the sisters re-establishing a relationship with him given that he cannot remember, and is consigned to a very limited world within the household he has established with his second wife. The house may be large but the world within it is small.

In *Was Spring*, Kitty recalls that every Saturday she and her mother went into town. She says that these trips to town were "mostly to get away from Dad I guess. I had a mean old Dad" (5). Little more is offered about the specifics of Kitty's relation with her father. Kath suggests that society fosters a divide between boys and girls, which is sustained as they grow up. She says:

> And the girl babies start to grow into little Princesses that they've learned about from stories of pumpkin coaches and talking mermaids and flying godmothers.

> And the boy babies start growing into nicknames like Junior or Slugger or Buddy or Champ and dreaming of race cars and home runs and fire trucks and zombies.

> And the little Princesses begin to live in hope that someday there will be a Prince in the shape of a man, who will save her from feeling like her daddy didn't love her. But the thing is the boys don't grow into Princes like the girls need them to—and they do need them to because what good's a Princess without a Prince? The problem is that the boys, as they grow, don't want to be Princes they want to be Kings. (25–26)

Kath's account of how boys and girls are socialized carries undertones of Freud's theory of the Oedipus complex in which a male child experiences his relationship with his mother as exclusive. At some point, the child realizes that the mother has a relationship with the father, initiating the crisis that is resolved by the child acknowledging the authority of the father, and because the child does not meet all the needs of his mother, he experiences a sense of lack (Freud). Masculinity is always marked by lack, a point that MacIvor indicates when Kath says,

> But of course the boy can't become King because Daddy is King and there can only be one King. Of course the truth is that even

Daddy isn't King because Daddy's Daddy is really King. And of course
Daddy's Daddy isn't King because really Daddy's Daddy's Daddy is
King. And it goes on and on and on like that until it turns out there
really isn't any King at all. (*Was Spring* 26)

Woman, shaped by the aspiration to be a princess, seeks fulfillment through
having a man be her prince, a role that "Slugger" was not socialized to realize. The possibility of fulfillment in a relationship with a man gives way to
disappointment and an experience of wanting.

In both *Marion Bridge* and *Was Spring*, each of the characters is defined
by lack to which each responds differently. Louise, the youngest in *Marion
Bridge*, largely seems to live vicariously through the improbable world of
the soap opera *Ryan's Cove*, although she recognizes that the plot lines of
the show are contrived, noting that half "the stuff" on the series is made up
(31). In conversation with her sisters Louise seems disengaged, although she
is occasionally capable of making insightful observations, as is evident, for
example, in the exchange with Agnes over her drinking.

LOUISE: You drink so much it makes you stupid—and if you are not
drinking it makes you sick—and if you're not sick or stupid, you're
surly. What's the fun of that anyway?
AGNES: I guess I'd be better off sitting in front of the TV all my life.
LOUISE: Maybe you would be. Gimme that. (39)

Louise's seeming disengagement, or being "strange" (19), means that the
expectation that she will have close relationships is reduced. She joins a
prayer group that Agnes attends to get a sense of what the apparently vulnerable "Louise was getting herself into" (53). Agnes notes that at the prayer
meeting, "people are awfully affectionate. Lots of hugging and hand holding
and so on" (54). At the meeting, Agnes meets Dory, who has been teaching
Louise "all the Patron Saints in alphabetical order of what they're patron
of" (54). Agnes suspects that her sister may have an interest in Dory beyond tutoring in saints, and urges Louise to socialize with Dory because,

as Agnes explains to Theresa, Louise "doesn't have any friends. She should have some friends" (57).

Theresa, like Louise, is isolated. She has become a nun, which means that she lives like other members of her religious order—the sisters—in a community of faith in which she is "wed" to God. In a monologue, Theresa tells the audience that she lives on a farm with animals because

> the Sisters there believe that it's best to use living things to make living things. Of the earth, for the earth, from the earth. . . . Farming is wonderful: getting your hands down there in the beautiful dirt. When you're working in it up to your elbows it starts to feel like liquid, thick dark liquid, like the blood of the earth. And that's really all I've got: the farm, the animals, the earth. And my faith. But lately I've been wondering if I'm there more for the farm than the faith. (77–78)

Later in the play, Theresa amends her depiction of life on the farm. She and Agnes are having a confrontation in which the elder sister lashes out at the younger, "Holy Saint Theresa all giving and kind but really you just don't want anyone to have a life. Not me not Louise. You don't want anyone else to have a life because you don't have one. That's why you're such a bitch" (106). Theresa responds that Agnes does not know her nor does she know anything about her life.

> And I'm supposed to believe that God is everywhere, in everything, in everyone—but sometimes I just don't see him. Imagine how that makes me feel—just as a person—as a person who made a decision and a promise to believe—to see God everywhere. But where is he? Every day—every minute of every day I have to ask that question because of the choices I've made. And you don't think sometimes I don't just feel like a fool? But I've got to keep believing and I've got to keep loving and giving and helping. But it's all such a mess and I don't know what to do about it. I don't know how to make things

right. I don't know how I got here. There's no room Agnes . . . I have
no room for anyone else . . . (106–07)

Both Louise and Theresa protect themselves from the risk of relationships, particularly with men, by isolating themselves, but so too does Agnes,
the oldest sister. As noted earlier, Agnes is an unsuccessful actor who drinks
heavily. When Theresa suggests that Agnes has friends, which would distinguish her from her sisters who do not seem to have friendships, she replies,
"My friends are all alcoholics and drug addicts to whom I owe money" (46).
None of the three sisters seems capable of an intimate relationship with another person, a point signalled from the opening of the play in which Agnes
recounts a recurring dream in which she drowns:

Every time I dream the dream I'm drowning and every time I dream
the dream I forget. Fooled by the sound of water I guess and I imagine it's a dream of a wonderful night on the beach, or a cruise in the
moonlight, or an August afternoon in a secret cove—but a moment
after having been fooled into expecting bonfires or handsome captains or treasures in the weedy shore it becomes very clear that the
water I'm hearing is the water that's rushing around my ears and
fighting its way into my mouth and pulling me down into its dark,
soggy oblivion. No captains, no treasures, no bonfires for me, in my
dream I'm drowning. (9)

For Agnes, there are no captains, or princes for that matter, to refer to the
absent masculine figure identified by Kath in *Was Spring*.

The sense of fractured family relations is signalled from the beginning
of *Marion Bridge* when Agnes recounts that in her dream she sees a family
on the beach. In her dream she musters her energy to wave to them, trying
to get help, but they misread her gesture, wave back as if she were offering a
friendly greeting and then they return to their picnic, oblivious that Agnes is
drowning (11). The dream is open to interpretation, but an obvious meaning

shows Agnes as not part of the idealized family at the beach. Indeed, if the MacKeigan sisters are seen as having a common sense of deep isolation, the remove that Agnes articulates is also true for both Theresa and Louise. The sisters have no father in any meaningful sense because they were estranged from him, and he is now too frail to re-establish the relationship with his daughters, apparently having replaced them with his new wife who calls him "Daddy." Theresa and Louise, to a lesser degree, seek to forge a relationship with God, the Father, but neither seems successful. Louise's faith seems to amount to the recitation of the names of patron saints, alphabetically; Theresa cannot find God (106–07).

  Marion Bridge gives few clues about the nature of the relationships the sisters had with their mother before her illness. The dying mother is off-stage, depicted as too weak to leave her room. She can only communicate by writing single words, single letters, and symbols on Post-it Notes (20). Like her former husband, the mother is losing her capacity to use language and therefore to share memories which are keys to forging relationships and, by extension, identity. While Theresa seems genuinely attentive to her mother, her confession to Agnes towards the end of the play opens the possibility that Theresa, in attending to her mother, was acting less from genuine care and more out of a combination of duty and the need to perform faith in light of her questioning whether there is a God, a Father, who is evident everywhere in His creation.

  Given that Agnes has come from Toronto to care for her mother, it is curious that Agnes is reluctant to enter her mother's room. The audience learns that Agnes had a daughter whom she gave up for adoption. Agnes says:

I made a big terrible mistake. I should have kept her. I wanted to keep her. But they wouldn't let me. Shipped me off to that bloody convent for six months to keep me out of sight and then when she was born, that was that, she was gone and I was supposed to forget about the whole thing. And the worst of it was they let me hold her before they took her away. I don't know if it was cruelty or stupidity—but they brought her in to me for five minutes and I held her and I felt how

right that felt and nothing, nothing has ever felt that right again. The
next day Mother came to get me and all the way home in the car all
she talked about was the goddamn weather. And that's why I can't
go in and see her . . . (49)

The trauma of carrying a pregnancy to term, giving birth to the infant,
and holding the baby is acute because in those few minutes of holding the
baby, a bond and the commensurate horizon of possibility of loving a child
are opened. An audience, in responding to Agnes's sense of loss—a mode of
absence or lack—should not overlook her use of "they," which has no gram-
matically clear referent. Within the context of the speech, it is clear that Agnes
uses "they" to refer to her parents, and to her mother in particular, and then
uses "they" to refer to the staff—presumably nuns—who oversaw much of her
pregnancy and delivery, and brought the baby to her to hold. "They" is conflated to signify figures who had authority over the young, vulnerable Agnes
and who were incapable of hearing her needs. This incapacity deforms Agnes,
turning her into a difficult woman who escapes her pain by drinking to excess,
and being an actress, performing the lives of others, which have been scripted
by playwrights. Agnes says, "I'm just trying to make some kind of story. I've
spent so long trying to tell other people's stories. . . . I want my story" (104).

Agnes recognizes that she has made a mess of her life, but she is trying to
rectify the mistakes of the past (104). She has not had a drink since the funeral
(84) and she attempts to address the loss of her daughter, whom she learns
is named Joanie and lives in Cape North where she and her adoptive mother
run a craft shop (49). Agnes has made a number of trips to Cape North, as
many as six, during which she has surreptitiously tried to establish contact
with her daughter by taking pottery classes run by Joanie's adoptive mother,
Chrissy (82). In Agnes's view, Chrissy is a neglectful mother who favours her
two biological children over her adopted daughter (80, 81). MacIvor allows
ambiguity about the accuracy of Agnes's account of the relationship between
Chrissy and Joanie: it could be that Agnes is being harsh in her assessment as
a way of rationalizing her establishing contact with her daughter after such
a long period of time. Towards the end of the play, Agnes tells Theresa that

Chrissy and Joanie "had words and Chrissy put her out of the house and Joanie has nowhere to stay," prompting Agnes to suggest that Joanie should come to stay in the MacKeigans' home, an offer which Theresa initially does not support (101).

From here on, the sentimental strain that has been running through *Marion Bridge* becomes pronounced. Theresa goes to Cape North to assess Joanie's situation. She tells Agnes, "You're right. It's not good" (114). In acknowledging that Agnes's assessment was right, Theresa relinquishes her oppositional stance to her sister, making amends with her in ways that parallel their mother's urging for the sisters to repair their relationships with their father. Further, Theresa tells Agnes that Joanie is in the first trimester of a pregnancy and is not taking good care of herself and needs support (116). Theresa reiterates the offer that Agnes wanted to make by extending an invitation to Joanie that she live with the MacKeigan sisters. Agnes asks, "Can we do this Theresa?" (116). Theresa responds, "Well I was thinking about it on the way home and I figured the best thing to do is just pretend it's a movie and hope for a happy ending" (116). It is as if MacIvor slyly signals that he is aware that the reconciliation of Agnes and Theresa, and the embrace of the pregnant Joanie, is sentimental and contrived in offering renewal to this family through the birth of a baby.

On the day that the three sisters travel to Cape North to bring Joanie home, Theresa makes sandwiches. The sisters stop at Marion Bridge, returning to the place where they visited with their family, an event each remembers differently. Louise insists that she was excluded from the initial trip because she had chicken pox:

> Mother said we'd wait till next week but Dad said no you were going anyway and you two made egg salad sandwiches and went off without me. . . . [T]hen you all came back and you gave me the egg salad sandwiches to make me feel better but I couldn't eat them because they were all sat on, and I was sick right, I couldn't eat them anyway even if they weren't sat on, and I ended up getting sicker on top of

the chicken pox because Deena Jessome's boyfriends kept me locked
out of the house all afternoon and it rained. (86)

For Louise, the memory is painful because it is a reminder that she never gets
"to be part of nothing" (86).

On the second visit to Marion Bridge, one which includes Louise, Theresa
counters her sister's recollection, telling her that she had recovered from the
chicken pox. She asserts that Louise chose not to make the trip "because Deena
Jessome was coming over to babysit you" (123). Agnes's recollection of the
day was that it was unpleasant because she was bitten by a dog that she had
been chasing on the beach but Theresa corrects, saying, "Yes I know that's
your story but what happened was you stepped on a nail chasing the poor
little thing" (124). It is unclear whether Theresa's memories are accurate, and
perhaps the reconciliation of divergent memories is the issue rather than the
accuracy of the memory. The congruent memories shared by individuals are
a key in the formation of identity. Standing on the beach at Marion Bridge,
Theresa recalls the first visit:

> It was lovely. Mother was so happy. Just staring out at the sky, lost
> in her dreams. But Dad didn't like that, no, he never liked seeing
> Mother content, and started in on her. Just after that it started to
> rain. The rain followed us all the way home. And then it stopped.
> And the four of us, us and Mother, we stood out in the backyard and
> saw the rainbow. (124)

Now, as then, the three women look to the sky, this time seeing clouds form-
ing a girl, happily riding her horse, as if she is flying freely (126). Theresa
"takes a huge pile of yellow post-it notes from her pocket" and divides them
amongst the three sisters (127). *"The three women throw the notes high into
the air. They stand each with an arm above their head as the notes fall around
them and the lights fade"* (127). As Cynthia Zimmerman notes, "The ending
of the play reconfigures its beginning" in which Agnes recounts her dream

of dying (264). Perhaps the "girl" the sisters see formed by the clouds is their mother, now free and happy, or perhaps it is any one of the three MacKeigan sisters who have reconciled, and in so doing have found a freedom that allows them to reconfigure the family to welcome Joanie and her yet-to-be-born baby. *Marion Bridge* ends with a sense of release from being held down by the past, as if drowning, by the weight of unresolved memories of the past, concluding with a sense of celebration, promise, and renewal.

The three sisters are each discrete individuals, but they are aspects of each other, sharing in a deep sense of isolation and loss that they are at the cusp of overcoming through the integration of Joanie in their family. In *Was Spring*, MacIvor returns to the theme of isolation arising from loss. Kit, the young girl, is isolated in her family life because she was "born into a certain unhappiness" occasioned by her parents' drinking heavily and their arguments fuelled by drink (48). Young, naive, and desperate, she believes that she has found release in David, a young man who is himself something of an outsider, but

> a boy who danced like elastic and joy. . . . And he took you. But he wouldn't keep you. And there was nothing you could do. And there was no one you could tell. You were gone. You looked in the mirror and you were no longer a child.
> KATH: I was a woman.
> KITTY: A woman with a baby in my belly and no man to name it. And then came Bruce. Bruce, a man physically yes, but if you were to imagine gallant or steadfast, heroic or stalwart as the making of man, he was none of these. Although he had ambition and was well set to climb a ladder at the bank. So let's call him at least male. He was the other side of David in all ways. But Bruce was lonely enough to be willing, and concerned about appearances enough to be quiet. (49)

Like Agnes, Kit/Kath is pregnant, and unmarried. Whereas Agnes's pregnancy is addressed by her being forced into the care of nuns for whom the adoption of the infant is the only viable way to address the birth of a child outside marriage, Kit/Kath chooses to marry a man whom she does not love in order to attain security. She does become financially secure, indicated by her having a generous house, with "a big veranda. . . . That house was so big it blocked out the view for people across the road" (42).

There is a cost for Kit/Kath in choosing financial security over love: Kit forfeits innocence and becomes the "acidic" Kath, who says to Kit, "You abandoned me! You left me bitter and biting. That's what you did. And here I end up stuck in the middle, I'm the one who has to live with it all. It's easy for you you're an idiot. [re: Kitty] And it's easy for her, she's drowning in denial" (31). In *Marion Bridge*, Agnes has no agency around giving up her child for adoption—decisions are made for her; in *Was Spring*, Kit exercises agency by choosing to keep the baby fathered by David, her "only love" (20). The consequence of her choice is that she unwittingly alters the dynamic of the Oedipal relation because she forfeits her connection with the father of her baby by substituting Bruce for David. Bruce is the surrogate who stands in, at least socially, as the father, but the reality is that in making the choice, Kit becomes Kath, a nasty, cynical woman. She has no deep affective bond with Bruce, who seems to be little more than a source of financial security and a reminder that she was abandoned by David. Kath focuses on the child of her union with David as if the baby is her only connection with him. Kitty speaks of "Love. The Love. Real love is when you can for a moment see outside yourself. Hold everything in your hands," which Kit understands as referring to David (29). Kath tartly corrects her, saying that Kitty is not referring to David, but to a mother's first encounter with her newborn child (29), a description that is reminiscent of Agnes remembering first holding her baby, and "how right that felt and nothing, nothing has ever felt that right again" (49).

In *Was Spring* MacIvor presses on the possible implications of that bond, suggesting that the intense exclusivity of the mother's bond to her child is a mode of selfishness that results in love becoming "twisted by . . . expectations," and "poisoned by . . . clinging greed" (30). Before the child becomes aware, Kath suggests "that all anybody really cares about is what they can get from her. The baby that exists in the calm centre of the storm of our selfishness. While she's this guileless 'gift from above.' Before she grows up to turn on us.

To hate us with justification. To abandon us with such malice" (30). Kitty at-
omizes the abandonment this way:

> This is what happens, and when this happens, when Want enters,
> leaning just over your shoulder, whispering in your ear, "What I
> want, what I want, what I want." That's when the separation starts.
> Oh there are the lovely days, the tiny tendernesses, you and her on
> the big veranda, the view of the lake. But the child, the gift, the hope
> of hope, who once crawled across these floors, slept in your lap on
> the big veranda, marvelled at your beauty, begins to move away. And
> the more she moves away, the more she fights against your want, the
> harder you hold. (38)

The daughter whom Kath loves so fiercely, whom Kath hopes will complete
herself, dies, separating herself from her mother through action that the mother reads as suicide (50). Like Agnes who drinks to erase the loss of her baby,
Kath drinks:

> And the darkness is everywhere. Tiny and finite but endless. All
> that's left now is whiskey in the morning, scotch for lunch and wine
> with dinner, but dinner is ruined, what to do now don't worry drown
> your disappointment with vodka and ice. These are the days, the
> days become numbers the numbers just ounces in bottles, and these
> are the every damn day is the same days. No daylight, no dusk, no
> midnight, no dawn, no person friend or foe, no God either of mercy
> or vengeance. I am hopelessness. My child is dead and I feel more a
> mother than I ever did. (51)

MacIvor avoids the contrived, sentimental resolution of *Marion Bridge*.
There is hope in *Was Spring*, but because the play is more lyrical in style than
Marion Bridge, the optimism is suggested rather than realized through image
and gesture. Kitty, Kath, and Kit go to the lake, perhaps only in memory. It is
at the lake that Kitty can make amends with her earlier selves, the innocent Kit

and the bitter Kath. As Kit and Kath *"quietly sing the song from their youth,"* Kitty speaks (55), then Kit and Kath disappear, perhaps into Kitty who says, "I do believe in something. / I believe in Spring" (56). The final line of the play is "it is Spring" (56), the time of rebirth as if this final trip to the lake—real, remembered, or imagined—has allowed the old, frail Kitty to be reborn by being reconciled with her earlier selves.

In Winter 2009, Daniel MacIvor was the writer-in-residence at the University of Guelph. In an interview with the University's publication, *At Guelph*, MacIvor told interviewer Teresa Pitman, "I was raised by my mother and my sister, and my grandmother was very involved. My father was absent. So what I understand of men, I understand from myself, and what I understand of women comes from the world I grew up in." This biographical detail explains, to some degree, why MacIvor explores identity through female characters, and the absence of father figures. It explains why absence—or more broadly lack—figures strongly in his plays. MacIvor's writing may be informed by his personal experience, which, likely, is true for most playwrights. MacIvor's gift is his understanding that lack is a key to understanding identity, and that people strive to have cohesive identity that, in MacIvor's world, is forged through relationships that involve sharing memories with our intimates. The experience of loss is one that can cause each of us to respond by isolating ourselves. In *Marion Bridge* the sisters come to realize their latent love for each other by arriving at the shared understanding of a family trip. In *Was Spring*, MacIvor offers a more harrowing perspective: each of us is not singular, but at different stages of life we are different selves, and the charge is to reconcile and embrace the histories which are offered at each phase of life so that each of us is not fractured, but whole, having made amends with our earlier selves.

REWRITING SELF AND MEMORY IN *THE SOLDIER DREAMS*

WES D. PEARCE

After three years of workshops and variant stagings, *The Soldier Dreams*, written by Daniel MacIvor, directed by MacIvor and Daniel Brooks, and produced by da da kamera, premiered at Canadian Stage on March 26, 1997. It is one of the last, if not the last, Canadian plays to deal with the AIDS crisis,[1] and it went on to win Dora Mavor Moore Awards for best production (shared by Canadian Stage Company and da da kamera) and best direction (shared by MacIvor and Brooks). Yet regardless of the awards, audiences, critics, and

---

1   *The Soldier Dreams* is representative of the third, or possibly fourth, generation of AIDS drama. The first generation of AIDS plays, as represented by Larry Kramer's *The Normal Heart* (1985) and William M. Hoffman's *As Is* (1985) are anguished howls from ground zero. They are radical and loud condemnations of existing government and health policies. Within a couple of years a second generation of AIDS plays appeared, plays that were less political and more educational. AIDS remained the focus of these plays but plays like Gay Sweatshop's *Compromised Immunity* (1987), Lanford Wilson's *A Poster of the Cosmos* (1989), Colin Thomas's *Flesh and Blood* (1991), and Michael L. MacLennan's *Beat The Sunset* (first produced in 1993) are written to inform and educate the audience and propose that empowerment will be achieved through knowledge of the disease. The third generation of plays, as exemplified by Paula Vogel's *The Baltimore Waltz* (1992), Brad Fraser's *Poor Super Man* (1994), and Terrence McNally's *Love! Valour! Compassion!* (1994), begin to move away from AIDS as a primary subject and/or focus of the play, resulting in works that are creative and dramaturgically daring in dealing with the disease and its aftermath. Finally, and perhaps unfairly, are the plays that were written after Tony Kushner's epic *Angels in America*. The critical, artistic, and scholarly attention that Kushner's *Millennium Approaches* (1993) and *Perestroika* (1994) generated overshadowed, until nearly the end of the first decade of the twenty-first century, most, if not all, of the HIV/AIDS drama that followed.

scholars have never genuinely warmed to it. The play has been referred to as one of MacIvor's "lesser scripts . . . [one that] doesn't show MacIvor at his best" (Thomas, "The Soldier") and has been burdened with an uneven production history.[2] Since its premiere, *The Soldier Dreams* has become, or perhaps remains, one of MacIvor's lesser-known works. Stylistically the play shifts between realism, minimalism, and MacIvor's own brand of physical theatre. Although the play retains many of the metatheatrical qualities present in earlier works such as *Never Swim Alone*, *2-2-Tango*, and *House*, it seems

---

2   When the play opened at the Canadian Stage Company in 1997, Robert Cushman, writing for *The Globe and Mail*, noted "the form is often brilliant, the content banal to non-existent" ("Soldier"). Referring to *The Soldier Dreams* as "a performance piece rather than a play," and comparing (unfavourably) some of the visuals to those of Robert Lepage, he then complains that he is bored with another "deathbed vigil play . . . [without] a compensating identity of its own." It was apparent that Cushman was expecting much more from a production that had three years of development prior to its premiere. The uneven reception that greeted the first production and a number of other factors, including the play's relatively large cast size, the success of Tony Kushner's *Angels in America*, and the rapid development of HIV/AIDS medicines (such as antiviral cocktails) sidelined MacIvor's play. As a result, *The Soldier Dreams* did not receive many productions after the premiere. A notable exception is Subterranean Theatre's warmly received 1999 production in Austin, Texas. In 2006, it was included in *I Still Love You: Five Plays*, a collection of MacIvor plays published by Playwrights Canada Press. The collection won the Governor General's Literary Award for English Drama, but critics were still unkind: "In most respects . . . *The Soldier Dreams* is a fairly typical entry in the elegiac genre" (Morrow, "MacIvor's" 45). Regardless of the criticism that followed its republication, productions of *The Soldier Dreams* have been more frequent since then. Strangely, most of the post-2006 Canadian productions have been in university and community theatres (Project X Theatre in Kamloops, I'm a Little Pickled Theatre Company in Vancouver, King's College in Halifax, and even the Banting Memorial High School Drama Club in Alliston, Ontario), whereas most, if not all, of the professional productions have been produced in the United States. Theatre East's off-off-Broadway production in 2011 was generally well received, although at least one critic took exception to the tone of the production, writing, "The play contains some elegantly written passages, but unfortunately director Judson Jones tends towards the overly sentimental in the production, which in many ways seems at odds with the tone of MacIvor's actual play" (Bacalzo). A production of the play at Baltimore's Iron Crow Theatre in 2012, however, garnered enthusiastic and nearly unanimous praise.

to mark a dramaturgical shift towards a greater sense of naturalism as later evidenced in *Marion Bridge, How It Works*, and *His Greatness*. These "slippages" might account for some of the critical and scholarly uncertainty around *The Soldier Dreams*, yet it is difficult to argue that MacIvor has ever restricted himself to one style or dramaturgical form with any of his plays and, furthermore, this conscious juxtaposition is central to MacIvor's oeuvre. What is more challenging, and perhaps consistent in his work, is MacIvor's use of autobiographical self-rewriting, confessional tropes, and memory/nostalgia within the play. None of these ideas are unique to *The Soldier Dreams* insofar as self-rewriting/confession are central to many of MacIvor's plays and the role of memory both in constructing and de-constructing identity surface in a great number of his plays.[3]

This essay suggests that the complex dramaturgical structures found in *The Soldier Dreams* had their genesis in earlier plays: *See Bob Run, Here Lies Henry*, and *House* can all be considered experiments with autobiography, confession, and memory. Unlike these earlier solo performance plays in which the protagonist self narrates her/his story and in doing so constructs an identity

---

3   MacIvor's *In On It* (2001) features two characters, This One and That One, rewriting and, to a certain extent, inventing identity through the staging of their memories. The telling and retelling of the past serves as a futile attempt to understand the unknowable and perhaps change the course of the characters in the play. Both *You Are Here* (2000) and *Cul-de-Sac* (2005) are narrated by characters who are dead but who nevertheless seek to understand the meaning of past events and, particularly in the case of Leonard in *Cul-de-Sac*, reclaim his identity after his neighbours rewrite his story after his death. *A Beautiful View* (2006), a play of memory, lies, the unknowability of "others," and identity construction as L and M recount their tumultuous and yet remarkably ordinary friendship, echoes *The Soldier Dreams*. With *How It Works* (2006) MacIvor again confronts the difficult choices and lies that victims of childhood sexual abuse tell themselves in order to survive. Denying her own memories and rewriting herself is the only way that Brooke deals with the traumatic effects of the sexual abuse she suffered at the hands of her father's best friend. *His Greatness* (2007), a fictionalized story inspired by Tennessee Williams's 1980 sojourn to Vancouver, more than echoes Williams's *Sweet Bird of Youth*, as the Assistant's carefully constructed reality, a reality maintained only through deceitful memory and deceptive self-rewriting slowly crumbles around him.

through selective editing of memory, *The Soldier Dreams* problematizes auto-biography, confession, and memory in unexpected ways. Within this domestic drama MacIvor introduces multiple characters and multiple voices, each seeking to rewrite themselves into David's life. Juxtaposed to the mundane events surrounding his impending death are David's own elusive and fragmentary memories of a particularly significant, yet seemingly insignificant moment in his life. Playing with time in a fluid manner MacIvor presents multiple perspectives of events and people resulting in a growing awareness of the futility and impossibility of understanding the self, let alone "even a tiny part of another human being" (Denton). *The Soldier Dreams* demonstrates that in moments of crisis one's past can easily be claimed by others. Autobiography is often rewritten to appease those who remain and memory itself is subject to manipulation and exploitation. Death obliterates and yet, MacIvor believes, hope remains.

The Soldier Dreams focuses on the last days, or possibly hours, of David—a young gay man who is dying, and although no cause or disease is ever discussed, Dirk Gindt argues, that "HIV and AIDS are so omnipresent that they never need to be mentioned" ("Queer" 131). David is represented by two actors. David of the present (DAVID 1) lies in his bed, mostly comatose, for almost the entire play, occasionally uttering a few disconnected words—"Ottawa," "matchbook," "German doctor," but nothing coherent.[4] David of the past (DAVID) appears as a memory, a dream, possibly even a ghost of the dying David, and in these remembered moments captures a one-night stand that David spent with a young German medical resident while in Ottawa on the eve of his sister's wedding.[5] As David's past and present collide on stage, the

---

4   Although it is never stated, most critics agree with Dirk Gindt's analysis that "we can assume that it was on this particular occasion [and with the German student] that David was infected with HIV" ("Queer" 131).

5   The genesis for this staging was certainly influenced by MacIvor's work with DNA Theatre's 1991 AIDS project entitled *SICK: A Chamber of Horrors*. As described by Richie Wilcox in his paper "Daniel MacIvor Is Dying," *SICK* was part of a year-long AIDS project undertaken by Hillar Liitoja's DNA Theatre in response to the ongoing and continual cultural apathy and political/societal horror(s) and attacks that communities affected by

"real" world (i.e. David's bedroom and house that he shares with his partner Richard) is invaded by David's uncomprehending but well-meaning siblings: older sister Tish and her husband Sam, and younger sister Judy. As the family prepares for David's death it quickly becomes apparent how little any of them, including Richard, really knows/knew him and how ill-prepared they are for his impending death: Tish is obsessed with making Jell-O for everyone, but especially David, while Sam attempts to work through the situation by writing poetry. For much of the play the characters are committed to a rewriting of self, and whether conscious of it or not, each individual seems to be attempting, with varying degrees of success, to write themselves back into the history of David's life while at the same time claiming David's past and his memories as theirs.

The strained relationships between Tish and Richard and Tish and Judy are readily apparent from the beginning of the play and intensify as David's death approaches. MacIvor breaks these naturalistic scenes by freezing the "now"; allowing the characters' confessional monologues to morph into self-rewriting. These seemingly "authentic" confessions complicate our knowledge of David for they implicate him in an ongoing series of lies and deceit. The most egregious of these lies excluded Richard from attending Tish and Sam's wedding:

> TISH: Okay David says to me:
> RICHARD: David says to me:
> TISH: David says: "About the wedding, Richard's not coming."

AIDS found themselves under. Of the three pieces that made up the project: *The Panel, SICK,* and *The Last Supper, SICK* was the most graphic:

> a sensory overload spectacle and melodramatics replacing any cohesive narrative and form. *SICK,* staying true to its subtitle, featured numerous simultaneous acts such as a man confessing he has AIDS on a telephone, a woman killing herself before a picture of Jesus, a naked man being spread-eagled and tied up by his penis and other horrors. . . . At the center of this metaphor for death was one man lying on a hospital bed dying of AIDS. This man was performed by Daniel MacIvor.

RICHARD: David says: "About the wedding, you're not invited." And
I think:
TISH/RICHARD: Okay. If that's the way Her Majesty wants it that's
the way it's going to be. (39–41)

As for so many of David's actions, there is no explanation provided, but
certainly one possibility is his need to maintain a separation between carefully constructed identities—David the golden son and David the promiscuous
party boy. As the play progresses our understanding of David unravels and in
many ways, as an audience, we have just as little knowledge and understanding of him as does his family. The understanding we do have of him is then
further disrupted by David's dreams/memories/hallucinations, which present
a different version of the "domestic" David, and yet they are equally problematic insofar as they may not reflect a version of him that is any truer than
the stories of special bonds that Tish, Sam, and Judy share with the audience.

The past, and more importantly reorganizing and reconceiving memory, is central to *The Soldier Dreams* just as it is in so many of MacIvor's
other plays. These are never simple "flash-back memory plays," for MacIvor
uses time in a postmodern and self-conscious manner that echoes Andreas
Huyssen's observation that "[we are] at a time in which simultaneity seems to
have obliterated distinctions between the past and the present and in which
the future seems to fold itself into the past, memory becomes attenuated *and*
the object of obsessive quests" (1).

MacIvor's non-linear and non-narrative use of time often challenges audiences and characters. In plays like *Cul-de-Sac, Monster,* and *The Soldier
Dreams,* MacIvor creates a sense of "dislocation that makes memory both difficult and desired" (Radstone 26). Within these sometimes conflicted spaces of
memory, MacIvor's characters often perform a sort of confession or, perhaps
more precisely, they engage in what Susannah Radstone would term "autobiographical self 'rewriting.'" In many of MacIvor's plays characters engage in
these acts of self-rewriting in an attempt to both contextualize and understand
their relationship with, and to, a "history that has now become beyond reach"
(Fredric Jameson, cited in Radstone 25) and in doing so, reaffirm, though not

necessarily stabilize, their identity in the present. MacIvor's first major play, *See Bob Run*, plays with variations on autobiographical self-rewriting, and while many of the plays that are written after *See Bob Run* also use it as a dramaturgical device, it is an idea that he exploits to greater degrees in *The Soldier Dreams*. Briefly exploring how autobiographical self-rewriting functions in *See Bob Run*, before discussing *The Soldier Dreams*, seems prudent and useful.

In *See Bob Run* (1986) Roberta (Bob) slowly reveals her story to a series of drivers as she hitchhikes away from the "big weird animal" in the closet towards her "father at the water" (30). The world that Bob first allows the audience into is a world of fantasy and make-believe:

> Once upon a time there was a king and a queen. And they were married. The king was handsome and strong and everybody thought he was good 'cause he was, most of the time, and he was good even to the queen who was a witch. . . . Aaaaaaand . . . all the king wanted was a princess. He wanted a princess so bad. A little princess that he could put on his knee and give big wet kisses to. And the queen says "No." "No way," she says. She doesn't want a princess 'cause she knows what'll happen. She knows that the king will end up lovin the princess so much that he won't love her anymore. (7–8)

As the play progress we come to realize that the fantasy world that Bob has cast herself in is a mechanism to protect herself from the memories of the sexual abuse she has suffered at the hands of her father:

> There was this big weird animal in the closet. This big weird animal. And it was in the closet. The little girl who was born a princess and a pile of shit is always scared when she goes to bed at night because she knows it's there. She can see it peekin out and she can hear it breathin. It's real for sure. But no one else believes her and call her dreamin when she talks about it. A bad dream. And she says, "But there is an animal in the closet, I can hear it breathin!" And her mother says "Shut up. Grow up. Bad dream." And after a while she starts thinkin maybe

it is a dream. And just when she starts believing that, that's when the door of the closet opens and there it is. This big weird naked animal. And it's smiling. . . . And it comes over to her in her bed where she's starin at it and it says: "Hold on to my handle, do that. See it, there's my happy handle. Come on. Hold it and make me happy. So she does and it makes it happy. And the big weird animal is so happy that it never goes back into the closet again. It's always waitin for her. But it's okay for a little girl now. Now she knows, it's just a dream. (14–15)

As Bob matures she maintains, to the best of her abilities, the fairy-tale world of her youth; recalling how when she and Timmy Prince first met he called her "Princess" and how gallant he was when he talked of lilacs and Lake Bob:

All this perfect pretend.
And that's what was good see.
For a while
Everything was like walkin through the park and pretendin.
He never tried nothing. (22)

By carefully rewriting her past and allowing the present to exist only on her terms, Bob was able to reconcile the abuse and move on. Timmy's sexual assault of Bob shatters the world of "perfect pretend":

I don't remember it. I don't remember any of it.

Just after and how he looked like he was just a person . . . real . . .
Like it wasn't Timmy Prince holdin me so quiet and dressin slow
and leavin backwards out Tamara's front door. Just some person . . .
some guy. Like the ones in school and the ones on the street. (23)

Yet when Timmy presents Bob with a bottle of pink water from Lake Bob she agrees to reconcile with him and move in with him, as she says, "'Cause that wasn't real—see it was pretend and maybe he would be able to pretend forever" (23). The pretend and the rewriting of the past fails. Near the end of the play it becomes clear that Bob is unable to keep her "perfect pretend" intact as she rewrites herself once again and confesses to Timmy's murder:

> I think I'm cryin. Or my head is. I'm standing right in front of him now. I got it pointed at him. Right at his head. And he knows I'm there and he won't open his eyes and he won't stop singin and he won't stop singin that song . . . and what if it don't work . . . and stop. Stop. Stop! Stop! STOP! STOP . . .
> And it worked.
> Bang.
> . . .
>
> I think . . . you know . . . it's good we're stopping . . . I think maybe we should go someplace and I should tell somebody about Timmy. 'Cause he's there all by himself . . . it's so messy . . . You think? I better eh?
> I mean it wasn't like he was so bad or anything. (34–36)

MacIvor, however, denies a traditional reading of Bob's story as simply a loss of innocence; after Bob's confession and seeming acceptance of her actions, she returns to her world of perfect pretend, an act that embodies Radstone's notions of memory and dislocation.[6] MacIvor suggests that Bob is unable to "just [sit] in the 'is' of our lives. Because in that 'is' exists a kind of loneliness" (ix), rewriting herself and her story is an attempt to escape and reconnect with a past that seems so near to her and yet, as we have discovered, never existed.

This dislocation between the desire for particular memories, the realization that a given and specific past never existed, and the necessity to rewrite the self in order to reconcile these seemingly irreconcilable positions resurfaces in a number of MacIvor's plays. *House* (1992) is a play built around

---

6   Contemporary readers might read Bob's rejection of her earlier realization and acceptance of her past actions as being consistent with symptoms of post-traumatic stress disorder.

Victor's hypercritical rewriting of self, but unlike *See Bob Run, House* plays with this autobiographical self-rewriting in a manner that is darkly comic and completely self-aware. *Here Lies Henry* (1996) shares stylistic elements with *House*, but while the latter play is even more metatheatrical and self-aware than its predecessors, it is, in many ways, a play about the necessity of autobiographical rewriting:

My sister was really my sister but I thought it
would be more interesting if I said she was my
Mother.
And I can play the violin, some people call it the ukulele.
and my favourite song is "Finally" by Ce Ce
Pennison.
And my favourite movie is "Airport 75", because
Karen Black landed a plane in a skirt.
And my best day, if I had a best day, would be the
day Elizabeth Taylor came to the Bay and I got to
hold her dog while she went to the bathroom.
And I don't have a problem being a homosexual I
just have a problem with other people's problem
with my not having a problem, maybe that's a
problem, I don't know!
And I never meant to be mean, I was just trying to
be funny.
And I did write a book, it just hasn't been
published. There's always hope.
And no I didn't set the fire, there was never any fire,
I just wanted there to have been a fire because I
wanted something to end.
And I think that love is a very good thing.

He waits for the end to happen.

You know it just doesn't feel complete unless the
lights were to come up bright and there were to be
a slow slow slow fade to total black and Henry
"Tom" Gallery, the Second, were to disappear
forever.
But that's not going to happen.

He leaps out of his chair.
Light full bright.
He regards the audience.
Light begins slow fade.

I am such a liar! (54–55)

In *The Soldier Dreams*, MacIvor plays with self-rewriting in a time of
crisis, introducing multiple voices into this literary and dramatic form that
generally is understood as being pursued individually.[7] In the extended monologues that MacIvor gives to Tish, Judy, and Sam, and in Richard's aborted
monologue, each character attempts an autobiographical rewriting of the self,
reconstructing their histories and memories with and of David into something
tangible and valued. Simultaneously, they are attempting to collectively create
for themselves "the memory," to understand the event that David is fitfully
remembering and from which they are all so disconnected.

---

7   More recent plays like *Monster* (1999) and, more specifically, *Cul-de-Sac* (2005) further
MacIvor's experimentation with characters who are engaged in autobiographical self-rewriting. Many of the dramaturgical elements celebrated in *Cul-de-Sac* appear to have their
genesis in *The Soldier Dreams*. *Cul–de-Sac* is narrated by Leonard, who is dead, and along
with other residents of his neighbourhood bears witness to his life and death. Although
Leonard narrates the story in a manner that is similar to the counter narratives of David's
family, Leonard and his story are undermined, reinterpreted, and retold by Leonard and
his neighbours. The more characters that we meet, the more problematized Leonard's
story and our understanding of Leonard become. As in *The Soldier Dreams*, the multiple
points of view and the retellings of the same event complicate the notion of self-rewriting
and make manifest the disconnect between the desire for memory and the certainty of it.

Like many of MacIvor's plays, *The Soldier Dreams* is deeply personal. It was written during a time when AIDS and its devastating consequences continued to cast an hysterical pall over North America, but equally importantly it was also written while MacIvor was still deeply affected by the AIDS-related death of Ken McDougall, with whom MacIvor had collaborated on many projects.[8] In 2000 MacIvor reflected back, commenting that "the work [he] was seeing and doing that was influenced by AIDS had to do with loss and issues around blame and responsibility" (Nolen). In the introduction to her book, *Bequest and Betrayal: Memoirs of a Parent's Death*, Nancy K. Allen writes, "Reacting to loss can take the form of a literary obligation" (x), and MacIvor's literary obligation, in this case *The Soldier Dreams*, is one filled with contemplation of death, grief, love, hurt, pain, and the guilt of the survivor:

> RICHARD: You see we weren't *(Sigh.)* We weren't exclusively together. And we hadn't been for a long time. You know?
> SAM: Uh.
> RICHARD: We saw other people.
> SAM: Oh right of course. No I mean not "of course" I mean . . . Sorry. Go on.
> RICHARD: No it's just—I mean we always saw other people, and I mean maybe that's part of the reason we've stayed together all these years, maybe it was good for the relationship, . . . and I ask myself, or try to figure out what do I really feel about that, about David, about what's happening now— (28–29)

Trauma affects people in radically different ways. In *The Soldier Dreams*, as is often the case in real life, none of the family members can comprehend nor do they understand how to prepare for David's death. What emerges from these monologues, these moments of reflection and self-rewriting, is a chance to confess. Michel Foucault argues that confession is "a ritual in which the

---

8   Richie Wilcox provides a detailed analysis and chronology of their intertwined personal and private relationship in his paper "Daniel MacIvor is Dying."

expression alone . . . produces intrinsic modifications in the subject who articulates it: it exonerates, redeems and purifies him, it unburdens him of his wrongs" (62). In turn, the confessions of Tish, Sam, and Judy, also serve as "memorial speeches for David . . . turn[ing] the spectators into participants at his imagined future funeral . . . [and become] a potent theatrical device to create community" (Gindt, "Queer" 132). Tish, Judy, and Sam's confessions also serve to exorcise feelings of guilt but simultaneously, by defining David only through his special relationship to each speaker, everyone makes "David's moment" entirely about themselves:

> TISH: We weren't allowed to talk at the dinner table—and then it turned out that in Girl Guides I learned the sign alphabet—which was one of the few things I managed to learn from Girl Guides other than don't even think about putting me in a beret. . . . So I taught David how to sign the alphabet and then at dinner we were able to communicate—you know very surreptitiously, just small, like this. Not whole phrases or sentences or whatever of course, just . . . like a code. . . . The point is about the connection that David and I have. (21–22)
>
> . . .
>
> SAM: And I mentioned that I could sign and David seemed very interested in that and so I taught him how to do it—he actually caught on to it pretty quickly. Um but it became this thing we had that—I mean it became our own kind of thing—our own little code . . . something private, something special, something . . . you know . . . nice . . . (30–31)
>
> . . .
>
> JUDY: Yeah we used to go out and stand there in the middle of the dance floor and it would just be noise noise noise and you couldn't talk, you couldn't think, you couldn't even feel anything, except the beat—and that was so cool. And we had this way of communicating in this weird language we invented—see I taught David how to do the sign language alphabet—I learned it from this girl this deaf

girl in this welding class I took—and I taught him . . . well I tried to teach him but he wasn't catching on too quick . . . or maybe I was just a bad teacher—but we worked out this other kinda way of doing it. . . . Yeah, anyway . . . but it was our special, private, personal thing. Ours. And that was so cool. (41–42)

All three family members actively engage in a rewriting of their identity, their story, and their history. As remembered and told to the reader, all three stories cannot have happened and still all be true and yet to each of the speakers the memories and the stories are fact. Upon a cursory glance it seems impossible that David allowed Tish, Sam, and Judy to each teach him sign language—this seems like an extraordinarily generous act from a rather self-absorbed individual. Richard's disclosure about the fate of the family heirloom reveals a David who cared first and foremost about himself and who had no use for sentimentality:

RICHARD: Look, there's no carpet. He sold it.

Pause.

Got ten thousand dollars for it.

Pause.

He went to Europe and spent the whole thing in two weeks.

Silence.

SAM: Whoa.
RICHARD: And he didn't even take me. (55)

It is difficult to believe that all three speakers are lying, and in fact, they aren't lying but rather they are remembering in a way that asserts, or possibly reasserts, their importance as David's favourite. In these self-rewritings disguised as confessions "MacIvor . . . directs our attention to the unreliable nature of memories and how easily they can be whitewashed or manipulated" (Gindt, "Queer" 132). It is probable that David shared some form of secret communication with each family member and in the moment of crisis that particular memory comes to define their relationship. The fact that all three speakers use similar, almost identical, words and phrases in describing both the importance of using this special language and keeping it a secret from others suggests that David was not an innocent player and probably saw this manipulation as a bit of a game. Perhaps this assessment of David is too harsh and the playful deceit he employs does allow the three characters to believe they are the closest and most important person to him and maybe, while he was alive, that was enough. Further, and regardless of anyone's actual relationship to David, what these confessions reveal is that David told a lot of lies—big and small, not only to all members of his family, but also to himself.[9]

Traditional literary confession, Radstone argues, "produces self-transformation" (36), further arguing that "at the heart of . . . the confession is a subject on his way, a subject 'becoming,' a subject characterized, indeed, by this forward movement towards becoming someone identical [and] yet markedly different from his/her former self" (37). Yet none of the family members is transformed, nor even moved towards a sense of greater self-awareness, by their confessions. It seems that the flawed confessions offered up by the family members suggest that each individual is attempting to assuage their guilt, anger, and hopelessness rather than seeking transformation or redemption. These confessions then, become less about a public ritual and "the production of truth" (Foucault 59) and more about an inward rewriting of autobiography, "the means through which the sufferings of the individual can be healed" (Radstone 44), or as Peter Axthelm has argued, "confession answers to a need to find *within* the self 'new principles of order and meaning'" (cited in

---

9   The most egregious of these lies are the ones he separately told Tish and Richard in order to exclude Richard from Tish and Sam's wedding. These two lies give further support to my analysis that David was both petulant and selfish and that in telling these lies, for whatever reason, David did irreparable harm to the relationships between his family, himself, and his partner.

Daniel MacIvor as David and Volker Bürger as the Student from *The Soldier Dreams*. Photo provided courtesy of Guntar Kravis.

Radstone 44). Understood in this way, the confessions are not so much failed confessions but rather necessary attempts to come to terms with, to appease, and console the self when faced with the unknown abyss of David's death.

The attempt by Tish, Sam, Judy, and Richard to construct meaning and memory from the few words that David utters proves as futile as the individual attempts to reconnect with him. Tish believes that "Ottawa" and "matchbook" are David's memories of her and Sam's wedding, but even Sam is skeptical of this interpretation:

DAVID (1): Ottawa.
NURSE: Ottawa?
RICHARD: Ottawa right Ottawa.
SAM: Ottawa.
JUDY: *(TO NURSE.)* He's saying that a lot.
TISH: He's remembering our wedding.
RICHARD: Your wedding?
SAM: Did something special happen at our wedding? (14)

Repeatedly, these random words, which serve as David's final moments and should clearly belong to him, are continually reclaimed and rewritten by others. In the end, as Martin Denton suggests, "all the 'moments for David' are actually about the others":

DAVID (1): Matchbook.
TISH: Matchbook. *(Pause.)* Oh my God!
SAM: What?
TISH: He's remembering those little matchbooks we had made up for our wedding.
SAM: Really?
TISH: Well sure.
SAM: Do you really think our wedding was that important to him?

Silence. (32)

Tish's belief, perhaps even insistence, that David is remembering the most important day in her life echoes Bob's world of "perfect pretend." Tish's narcissism reveals "a world in which the reality of others cannot be perceived" (Radstone 47), but that being said, no one else is any closer to understanding David's experience. None can imagine a world without David in it but none of them, especially Richard, can really imagine a world with David in it either. What the family members can imagine is a life, their life and their life with David, reimagined as "the perfect pretend"; " 'Cause that wasn't real—see it was pretend" (*See Bob Run* 23).

Richard and David do not discuss their open relationship:

But see we never talked about it, it was just this unspoken under-standing—and I wonder why we didn't talk about it—but I never wanted to talk about it—and I mean David never brought it up and I mean I think about all that, about David. (28–29)

Richard is now more able to articulate what he wasn't able to while David was living: to discuss their relationship is to acknowledge that the relationship is anything but perfect. David's manipulation of Richard and Tish around the wedding (ensuring that Richard was excluded from the event), his treatment of Richard after selling the carpet, and his generally loutish treatment of Richard at the birthday party all indicate that the relationship was far from perfect. Richard's brief "confession" to Sam is Richard's first movement towards unwriting the history that he and David had constructed, and as the play progresses he becomes aware that the reason he and David avoided discussing their unhappy and at times dysfunctional relationship was to preserve the perfect pretend world they had constructed. Unlike the rest of the family, Richard becomes increasingly self-aware about the necessary impossibility and the great personal cost of rewriting the past and the self in order to maintain the charade of the perfect pretend:

RICHARD: I would like to take this moment for David . . .

Silence.

RICHARD clears his throat.

Silence.

Um.

RICHARD does not cry. (55)

The perfect pretend of the play extends beyond David's deathbed, as is evidenced by Tish and Judy's cousins, who send David lottery tickets in his get-well card and in the meaningless tasks the family occupies themselves with. As mentioned, MacIvor wrote *The Soldier Dreams* at a time when he was experiencing intense public and private grief, uncertainty, and fear. The play suggests that the AIDS crisis has witnessed far too many families doing everything they can to rewrite *a* history and maintain the illusion of the world of perfect pretend. The play implicates, but does not condemn, audiences in this general practice and MacIvor makes clear that the living remember the dead by rewriting history, by "forgetting the negative and grasping at the shiniest moments, the ones that make *them* feel good" (Segneri).

At the centre of all this activity lies the only person who can understand and articulate those memories, and that is David. Gindt argues that David resists these "attempts [by his family] to take control of his memories, past and legacy by assigning their own version of events onto his life and personality" (Gindt, "Queer" 133) and does so by actively participating in reanimating and reclaiming the memories of his dying self. In a particularly erotic moment, David is once again exposed to sign language, but this time the language is queered and owned entirely by him:

STUDENT: You have nice hands. You should speak with them.
DAVID: Speak?
STUDENT: I know the alphabet letters of hands. Shall I teach you.

Pause.

DAVID: Sure.
. . .
STUDENT: You are a fast learner.
DAVID: I'm good with my hands.
STUDENT: Oh, so you're the best man with his hands. (45)

In their exploration of the struggle around gay memory, Christopher Castiglia and Christopher Reed argue that "(queer) memory is an act of resistance" (11): as long as one can remember one can fight. David fights his premature death, the heteronormalization of his life,[10] and the power struggles

---

10   David and Richard's home is overrun by David's family, which upsets the homosocial/
normative world they shared. Richard is appalled when Tish tries to rewrite her wedding
onto David's memory and own it for herself, and as the play progresses Richard is moved
further and further from the narrative. Dirk Gindt suggests the possibility that David actually learned the sign language from the student and subsequently taught it to the family
after he was infected ("Queer" 132).

(the war) of his family by reliving his past and inhabiting his memories. Inevitably, with David's death this fight, this war, is lost and his active rewriting of his past is rewritten back into the heteronormative perfect pretend of the family. David, it seems, is no more successful at rewriting himself than Tish, Judy, or Sam are; to varying degrees, all lack the self-awareness that makes the manipulation of memory unnecessary.

Ironically, the play makes clear the dangers, or at least the impossible challenges, of autobiography, the rewriting of self, and, perhaps, the very act of memory:

> STUDENT: The water is so still.
> DAVID: The lights are beautiful.
> STUDENT: Yes. More so in the water. Of their reflection. This is the difference between reality and a memory. The reflection is the memory of the light. The memory is always more wonderful. (27)

So it is possible to question even what the dying David is seeing as the scene plays out in his memory: is he seeing the lights or their reflection? Is David reliving past events as lived or is he also reinventing and rewriting his perfect pretend, simultaneously dreaming into existence and holding onto a reimagined perfect past before AIDS? Gindt also plays with this *nostalgic* moment, arguing "we should, however, not assume that the ghost of the dreaming David is telling the truth; in fact, his recollections of the German Student might be equally idealized or false—yet, again, the unreliability of these memories should not divert us from their significance" ("Queer" 133). Near the end of the play, the student shifts from David's dream world into the "real" world, and when probed about his identity he responds, "I am nothing" (57). Nothing in this world? Nothing to these people? Or Nothing? Nothing because if David is now dead and the student lived only as a refracted memory then he would die again with David? Nothing because the memory of Ottawa is simply the romantic fantasy of a dying man? There is no answer but the German student's response is a lie. Whatever he is, he is central to David's ability to rewrite and remember as David desired. Tish remarks, "After college he decided he didn't like pictures[11]—he said he wanted to remember things just as they were in his memory" (53). Doing so enables David to re-arrange the past and to rewrite his autobiographical self, in life *and* in death as *he* wishes. The student cautions David, "Even when the soldier dreams the war goes on" (35), and as his family members feverishly construct, organize, and rewrite their memories onto David, David must do the same in order to survive the war and save himself.

The Soldier Dreams is set in a liminal space, "living between what was and will be" (Friedlander), but it does not provide an explanation nor a road map for how to successfully navigate the movement between these two states. MacIvor challenges understandings of memory, of autobiography, and of con-fession, suggesting that none of them are fixed, stable, or understandable, but that each of us has the capacity to use them in extraordinarily selfish ways. Seemingly insignificant moments and events resonate throughout life in ways and are inscribed with meaning impossible to decipher or comprehend. In the end, MacIvor reminds us that, unable to know ourselves, let alone our family, our lovers, our friends, we are alone and even David, the favourite son, passes away unnoticed. At the end of the play the family members seem more alone than ever; unable to comfort each other they are further away from each other than ever and quietly leave the stage. The final image of the play is David, also alone, as he "*spins and spins until it is as if he flies into the air and disappears*" (61), and in a bittersweet moment MacIvor finds hope: "The Buddhists say that the perfect way to view life is through tears, tears brought on by the beauty of all things and the knowledge that all this beauty is temporary. And in that is a kind of loneliness, but we can take great solace in the fact that we are all alone together" ("The Heart of the Actor" ix).

---

11   When Judy hears Tish and Richard talk about David's rejection of all things photo-graphic she replies, "I didn't know that." This seems extremely strange coming from the sister who claims to have known David so well. It also suggests a deeper understanding, if not relationship, between Tish, Richard, and David.

"HERE'S TO SHUTTING UP": LESSONS OF THE MU-KOAN IN *A BEAUTIFUL VIEW*

JENN STEPHENSON

"Some people say when you die you go to heaven, some people say when you die you go to hell, I say when you die you go to the theatre" ("Overview" 2). This quote from playwright Daniel MacIvor graces the top of one of the pages in the promotional package for the recent Volcano/BeMe Theatre production of *A Beautiful View*.[1] It is unclear who exactly MacIvor is condemning to theatrical limbo; the audience perhaps? Regardless of whether or not this is indeed to be our collective fate, the purgatorial blankness of an empty stage under the lights and surrounded by spectral witnesses is not an uncommon stopping place for a number of MacIvor characters—ghostly storytellers who find solace and redemption in the reperformance of their life stories. If the primary aim of autobiography is to harness the potentially transformative power of reperforming one's past to imagine new identities and engender new lived futures (Heddon; Stephenson, *Performing*), what is the impulse for the dead to take up the mantle of autothanatography?

Grateful appreciation is owed to Ross Manson, Meredith Potter, and AJ Laflamme for most generously sharing private archival resources pertaining to the Volcano/BeMe production.

1   This recent production of *A Beautiful View* directed by Ross Manson and featuring Amy Rutherford as L and Becky Johnson as M was co-produced by BeMe Theatre of Munich, Germany, and Canada's Volcano Theatre. Performances in Munich ran from 9–27 October 2012. The production was remounted at Factory Theatre in Toronto on 26 February 2014. The Toronto run was followed by an Ontario tour in March 2014, including performances in Kingston, Milton, Burlington, St. Catharines, and North Bay. Lighting design was by Rebecca Picherack, sound design by Michael Laird, and no set designer was credited. This is the production being discussed here.

In MacIvor's metatheatrical duet *In On It* (2001) only one of the two performers is a ghost. Invoking the near-divine power of a playwright to create worlds, Brian conjures his lover Brad who died in a car crash with a fateful blue Mercedes. Together they invent an identity and biography for the Mercedes's driver, a terminally ill man named Ray. By enacting interlaced scenes from Ray's life post-diagnosis and from the pair's romantic history, Brian with Brad's assistance strives to deflect the crash. Attempting to shift performative power from the fictional realm of their play to the superior actual-world, Brian as playwright tries to separate the two intersecting storylines and write a new ending. Through the spiralling, iterating pattern of the play, Brian confronts the inherent limitations of performative power outside fictional worlds and learns to accept his loss. *In On It* documents a recurring pattern of emptiness, tracing the experience of the negative spaces like the abandoned grey wool jacket that testify to loss. The play is itself in this respect an act of mourning. Although Brad participates as a co-creator of this autothanatographical play-within-a-play, the burden and benefit of autobiography falls primarily to the still-living Brian. He is the one who has been transformed by his journey through this recursive performance. In *A Beautiful View* (2006), which resonates as the female yin to the male yang of *In On It*, the two characters, equivocally named "L" and "M," are both dead, victims of a campground bear mauling. Unlike Brian and Brad who have rented the theatre and printed posters for the event, L and M are reluctant performers, having arrived on stage perhaps at the behest of unknown forces. Here, however, rather than leverage the performative power of autobiography to change the past, L and M apply various strategies to escape the stifling bounds of performativity altogether, to nullify the citational force of linguistic identity creation. From the performatively rich locale of the theatre, they try to open up a rift to an impossible space that resides outside the flow of world-creating discourse, a space where they can be truly no thing.

Like *In On It*, *A Beautiful View* retrospectively reframes the mutual history of its protagonists in a play-within as their reperformance of key episodes from their relationship are intercut with the present-tense work of staging those scenes and self-aware commentary to the audience regarding the play in progress. Also in a similar fashion to *In On It*, the audience's perception that they are witness to a supernatural encounter with the dead is not a given from the outset but emerges in hints and fragments as we go. In the first of the revisited moments, L and M initially meet in a camping supply store. M crawls out of a floor-model tent and L mistakenly thinks that she works there. This is the first of a series of erring assumptions the two each make about the other. Discovering a mutual sexual attraction, L invites M for a drink. Each woman, who thinks of herself as straight, concludes the other one is a lesbian. On the morning after, M flees, claiming that she couldn't "go getting bisexual on myself . . . I do not have the constitution for it" (220). Time passes and they meet each other again. Disentangling themselves from the co-constituting idea that they are both lesbians, they become devoted best friends. In this second part of their history, the performed inset scenes explore the quality of their intense connection, not as lovers but undoubtedly as a pair of some kind. After several years, L observes wistfully: "We're like a couple aren't we." M deflects this expectant statement with a joke: "A couple of what?" (236). The central crisis of their relationship unfolds at a Halloween house party where M discovers L in an upstairs room having sex with another woman, Sasha. M is devastated: "And I maintain that if she thought about me for one second, just one second, it wouldn't have happened." L: "Why are you so upset? Because it was Sasha?" M: "Because it was you" (237). After some period of coolness, L attempts to reconcile and the two meet at a campground. That night, M hears a noise near her tent and fear brings her to L's tent. Forced together, they take small steps towards reconciliation. When they both hear a noise, they decide to seek safety at the camp office. This episode ends with the stage direction "*Blackout. The bear growls ferociously*," delivering them full circle to the purgatory of the theatre stage.

In the context of their current liminal situation, the word "nothing" and the repeated mantra "nothing is enough"[2] accrue increasing significance

---

2   This mantra became significant to da da kamera, MacIvor's now-defunct company, as they had it printed on T-shirts, which made it a branded slogan for the show and collective.

throughout the play both in the present of the show and in their re-enact-
ments. On the night of their mutual seduction, M notices the phrase on L's
fridge.

> L: So you like "nothing is enough?"
> M: Yeah. Do you mean it in the good way or in the bad way.
> L: The good way definitely. (217)

Later, when L attempts a reconciliation with the emotionally wounded M, L
says: "Nothing is enough. *(A moment.)* Actually I had always thought of it the
bad way. Nothing will ever do. I like it better the other way. Upon considering
it. I like it better your way. Nothing is sufficient" (240). The original source
of this statement is the ancient Greek philosopher Epicurus, who declared,
"Nothing is enough for the man to whom enough is too little," expanding
the ambiguous sentence stem to read in the "bad way:" one is never satisfied
even when given everything. By contrast, the "good way" suggests that one
can be happy with nothing at all. Significantly, the main attention devoted to
L and M's juvenile philosophizing is not in the application of its intents but in
worrying at the undecidable ambiguity of its grammar. Focus is not on actual
material satisfaction but on the bifocal grammatical structure of the phrase,
which carries two concurrent and opposite meanings.

This paradoxical bivalent pattern constitutes a central feature of Zen
Buddhist practice[3] as evidenced in the koan called "Joshu's Dog." This famous
koan holds a primary place in Zen teaching, being the first koan case of *The
Gateless Gate*,[4] a thirteenth-century collection composed by Wumen Huikai
(1183–1260), and often marking the beginning of training. In the puzzling

---

3   MacIvor is an active practitioner of Shambhala Buddhism. On the blog site *nomorepotlucks*, MacIvor discusses how the Buddhist understanding of ego affects his theatre
work (Sasha).

4   The translation I am using by Robert Aitken is titled *The Gateless Barrier*, but *The
Gateless Gate* is also a very common translation for the title of this collection of koans. I
prefer *The Gateless Gate* because of its clearer articulation of the ambiguity on the word
gate as either a passageway or a barrier.

parable, a monk asks the revered master Joshu, "Has a dog Buddha-nature or not?" Joshu responds "MU" (Aitken 7). In ordinary parlance, "mu" is literally translated as "no," but it also carries the more profound connotations of nothing, non-existence, non-being, or that which is impossible (Keown). The answer to the koan is both yes and no, and also "not applicable." As both answers are correct and incorrect, attention is to be directed back to the question. In this vein, mu has been popularly translated as "unask the question" (Hofstadter 241). Mu, then, is variously nothing, no thing, and an instruction to reject the premise of the original problem posed.

With this pattern as a guide, I propose here to apply this understanding of mu—no/thing—to the desire of L and M in *A Beautiful View* to opt out of autobiographical performativity, to unask the question that troubles them: "A couple of what?" Although the production in my city (Kingston) was heavily marketed to the LGBT community, the problem of the play is not narrowly about how to construct lesbian identity or the public acceptance of such an identity marker. It is not a coming-out play. (Coming out is, of course, a performative par excellence.) The question with which L and M struggle concerns the general construction of identity, including sexuality certainly. But more than this, the play asks, "Who am I in relation to you?" To illustrate how the play both answers and defies this question through "unasking," I will first outline the persistent misfires by L and M to performatively co-constitute the other through autobiographical performance. Second, I will trace through the women's play-within the impulse of mu, the desire for no thing, for finding a way to reject the autobiographical project of performative self-fashioning altogether. Finally, I will show that L and M do impossibly break free of performative delineation, returning to an Edenic state, and that the murderous bear is not an arbitrary and tragic force but an incarnation of their transcendent release.

In our post-structural context, it is commonly understood that identities are not fundamentally biological and binary. Nominative categories like gender, race, sexuality, and disability are not autonomously pre-given; they are brought into being by a series of citational acts. Identity is a performative construct, iteratively created through everyday repetition, and as such is variable, malleable, and fluid. And yet, even with the rejection of innate fixed identity, the possibilities are not infinite. There are numerous ways for a performative utterance to fail. As J.L. Austin notes, for a performative speech act to be felicitous, that is, for it to be effectual, it must conform to certain rules, spoken using the right formula by the right person in the right context (15). Picking up this idea then of the "rightness" of these conventional and ritualized situations, Jacques Derrida ("Signature") secures the efficacy of the performative to its citationality. The parasitical nature of speech acts, which Austin initially rejects as invalid, turns out to be in fact an essential quality of its success. "Could a performative utterance succeed if its formulation did not repeat a 'coded' or iterable utterance, or in other words, if the formula I pronounce to open a meeting, launch a ship or consecrate a marriage were not identifiable as *conforming* with an iterable model, if it were not identifiable in some way as a 'citation'?" ("Signature" 18). The underpinning mechanism of citationality that makes the performative felicitous also limits its power. Noting with regard to the performance of gender, Judith Butler writes,

> That is not to say that any and all gendered possibilities are open, but the boundaries of analysis suggest the limits of a discursively condi-tioned experience. These limits are always set within the terms of a hegemonic cultural discourse. . . . Constraint is thus built into what that language constitutes as the imaginable domain of gender. (13)

As Butler stipulates for gender, the same constraints apply to any kind of per-formative identity position. I am rehearsing these well-established theoretical underpinnings here to tease out three key points in relation to the way *A Beautiful View*'s L and M engage with the problem of performing identity. One, identity arises only through performance. Two, the performance of identity is only efficacious by citation in accordance with hegemonic norms. Three, performative citationality is built on a void. As Derrida famously notes, "Il n'y a pas de hors-texte" (*Of Grammatology* 158). There is nothing outside of discourse. Performative constructions float free of the physical world and so are mapped onto empty spaces. As discursive constructions lacking signifieds, performatives refer to nothing, being structured solely in relation to other performative statements.

As characters sentenced to theatrical labour in MacIvor's performative purgatory, L and M frequently fail to execute successful performatives and by doing so expose the emptiness beneath the discursive surface. To begin, L and M, in contravention of the primary Adamic performative, don't even have names.[5] The published script recommends that the actresses choose their own names;[6] however, the names are never mentioned in the play. They are profoundly anonymous. Beyond the performative vacancy of their personal labels, L and M also tell lies about themselves, creating multiple free-floating identities. Neither woman has a malicious intent to deceive, but both tell white lies to buoy up their own social status and perhaps to please the other one. M claims to be the drummer in an all-girl ukulele-playing '80s cover band; L says she is a bartender at the airport. When they meet accidentally a second time at a club watching a live band, M backs awkwardly into a social lie, claiming to know more about the ins and outs of the romantic status of the band's drummer Sasha than she actually does (which is nothing at all). This leads to a third meeting when M treks out to the airport to undo her lie. She discovers that L is not a bartender but is in fact only the hostess and in a flood of confession also admits that she doesn't have a band. As L says, "Well, at least we've established that we're both liars." M responds, "I like to think of it as wishful thinking" (214). These inconsistent performatives arise out of nervousness, founded on a passive desire to fulfill the other one's assumptions by agreeing to the biography created by other. For example, L's

---

5   In his essay "Social Theory and Politics of Identity," Craig Calhoun writes, "We know of no people without names, no languages or cultures in which some manner of distinctions between self and other, we and they, are not made" (9).

6   In the original 2006 production, actors Tracy Wright and Caroline Gillis chose Liz and Mitch respectively. These are the names that are published in the *I Still Love You* anthology. In the 2012/2014 Munich-Toronto production, the actors significantly did not choose names. They are indicated in the prompt script only as L and M. In the show programs, they are credited simply as "Starring Amy Rutherford and Becky Johnson," cleverly avoiding any naming at all.

claim to be a bartender is prompted by M's question about her work at the bar. "Bartender?" L's agreement, "Yeah," spills out in spite of herself (208). As M says, this is the product of wishful thinking. It is aspirational, bringing into being, even if just provisionally, someone I want to be—someone I think you imagine me to be. Fanciful autobiography is born out of flawed biography. For L and M engaged in the creation of self, the processes and problems of their co-constitutive relationship displace any deference to an objective referential truth. Their attempts to paper over the void actually serve to expose the underlying precariousness of the autobiographical project.

Both women make "I am" statements where the characteristics of the actual-world (world^a) subject are not equal to the "fictional character" (resident in world^b) created via these self-narrating performances.[7] This misalignment between these two constructions triggers a failure of the autobiographical pact. Philippe Lejeune, in an attempt to differentiate autobiography from novelistic first-person narration outlines the principles of the contractual agreement between author and reader at the heart of autobiography (13). The core this pact declares, "In order for there to be autobiography, the author, the narrator, and the protagonist must be identical" (5). In a work of autobiography, these three ontologically distinct subject positions are co-joined by the phoneme "I," each one a version of the same historically verifiable person. As Lejeune stresses, "The place assigned to this name [the author] is essential: it is linked, by a social convention, to the pledge of responsibility of a real person . . . But his existence is beyond question: exceptions and breaches of trust serve only to emphasize the general credence accorded this type of social contract" (11). Autobiography is a truth-based genre, founded on this equivalency.

---

7   This is a system of notation that I have developed for describing the relative and equivalent ontology of metatheatrical frames. World^a refers to the actual world, the so-called real world inhabited by you and me and the play as an event. World^b, accordingly, is the first constructed fictional world. This is the world occupied by the characters of the play. Additional subsequent inset worlds can be denoted by world^c, world^d, and so on. Here, however, for clarity, I am eliding world^a and taking L and M to be "real" relative to their performed "show" selves.

In the context of theatre in general, and in the nested performance-within of *A Beautiful View* in particular, the contractual compulsion to actual-world truth is significantly diluted since neither L nor M exists independently as a historically verifiable person. Both are, even at their "highest" ontological level, still only constructions of discourse, birthed in MacIvor's text. What this means for the autobiographical pact is that their lies, rather than effecting a hard binary break between truth and not-truth, open up the "mu" pattern of bistable perception.[8] Their self-storying statements are concurrently both true and not true. L is a bartender *and* a hostess. M is a drummer *and* she is not a drummer. Both identities are in equal circulation, thinly masking the void beneath. Like the koan of Joshu's dog, the ultimate effect is to direct contemplation to the original question, not "Who or what am I?" but "How am I?" and more challengingly, "Can I not be?"

The opposing correlative to performative lying is misreading. Whereas lying is a failure of autobiography (what Susanna Egan delightfully calls "frautobiography" (46)), misrecognition is a kind of failed biography, the performative miswriting of the life story of another. When they first meet in the camping-supply store, L assumes M is an employee. Considering that M has just climbed out of the display tent, this seems like a reasonable conclusion; wrong but reasonable. A more extended meditation on the workings of how identity is constructed "correctly" or "incorrectly" through outside perception is presented in the scene when L and M are getting ready for a Halloween party. Their central worry is that other guests will misinterpret their costumes and "not know who I am." Outfitted in a plain man's shirt and tie, L chooses to dress as Norman Jones, a previously mentioned mutual acquaintance. (It is not clear what makes him distinctive or why she chooses

---

8   "Occasionally our sensory systems do fail to reach a single interpretation for a given input. Sometimes, our percepts fluctuate between two distinct interpretations or states, although more than two interpretations are also possible. This is called *bistable* (or multistable for more than two states) *perception*. The perceptual alternations are spontaneous and stochastic, and the alternating percepts are often mutually exclusive" (He). Well-known examples of visual objects that easily trigger bistable perception are the Necker cube and the famous two faces/vase illusion.

him to impersonate.) When they arrive at the party, L is fretful that the people at the party don't get it: "Not everybody knows Norman so when people ask me who I'm supposed to be most people think it's just a dumb costume. So I'm looking for Norman" (236). Those partygoing readers who don't know the world[a] Norman cannot connect the world[b] performance L-as-Norman to its world[a] referent, opening up alternate and unwanted identities. In her straw hat with attached ginger braids, M has the same concern that no one will know she's Anne of Green Gables. L here embodies the ignorant reader, insisting that she doesn't know the original and confuses M-as-Anne with Orphan Annie and Pippi Longstocking. L cannot align world[b] with world[a] again because she lacks knowledge of the world[a] original. In contrast to L's experience and encouragingly for M, people at the party do make the connection successfully; she is Anne. Positive or negative outcomes aside, this episode works to underscore the anxious necessity of social corroboration for felicitous performative generation. What other people think is absolutely critical but is also freighted with the fecund potential for multiplicity in misreading.

The most significant misreading in *A Beautiful View* is the mutual error by L and M in assuming that the other one is lesbian, a misreading that opens the seductive space for the genesis of their relationship. By "passing" as lesbian, L and M each cross the usual borders marking sexual divisions, allowing them to mix. Sara Ahmed notes, "Passing . . . allows a mobility precisely through not being locatable as an object that meets the gaze of the subject; passing . . . passes through the limits of representation and intentionality . . . so while passing unfixes by the impossibility of naming the difference, it also fixes" (95). Ahmed is talking about race, about passing for black or passing for white and the stakes of passing in highly regulated, hierarchical situations, but the same general principles can be applied to sexual orientation. Passing is not identity formation; passing is not becoming. Intentional or accidental misreading of status destabilizes the firm boundaries of a given identity position: What is a lesbian? How do I know? But simultaneously the act of passing also marks the boundaries of that fixity: "While identity may be dislodged through the act of theft and hence become subject to reiteration it also determines the economics of passing, that which it takes for granted as the measure of desire" (Ahmed 98). Like the other examples of performative instability and multiplicity above, passing also manifests as a both/neither/mu bistable phenomenon, which while admitting two exclusive answers, demands active consideration of the parameters of how identity is policed for perception in the first place.

Later, having shed their imaginatively imposed identities—"Have you switched over entirely?" "To what?" "Men." "I never left. Well I mean there was you." "Do you only sleep with other lesbians?" "I'm not a lesbian." *A moment. They consider this.* "That's funny." "Or sad." (222)—L and M are left with their relationship uncategorized. This problem of being innominate casts their relationship adrift. Although they are happy together, the lack of appellation, while freeing, also leaves them vulnerable and incomplete. Without knowing what they are, they cannot behave accordingly, protected by the security of social forms and expectations. Thinking about autobiographical imposture, Egan observes that "sexuality, ethnicity, and abuse involve their own secrets, their own taboos and therefore arouse keen interest, making fair game for the imposter with a finger on the pulse of public concerns" (2). And so, "What many impostures achieve by their mis-taking of 'identity' is renewed clarification of what particular identities mean in the world around them, what their value is, how they are read, whether they are individual, communal or national" (Egan 10). In the case of *A Beautiful View*, I would extend this line of thinking even further. Beyond the clarification of what particular identities mean, the performative struggles in MacIvor's play address the problems of fitting into preconstructed, preapproved performative identity slots, rebelliously wondering if we can just "not do" gender, disability, race, sexuality at all.[9]

---

9 I am struck by the evolving acronym for individuals who are non-heterosexual or non-cisgender from the L and G of PFLAG (Parents, Friends, and Family of Lesbians and Gays) founded in 1972 to LGBT (1990s), which is itself an adaptation of the earlier LGB of the 1980s. The recent 2014 WorldPride event in Toronto used the acronym LGBTTIQQ2SA—Lesbian, Gay, Bisexual, Transsexual, Transgender, Intersex, Queer, Questioning, 2-Spirited, and Allies—to describe its constituent communities ("About WorldPride 2014"). The perennially expanding length and diversity of these named

L's final address to the audience points to the pair's problem with naming and makes a plea for an alternative.

> I guess finally for me it's—I mean she says teach your kids to play guitar—I'd say, if I had to say something—and since I can, I'd have to say stop naming things. "I am a," "We are a," "She is a." If we could only let it be what it is and be okay with that. "A friendship." "A love affair." "A soulmate." These are just names so other people can feel comfortable. It's not about other people. Or maybe . . . I guess for me it was about her, at this point anyway. (241)

The failure of L and M to adopt a felicitous, culturally approved identity—"We are a couple." "A couple of what?"—fosters the fatal uncertainty that leads to L's tryst with Sasha and M's betrayed hurt. For this unique pair, existing identity descriptions don't fit. For their uniqueness there is no pre-existing vocabulary. To be "not that" is one kind of namelessness—a negative naming; however, L and M in their rejection of traditional naming seek a different kind of namelessness, to be "no thing at all." It is the essential hollowness subsisting discourse identified by Derrida that they wish to fall into.

In some late night philosophizing, L declares,

> And the silence is there, underneath all the blah-de-blah. But nobody can hear it. Silence is God. Silence is God saying "Shhh." But nobody can hear it. And even if they could hear it they'd be too busy listening for something to hear it. We'll never hear anything until we shut up and stop listening for something so hard we can't hear it . . . Here's to shutting up. (218)

The silence she advocates for is a true silence; the silence that no one can hear. This silence underneath the blah-de-blah of performative discourse rests

---

communities indicates a zeitgeist in popular desire for more and more specific and inclusive naming but also begs the question at what point can we eschew naming altogether?

not in "letting it be" characterized by the silence we are listening hard for, but rather in non-being, the silence of just shutting up. In an interview Robert Pirsig, author of the cult classic *Zen and the Art of Motorcycle Maintenance*, observes, "It is not good to talk about Zen because Zen is nothingness . . . If you talk about it, you are always lying, and if you don't talk about it, no one knows it is there" (qtd. in Tim Adams). The failures of performative discourse, discussed above, characterized primarily by lying and misreading, constitute one way of forfeiting the silence. This is L's blah-de-blah. The other mistaken path is through false silences, through being too busy listening to hear.

Mapping the landscape of the time that passes over their years together, M recounts that at one point L persuaded her to go to therapy, both attending the same therapist. "And he had this style. This don't say anything style. Which was kind of driving us both nuts" (224). Frustrated, the two concocted a mischievous plot to see if they could make him speak. At their separate sessions, L would never speak, sitting in total silence, and M would yap ceaselessly for the whole time. After many months, they encountered the therapist in a restaurant.

> M: And that was something, but the really something was when he
> saw us. Her and me, the silent one and the mouth, sitting together.
> L: *(off)* Flipped a nut.
> M: They had to lock him up.
> L: He took a break.
> M: He quit.
> L: He opened up a B and B.
> M: And there we were, suddenly out of therapy. (225)

The mu silence, the silence of "just shutting up," is something they desire, but also as evidenced by their choice to tell this anecdote, is something they fear. The impulse to fill silence with blah-de-blah is materially embodied in the performance of *A Beautiful View* by an artificial fig tree. M brings on the prop ficus plant in the set-up for scene four, the seduction scene in L's apartment. Apart from two pillows on the floor and a stuffed bear, this is the only indicator of the setting. After commenting on the phrase "nothing is enough" on the fridge, M takes note of the ficus: "That's one sick fig."[10] "*L shrugs. (finding the idea delightful)* Should we not talk? *L shrugs. M is silent. She finds it weird and delightful. The silence reaches another level. And another. The women are about to kiss*" (218–19). Before they actually kiss, M stands up quickly, the lights shift back to the frame state, and she defends her choice to include the plant in the scene. What is important to her is "what it represents" (219). She claims that her random comment on the fig is not at all significant: "That's just what came out, it was something to say . . . Sometimes we're just looking for something to say. And I just think that's funny" (219). M's interruption of the silence crosses two theatrical worlds. Her first comment—"That's one sick fig"—skittishly invades the silence blossoming between the two women in L's apartment. Her second comment justifying her first comment cuts off the moment of the kiss in the relived performance of the scene. What the fig tree represents then is both the existence of and M's fear of that deepening silence.

In addition to sharing a birthday and an inability to swim, L and M share a terrifying fear of bears: "If fear had four legs it would be a bear" (216). In the end, it is a bear that kills the two women, manifesting their competing desire for and fear of the performative silence of non-being. M's response to L's metaphor of four-legged fear is to call her a nerd. L shoots back: "Nerd? Prophet" (216). Indeed L channels the performative logic of prophecy—a propulsive teleology that is especially potent in fiction. If you say it, it will happen. Perhaps not in the way you expect, but it does happen. L and M summon the bear in their very first meeting, bonding over a shared recounting of the recent news of a pair of foolish campers who lured a bear with peanut butter on their

---

10   The sick fig in L's apartment finds a parallel in the New Testament account in the gospels of Mark (New International Version 11:12–14 and 11:20–25) and Matthew (21:18–22) of Jesus's cursing of the fig tree. Seeing a barren fig tree on the side of the road, Jesus cursed it, saying, "May no one ever eat fruit from you again." At this, the tree immediately withered. Jesus explained that this exemplified the power of prayer. What you say with full belief in your heart will actually come to pass. In this context, the sick fig might be seen as an example of performative power.

hands, only to be mauled and eaten (208). Desire and fear are two sides of the same coin, marrying things we want to things we don't want. In the beginning, L and M are pulled together by desire, and in the end "it was fear that brought us back together" (241). The answer "MU" is the bear, containing the opposing drives of fear and desire, and unasking the question about what it is that they are together. Mu is, in Zen practice, a barrier but also a gateway to insight, a path to transcending the everyday. Mumon Yamada's commentary on the koan of Joshu's dog in *The Gateless Gate* elucidates this quality of mu. "Enlightenment always comes after the road of thinking is blocked . . . This one word, Mu, is it. This is the barrier of Zen . . . When you enter this Mu and there is no discontinuation, your attainment will be as a candle burning and illuminating the whole universe" (Aitken 7). The bear is the gate, read bivalently as opening and barrier, to the bright and beautiful view.

For L, bears are impractical but inevitable. In one of her long addresses to the audience she explains,

> Feelings develop because needs aren't met. Feelings are not practical . . . I've always been drawn to practical things. Like camping. Camping is very practical. How you pick a site, the best time to arrive, planning meals, organizing hikes. You rise with the sun you sleep with the moon. All very practical. Of course there are the odd impractical things like mosquitos or poison ivy. Or bears. Especially bears . . . Feelings are like bears. (214–15)

The result of this syllogism is that bears develop because needs aren't being met. Needs are defined concretely by L, reflecting on her preternaturally practical seven-year-old self who knew the phone numbers for Chickees Ribs and Wings (food), Goldman Locksmiths (shelter), and Yellow Cab (transportation) (215). When she loses M, she discovers another need.

> L: Why didn't you say anything?
> M: What did you want me to say?
> L: Whatever you were thinking?

M: What did you want me to think?

L: I wonder if she's lonely. (240)

Completing the pair, not being alone, is another practical need. This same idea is expressed in M's breakup song, written for the production by Tucker Finn of the Jane Waynes. "If I had to gamble my heart on one person / I know where I'd lay down my cash / Because you're the one in my only / The two in my gether / and if there is such a thing / you're the four in my ever" (238).[11] The chorus of the song makes nonsense of the words "one and only," "together," and "forever," breaking them into halves, duplicating the patterned need for wholeness in both form and content.

Ambient noises specific to the historical settings—the Outdoor Outfitters store, a dance club, the airport bar, a forested campground at night—broadcast from a portable boom box—underscore each of the inset scenes. As mimetic representations, these sounds function in the same manner as performative naming, using audio tracks to semiotically manufacture the physical site. This is another instance of citational blah-de-blah discursively masking the referential void. The bear, however, lives in the silence, always there, like the silence under the blah-de-blah. In the Volcano/BeMe Theatre production, audio tracks of pink noise were used in conjunction with references to the bear and also layered under the growling, wind-rushing sound used to represent the bear. A static low hissing, pink noise is produced by filtering white noise containing all frequencies audible to humans.[12] It sounds like crashing waves or the sound of your own blood in your ears when you block your ears with your fingers. (Try it.) Whereas white noise has equal power at all frequencies,

---

11 There is a typo here in the published script which rationalizes the nonsensical line "The two in my gether" to "The two in my ever;" however, this obviates the verbal play of two/together. The Toronto prompt script contains the correct lyric.

12 "Pink noise or $1/f$ noise (sometimes also called flicker noise) is a signal or process with a frequency spectrum such that the power spectral density (energy or power per Hz) is inversely proportional to the frequency of the signal. In pink noise, each octave (halving/doubling in frequency) carries an equal amount of noise power. The name arises from the pink appearance of visible light within this power spectrum" ("Pink Noise").

in the case of pink noise, power decreases as frequency increases. Pink noise is ubiquitous in nature. The mathematical pattern emitted is found in heart-beats, neural activity, and the statistics of DNA sequences ("Pink Noise"). In Manson's *A Beautiful View*, pink noise is used, I suggest, as a special kind of noise/silence representing the desirable state L describes as "God saying 'Shhh'" and the silence we hear when we "just shut up." The production be-gins with just the boom box on stage emitting a steady stream of pink noise, it shuts off with the first cue and we are plunged abruptly into blackout with the sounds of the bear and the women screaming. The bear and screaming sound cue is repeated again later as part of the bear attack sequence, but also significantly immediately after M's line explaining why she was so upset find-ing L with Sasha: "Because it was you" (237).[13] Two other incidences of pink noise are associated with desire rather than fear. Notably one of these fills the deep silence from "Should we not talk?" to just before the interrupted kiss.[14] The conflation of the sound of pink noise, the immanence of the bear, and the silence of shutting up work to open up a space between fear and desire, an impossible space exempt from the necessity of performative speech. As Kwame Anthony Appiah writes in *The Ethics of Identity*:

> A tree, whatever the circumstances, does not become a legume, a vine, or a cow. The reasonable middle view is that constructing identi-ty is a good thing (if self-authorship is a good thing) but that identity must make some kind of sense. And for it to make sense, it must be an identity constructed in response to facts outside oneself, things that are beyond one's own choices. (18)

---

13   This is what happens in this particular co-production directed by Ross Manson. In the printed text, the lights go to black immediately after this line and then restore. "L and M haven't moved" (237).

14   It should be noted that these two examples did not actually appear in performances in Toronto or on the subsequent Ontario tour. The stage manager's call points for pink noise on and off that I am referring to were erased from the prompt script. It appears that they were included in technical rehearsals and then omitted prior to the opening performance.

Without solid recourse to a preconstructed identity group, L and M "shut up."
They decide that constructing identity may not be a good thing, or at least
not for them a possible thing.

The identity beyond words that L and M seek has yet to be created. It
is still outside of the sense endowed by outside corroboration and so must
be deferred in this world. "Like a Rwanda full of Hutsis [a neologism for the
offspring of mixed-race marriages between Hutus and Tutsis], it exists only
in the imagination. That does not necessarily mean that such a society could
not or should not emerge. But 'the facts beyond one's own choice' do not yet
allow it" (Younge 88). Disallowed a viable identity in the world, L and M escape through death, through the gateless gate.

The penultimate scene of the play-within revisits their emotionally brittle meeting in the campground. L wants to be forgiven and to renew their
relationship. M is not so sure: "It's all become a bit 'here's to shutting up' to
me" (240). The very last scene, however, differs substantially from the rest. L
and M are silent. The boom box, carefully placed centre stage, plays a recording of their final conversation. We hear M's fearful arrival in L's tent because
she heard a noise in the woods, their peacemaking decision to blame it all
on Sasha, the shared singing of M's song, and finally the bear attack. In the
published script, L and M set up the props of the campsite and then sit and
listen attentively to the recording. In Manson's production, the two actors
fill the space of this scene with a choreographed dance-like blocking series.
The movements are strongly coordinated, being sometimes, but not always,
symmetrically mirrored. As an audience member, my sense of this was to feel
some recognition of familiarity that I had seen these gestures before, and also
a sense of storytelling, although the gestures were not literally communicative
as mimesis. Looking at the prompt script, I learn that this is an improvised
section where the two actors work from a set list of gestural vocabulary. The
gestures are iterative, having been culled from the previous scenes of the
play-within. This is neither blah-de-blah nor denial in silence but an attempt
to again embody their history. Coded as autobiography, the approximately
two dozen gestures have names—"peanut butter hands," "pathfinder," "Dixie/
audience hello," "inventory of damage"—but we don't "read" this language.

Emphasis is not on performative communication but simply on connected-
ness. The improvisation is structured so that one actor begins and the other
is her mirror and at certain points they switch. The ideal is an invisibility of
leader and follower in making these shifts, which fosters an intense unspoken connection and creates a kind of unity where two become one. At the
end of her speech asking for a halt to naming things, L hints at a recognition that the naming she seeks to avoid might be viable, even necessary, on
a small scale. "Those are just names so other people can feel comfortable. It's
not about other people. Or maybe . . . I guess for me it was about her" (241).
The change in impulse marked by "Or maybe" is important. Although performativity depends on communal citationality, it might be possible to create a
microcommunity of two people. The improvised gesture sequence might be
understood to express this kind of almost private communication. Between
them, they completely contain their own story.

A key feature of performative naming is that it is self-reflexive. Not only
does the performative utterance create the thing or the effect in speech, it
also concurrently brings into being the speaker herself as a speaker. Through
this reflexive implication, both identity and agency arise simultaneously. "I"
and "you" are mutually interpellated through deictic pointing. Throughout
A Beautiful View, L and M are figured as mirror images. In the euphoria of
their first meeting, they revel in perceived points of identity:

M: We both have the same birthday.
L: *(to M)* Do you know anyone else with the same birthday?
M: *(to L)* Just you.
L: I know. Me neither. Just Martin Landau, and I don't even know
Martin Landau. (216)[15]

---

15   Martin Landau (b. 1928) is a well-known American television and film actor. In the
Toronto prompt book, Martin Landau is changed to Canadian superstar singer and icon
Anne Murray (b. 1945). Both Landau and Murray share the same birthday of 20 June.

Frequently, their dialogue is mirrored as they both repeat the same sentence or phrase. It is through this mirroring that they are able to create a shared identity outside of discursive performativity. When they pass through the gate, they are released into the epilogue. Facing each other, L and M ask again the same question that began the prologue, "What do you see?" (243). The beautiful view they encounter is the same one that L proposes on the night of the Halloween party as her vision of what happens after they die. Emanating from L's power as a performative prophet, her vision is materialized. Like the bear, it is summoned into being. She describes a pristine forested wilderness vista with a river, a waterfall, and a pond "where no one has ever been. And then we're there, the first person ever there, and we turn and see someone, and we look into their eyes and we see all of our history. Something about ourselves, something good about ourselves. Our best self" (235). Curiously but consistently with the idea of L and M as consubstantial, L conflates herself and M into one: "We're . . . the first person there." Then this combined identity sees someone else who reflects back "our best self." The word "identity" denotes sameness, an equivalence between two things, such that one interchangeably defines the other. Identity is a bridge, forging the representational relationship between self and the discursive enactment of that self. In *A Beautiful View*, ultimately L and M conclude the search for identity in the closed loop of an infinitely reflecting mirror, collapsing two into one: "What do you see?" "My best self." In the end, the answer to the identity question: "A couple of what?" is that they are not a couple at all but a singularity in an Eden prior to Adam's naming of all the creatures, a garden where even the pronouns "you" and "me" cease to have meaning. They successfully (impossibly) become truly no thing; blissful because they are nothing together.

SEARCHING FOR THE MUSE: CHANGING INSPIRATION

CAROLINE GILLIS

When I met Daniel MacIvor in the Arts Centre at Dalhousie University in 1981, where I was getting my bachelor of arts in theatre and he was in the acting program, I had little idea of where this friendship would lead. Thirty-three years later we are still friends and I have appeared in many of his plays, including *Never Swim Alone*, *Jump*, *The Soldier Dreams*, *Marion Bridge*, *How It Works*, *A Beautiful View*, *Communion*, and *Was Spring*.

We both grew up in Sydney, Cape Breton. Daniel was a year younger than me and in a different grade. We went to the same schools, St. Joseph's Elementary School and later Sheriff Junior High, although in high school I opted to attend the all-girl Holy Angels High School and he attended Sydney Academy. We lived about five minutes away from each other and we both attended mass at St. Joseph's Roman Catholic Church, which was right across the street from my house, but we never spoke. MacIvor being a boy and me being a girl in a different grade in Sydney meant not speaking to one another. So when Daniel and I met on that fateful day in the purple-carpeted halls of the Dalhousie Arts Centre we connected almost immediately and laughed about the fact that we had known each other for years but had never spoken. We shared one class together at Dalhousie but we really bonded when we decided to hitchhike to Sydney from Halifax one weekend. It's normally a five-hour drive and maybe a seven-hour hitchhike, but it took us about eleven hours and we eventually caved in Port Hawkesbury (about an hour

This essay was excerpted and adapted from Caroline Gillis's M.A. thesis in Theatre Studies, University of Guelph, September 2014.

or so from Sydney) and had to call Daniel's mother to pick us up. We failed miserably on the road, but the friendship was cemented.

Daniel ended up leaving the acting program at Dalhousie and eventually moved to Toronto and attended George Brown College. By then I had graduated and was living with my musician boyfriend in Halifax, but we stayed in touch, and Daniel kept asking me to move to Toronto. "I'll write you a play. I'll write a play for you if you come." It took some persuading, but in 1985 I decided to move to Toronto. We started doing some small theatre stuff together. AIDS was raising its fatal spectre and I remember one of my first big moments on stage was as part of the Safe Sex Cabarets that Buddies in Bad Times Theatre was hosting in the mid-eighties. I performed in one of four monologues Daniel had written called *Different Kinds of Dancing*. In 1986 we did a tiny production of MacIvor's original script *The Never Broken Heart* at the Rivoli Café for two nights only. However, for the most part, I was working at the By the Way Café, where I had graduated from dishwasher to counterperson/cook and finally to waitress. In 1987 I was working there when my Halifax ex decided he was going to marry his new "working" actress. I was traumatized and it spurred something in MacIvor—my friend and playwright. He showed up at the café one afternoon when I was working and said he had written me a play. I was very excited about the prospect of being in a rehearsal room and working with a full cast of actors with a part for me—at last! "But there's a catch," he said. "What's that?" I replied. "It's a one-woman show." Our accounts vary on this part of our history. He says I told him I wouldn't move to Toronto unless he wrote me a one-woman show, but I *know* that I was terrified at the prospect and I distinctly remember standing there with my black waitress belt tied around my waist (ignoring my customers) and saying, "No, no, no, I can't do a one-woman show. I'm too scared." But I did do it. The play was *See Bob Run*. I was to play the titular role of Bob, "short for Roberta."

We worked with the late Ken McDougall as director on the play and I think Daniel and me owe a lot of what we know about theatre to him. Ken was also an actor with some background in dance and choreography (which would really come into play in later works of MacIvor's, including *Never*

Swim Alone). I really had no idea of how to be an actress beyond producing emotions of "happy" or "mad," and Ken opened my eyes to an honest and simple delivery of MacIvor's words. Ken's most memorable direction to me was to "not feel sorry for myself" on stage and I think that's something that MacIvor and me both take to heart in our work. *See Bob Run* managed to be staged because of Ken's participation, not to mention the work of the late Albert Chevalier (Daniel's partner at the time). We got two thousand dollars in seed money from Buddies in Bad Times Theatre and we opened at the Poor Alex Theatre, which was basically across the street from the By the Way Café. The Buddies seed money combined with Albert's credit card basically got the production on stage.

See Bob Run was a turning point for both me and MacIvor. The reviews for the play were raves and we ended up taking the play on a tour across the country starting with the Edmonton Fringe Festival in 1987. We also took the show to Halifax, Montreal, and Vancouver—and eventually remounted the show in Toronto at the Theatre Centre. The play opened doors for Daniel as a writer and for me as an actress. Daniel joined the Playwrights Unit at the Tarragon Theatre and I started getting auditions. Daniel wrote *Somewhere I Have Never Travelled* for Tarragon Theatre and I played the role of Dolly in the play about a Cape Breton family dealing with the death of their alcoholic patriarch. The show was brutalized by the critics and this marked a change in MacIvor; he started to explore new ways of how to write a play. When he brought a first draft of the play *Never Swim Alone* to the Playwrights Unit it was deemed good writing, but "not a play."

Never Swim Alone was produced as a play, not by Tarragon but by MacIvor's recently formed company da da kamera and Platform 9 Theatre. Platform 9 was Ken McDougall's company with playwright Robin Fulford and was known for innovative plays such as Fulford's *Steel Kiss*. *Never Swim Alone* was performed at the Theatre Centre in 1991. It was February and I was wearing a bathing suit. Sometimes I wonder if, as a friend, MacIvor wasn't only challenging me as an actress but helping me to overcome my own fears on stage, by presenting me with personal challenges. A bathing suit. Of course, at the time, I thought I was fat. I was not. But there is something about the stage that changes you . . . you might find yourself modest at the Scadding Court public pool in downtown Toronto sporting a bathing suit with pasty skin and an imagined pot-belly—quickly hiding yourself with a towel when you come out of the water—but on stage there's a magic that takes place that enables you to own and honour certain aspects of yourself that you might not necessarily feel in real life. I wore that costume with confidence as the character of Referee/Lifeguard in *Never Swim Alone*—perched upon her chair, towering above the two businessmen who looked to her to decide their petty arguments in a tense game of one-upmanship.

After working with directors like McDougall, Ed Roy, and Daniel Brooks, MacIvor did his first full-fledged gig as a director for his play *Jump* in the Backspace at Theatre Passe Muraille with his company da da kamera. It was a non-speaking production set to music with a large cast and no words save for one at the end of the play. I was a bride, Ken McDougall was the groom, Judith Orban was my mom, Tracy Wright and Nadia Ross played my twin daughters, and Ed Roy was the host for the silent ceremony that ensued. In the end Wright's character climbs a ladder until she is out of sight of the audience and Ross's character looks up and whispers, "Jump." It was a fitting title for MacIvor's first endeavour into the world of direction, and not everyone in that position would have been brave enough to cast two of their former directors in the play. As a director MacIvor has become assured and confident. He knows what he wants to see on the stage, in the same way he knows how he wants his words to be on the page. He is very precise and if something is not working, even a tiny moment in a scene, he will take the time it needs to fix it or find the answer. If he doesn't find it that day, it will stay on the edges of his thoughts and he will usually come back the next day with a solution. The precise nature of what he demands from the actor on stage ends up looking like the most natural thing in the world when it is delivered. It is a kind of precise and deceptively casual kind of performance.

When Daniel knows what he doesn't want he makes the decision swiftly and emphatically. I remember one example of this was when we were rehearsing *Communion* at Tarragon Theatre in 2010. The character I played, Leda, has cancer. Her hair is growing back after chemotherapy and in the first scene of the play, she is wearing a tam to hide her baldness. In the second scene we find her in a hotel room wearing a wig as she waits to meet with her estranged daughter. The wig prompts her daughter to say, "Your hair's different," and Leda just brushes the comment off. The intent was that after an exhausting meeting with her daughter, which ends with her daughter leaving, Leda slumps down on the bed and pulls off the wig to reveal her very short hair. I went with the designer and the head of wardrobe at Tarragon to a shop to try on wigs—MacIvor had to stay in rehearsal. We spent a lot of time trying on the different hairpieces and we sent pictures of our three choices to MacIvor. You can't return a wig. Understandable. He picked one and we paid for the expensive wardrobe piece and headed back to the rehearsal hall. We arrived, I donned the wig, and we started the scene—and after about forty-five seconds MacIvor stopped everything and said, "No, no, I hate the wig. I don't want you to wear a wig at all—I just want you to have the short hair." The wig was instantly discarded. It lived on the props table for the next couple of weeks, never to be used except as a gag when on occasion MacIvor would don it to deliver his notes or to demonstrate blocking that an actor (usually me) couldn't get right. In a play about cancer, alcoholism, estrangement, and death, the laughs delivered by that wig were a welcome distraction.

In MacIvor's two-woman play *A Beautiful View* I went shopping with Sherrie Johnson (Daniel's producing partner in da da kamera) to find a shirt for my character Mitch to wear. We found a dark brown cotton blouse with long sleeves with a kind of retro western feel, and instead of buttons down the front, the blouse was kept closed by one single long lace crisscrossing through the eyelets. MacIvor hated it. He joked about it. He kept pulling at the lace. His direction during rehearsals kept coming back to "that shirt, I don't know . . . that shirt." After a couple of days of his quiet obsession with the laced-up shirt we were rehearsing a seduction scene between my character Mitch and Tracy Wright's character Liz. Daniel came on stage—he likes to come on stage to demonstrate—and he started pulling at the lace. The scene involved Tracy and I slowly moving in a circle to a very slow and sexy cover of Madonna's "Crazy For You" without actually touching. MacIvor started to circle with me; he untied the lace at the top, then he reached down and pulled at the lace from the bottom of the shirt and the lace gave way and came sliding out from the eyelets, leaving the shirt open, and then he tossed the lace on the floor. It became a brilliant part of the seduction scene and Tracy rendered the movement beautifully. And suddenly the shirt that obsessed him made sense. MacIvor hates having anything on stage that doesn't have a purpose and the lace in that shirt looked like an unused prop to him. The seduction scene is quickly followed by an uncomfortable Mitch, dimly lit, putting her shirt back on and delivering a monologue to the audience about guiltily sneaking away after her one-night stand with a woman. I am never adept at choreography, and trying to put the lace back into the eyelets of a shirt while speaking to an audience nervously, on what was basically a dark stage, was pretty tricky at first—but the fear of not getting my shirt back on properly for the next scene gave the speech an undercurrent of true anxiety that brought the scene to a whole new level. A part of me thinks that MacIvor took a secret pleasure in my anxiety over getting the shirt laced up correctly—a kind of punishment for choosing it in the first place.

As MacIvor and I changed, the characters in his plays reflected our changes back to us. Even though Bob, in *See Bob Run*, had killed someone, she had an innocence about her and a sense of humour that endeared her to the audience. In *Never Swim Alone*, Referee/Lifeguard's innocence was taken along with her life in drowning as a young girl, and in her reincarnation as the Lifeguard she possesses more power and savvy and wields it over the men who look to her as a judge in their never-ending competition. Certainly these changes were taking place in MacIvor and me as we slowly started to gain confidence and experience in our field. By the time I performed the role of Agnes in *Marion Bridge* cynicism was creeping into my characters, but not without humour. Never without humour. As the failed actress and recovering alcoholic we could see in Agnes the edges peeling away from the innocence of her youth.

By the time *Was Spring* was produced in 2012 at Tarragon Theatre's Extraspace, I was fifty and playing Kath, a character in full-blown anger mode. Kath was a recovering alcoholic, but recovering her sobriety didn't alleviate her anger. This was also the case with the character of Leda in *Communion*, who also quit the booze and sought help for her anger and fear (she also had cancer) from a therapist. Leda loses a daughter to religion, and Kath loses a daughter to addiction. These themes of addiction and recovery were starting to permeate MacIvor's plays, fitting in with his continuing preoccupation with death and dying. MacIvor writes from a very personal place, trying to understand what's going on around him. Certainly, we experienced the death of a lot of friends from AIDS when we were in our twenties (which MacIvor beautifully explored in his play *The Soldier Dreams*), and in our middle age we are dealing with the loss of friends to cancer and other ailments, as well as watching parents start to succumb to old age. All of these changes have no doubt affected us both as theatre artists, but MacIvor has always been interested in exploring "why we are here" in his writing, in what he has described as "a very, very gentle existentialism."

Throughout our intertwining careers I believe what has kept us together as friends and co-workers is our shared background and sense of humour. This creates a shorthand in our communication that goes a long way in rehearsals and is also part of the reason he writes some of his plays with me in mind. I think Daniel often writes with the image of an actor for a character in his head. It helps him to propel the piece forward even if that actor doesn't end up performing the role. MacIvor will even adapt a previously written role to more fluidly incorporate a new actor in a piece or an actor taking over a role originated by another. He's always open to development and change, constantly shifting and adapting his work depending on what might be preoccupying him at the time, or what inspiration he is drawing from his surroundings.

A Beautiful View is an interesting example of a play that was eventually propelled forward by his friendship with me and the late Tracy Wright. The play follows the friendship of two women, Liz and Mitch, starting in their early twenties, and it follows them through to middle age when they meet an untimely end after encountering a bear while on a camping trip. But it's funny. Really. The two meet and have a one-night stand, and when they meet up again a year or so later they discover (while talking across a tent) that they each mistakenly thought "the other one" was a lesbian. This was invariably one of the biggest laughs of the show, and it sets the stage for the long-term friendship that ensues.

The play developed over the course of a few years and went through a lot of incarnations before it was premiered as a two-woman play, with Wright and me, at the Wexner Center in Ohio in 2006. It started as a play with six or eight characters that MacIvor had workshopped with students at the Wexner Center. In the first version of the play that I read the piece was cut down to three characters. Wright and MacIvor would be playing a straight couple, and I was to play MacIvor's wacky and neurotic sister who popped into their scenes occasionally. My other role was a bear who hovers "ominously" over the couple as they get together and their relationship develops. In a one-night workshop performance in the back room of the Cameron House in Toronto, I had to open the show decked out in my bear costume while dancing to Mary J. Blige. We rented a bear costume from the Stratford Festival. The bear was, I believe, representative of the inner fears of the couple played by Wright and MacIvor. Every time the couple reached a critical turning point in their relationship the bear appeared looming behind them, and even physically enveloped them in some cases. It should have been scary and foreboding on some level when the bear appeared, but the only bear costume available from Stratford was a female bear complete with a tiara and long beautiful eyelashes framing her very kind eyes. We were able to remove the tiara but there was no getting around the fact that this bear was very pretty, and extremely non-threatening. But this is the beauty of bringing things out in a workshop. The bear costume was probably not going to make it to full production. (The costume was returned to Stratford but the "bear" theme remained.)

Shortly after the workshop at the Cameron House, MacIvor went on a retreat to meditate for ten days. When he returned to speaking society, the new play flooded out of him. The piece had transformed into the two-woman play. Tracy and I were actually rather shocked by the change and, I think as friends, we were a little wary of the ambiguous relationship between the two characters. But MacIvor's instincts were right, and even though the plot of the play was not the story of our lives, by using the friendship that Tracy and I had established over many years the play had a resonance of truth that coursed beneath the words that Daniel had written. The bear costume disappeared, but sadly Mitch and Liz still encountered a bear (that turned out to be very ominous in sound effects) that ended their lives, but in effect, ignited the story of the play. Their death made them examine their lives and their relationship.

MacIvor couldn't have known the future, that we would lose Tracy to cancer in 2010, but this play was a gift, one that I will never forget.

The common ground Daniel and I shared growing up in Cape Breton gives us the same sense of place. Sydney Academy, Holy Angels, the heavy-set girl who tap-danced till she was out of breath at every school variety show, the Mayflower Mall, Smoothermans Lounge, Meat Cove, fries and gravy at the Maple Leaf Restaurant, Whitney Avenue, the ocean at Inverness Beach, and the Vogue Theatre were all part of our fabric even if we never spoke to each other growing up. This shared history has continued as we collect experiences along the way as co-workers and friends.

Gillis Journals
June 8, 2006

Last night we opened [*A Beautiful View* at the Spoleto Festival in Charleston, SC]. The show went really well. A more cavernous space than we're used to but we handled it well. We were a little worried about how a more conservative audience might handle the play, but they were surprisingly supportive. [. . .] Daniel, Tracy and me went to Folly Beach about 20 minutes outside of town today. The ocean was beautiful. White fine sand that is still covering my body. I'm finding it in my ears. There was a wind that felt warm and luscious and the water was so warm. The waves and the undertow were stronger than I've ever felt in the ocean . . . even in Nova Scotia. We stayed fairly close to shore and were quite buffeted by the waves there. They just knock you over and we all got some sand burns from the force [. . .] The waves turn you into a kid again. You have no control. We screeched and we laughed. I'm pretty lucky in this life I have to say.

DANCE PLAYS ON THE CANADIAN IMAGINATION

RAY MILLER

Dance has enjoyed a long and varied collaboration with theatrical histories of all kinds—from the most traditional of dance-dramas from Africa and Asia to the most recent and often experimental, such as those of Robert Wilson, Martha Clarke, and Théâtre du Soleil, among many others. As we look at the work of Daniel MacIvor, it is important to place how he employs dance in his dramaturgy within a convention of "spoken drama," that is, plays that rely primarily on language rather than music and plays that often engage characters in clearly delineated situations (realistic and absurdist) as opposed to those in which movement or shifting scenographic elements define the primary theatrical language of the production. In that regard, MacIvor's plays are closer to those of Wole Soyinka or David Henry Hwang than those of Wilson or Julie Taymor. A contemporary of MacIvor is the self-exiled Chinese Nobel laureate, Gao Xingjian. Influenced by modern dance, Chinese acrobatics, Beijing opera, European absurdist drama, and the movement theories of Jacques Lecoq, Xingjian incorporates movement and dance into the very centre of his modernist aesthetic. The stage directions in his plays, like those of MacIvor, or Soyinka, or Mary Zimmerman, are written for "choreographers" so that the physical and kinesthetic aspects of his dramaturgy will be clearly understood and incorporated into the production of the plays. For these playwrights, including MacIvor, dance is not so much a separate and stand-alone art form as it traditionally has been viewed by many playwrights in the Western tradition; rather, they see it as another aspect, or tool, or extension of their dramatic vision. They see the visual and kinesthetic aspects of theatrical production, which include dance, not as *additions* to a literary text but at the very core of their understanding of what it means to create theatrical language unique to each play that incorporates text with movement with other carefully selected scenographic elements. In this regard, MacIvor and his contemporaries have been exploring and defining a contemporary theatrical language that better addresses the postmodern theatre in which they work. Many of them have found very specific dramaturgical reasons for employing dance in their playwriting—Daniel MacIvor being a prime example.

MacIvor, a prolific Canadian playwright, continues to include dance sequences and choreographed movements in his varied repertoire of plays. This essay only begins to investigate his use of dance in plays such as *The Soldier Dreams*, *2-2-Tango*, *In On It*, and *Never Swim Alone* but hopefully opens avenues for scholarly investigation into the dramaturgy of dance in his newer works such as *Bingo!*, *Arigato, Tokyo*, and *Who Killed Spalding Gray?* This examination of MacIvor's work from a dance perspective demonstrates how as a playwright he is keenly aware of the role and function of movement as a plastique and helps expose dance as an important metaphoric element in the dramaturgy of his plays. MacIvor tends to use dance in his plays in subtle and nuanced ways. For him, dance as subject matter is often an adjunct to larger themes or dramatic explorations of characters or situations. For each of his plays, MacIvor searches for a theatrical language that is at once literary, kinesthetic, and unique to that play. Movements of the heart, the emotions, and the mind are intertwined in how he writes his plays.

There is a famous BBC series from the early 1980s called *Playing Shakespeare* in which members of the Royal Shakespeare Company under the direction of John Barton provide countless examples of techniques and approaches that the members of this company use to create productions of Shakespeare's plays. One of the mantras that is stressed over and over is the idea that the playwright—if you simply pay attention and ask questions—will guide you through the appropriate choices actors and directors can make when re-enacting one of Shakespeare's plays. The language, the juxtaposition of the words, the inherent rhythms in the construction of phrases, in the shifting tempos of beats and scenes, and so on, all provide clues and ways to approach the acting of his plays. The same can be said of the plays of Daniel

MacIvor. While his subject matter may range over a wide area, there is a deliciousness to how he mixes words and a joy-filled playfulness to how he asks actors to physically "get off their butts" and engage with the material at hand.

MacIvor incorporates and uses dance in many, if not most, of his plays. Many of them are written in a way that is often episodic. Each French scene might be only two or three pages in length. He explores simple ideas, or feelings, or perceptions and then he juxtaposes them in ways that encourage a more layered sense of who his characters are and the world(s) in which they live. Many of his characters struggle with sexual and personal identity and familial or societal expectations and conventions. For MacIvor, identity itself is up for grabs. It is a theme that he returns to over and over. His characters live in a postmodern world in which authenticity is not so much about personhood as it is about slivers of experience, the moment. American modern dancer/choreographer Erick Hawkins succinctly sums up this sentiment in his book titled *Here and Now With Watchers*.

For MacIvor, dance becomes a method by which characters take ownership of their lives. Sometimes he uses simple social dance forms to push and shove his characters into physical contact so that they might confront their frailties and the barriers that they must overcome in order to be able to simply communicate. This is certainly the case in *2-2-Tango*, in which the characters, James and Jim, tango, waltz, hustle, and Charleston with each other in their attempts to make contact. In other plays, like *The Soldier Dreams*, MacIvor is much more interested in dance as an ideal, a metaphor, a fragment in the life of the character of David as he struggles with AIDS and its dizzying repercussions in personal and social worlds. In *In On It*, what appears to be a simple and superficial dance to a song by Leslie Gore takes on both humorous and poignant qualities within the context of the play. And in *Never Swim Alone* there is fierce competition and violent confrontation between the two male characters in which one form of playful physical repartee between them explodes into fighting and battle.

THE SOLDIER DREAMS

Of the four plays examined in this essay, *The Soldier Dreams* is certainly the most conventional in dramatic structure and style. The play centres on the character of David, who is dying. He is in a coma-like state in a bed located in the centre of the stage. On stage right and left are platforms with microphones on them. There is an actor who plays the dying David and who remains in the bed until the end of the play. The other David, played by another actor, can move freely from one location to another and he personifies the memory of David. The other characters in the play consist of his older, cantankerous sister Tish and her nerdy, ineffectual husband, Sam; the younger, irresponsible sister Judy; and his live-in lover, Richard. Throughout the play, there are vignettes in which a German student, with whom he has had a liaison, makes appearances to the memory-of-David character. Family scenes around the dying David in his bedroom are punctuated mostly by individual scenes in which each character reveals some special aspect of her or his relationship to David and by memory scenes of David's encounter with the German student.

The play begins and ends with memory-David repeating, "And if I had my way we'd all be dancing" (41, 75). Throughout the play, each character reinforces David's propensity to engage in some form of social dance with his family and friends as ways in which to bypass the restrictive boundaries suggested by defining reality mostly with words. As his awkward brother-in-law Sam would put it, "Words. Words. Problematic. Words trap thoughts. Words are like little cages for thoughts" (54). His lines echo the famous line from Shakespeare's *Hamlet* in the titular character's dialogue with Polonius: "Words, words, words" (159). MacIvor problematizes the very element his artistry relies upon and subtly suggests that words—even words in plays—can only carry us so far. Sam reminds us as much when he says that "if David has his way we'd probably all be dancing—that's what he loved—he said it was good for the soul. Um. Yes. Um. Soul" (53–54).

This family was dominated when they were growing up by a soured and unpleasant father and a drunken, domineering mother. There was little in the way of meaningful communication. Each of the sisters and later Sam and Richard, and the German student, taught David how to use simple sign language and each developed their own unique shorthand as a way in which to communicate with David. None of them understood that this means of communication was also shared by each of the others in their relationships with David. That certainly provides some of the humour for the audience; at the same time, it underscores the desperate challenge in communicating and in the inadequacy of verbal communication to touch another human being in ways that are emotionally honest.

In this limbo land before death, the dying David is coming to terms with the homophobic world of his family, friends, and lovers with this German student who he happens to meet when attending his sister's wedding in Ottawa. After telling a conventional homophobic joke to his new German student friend, he is admonished for doing so. The German student goes on to say, "To me life is a war and it is very important what side you choose to be. . . . Even when the soldier dreams the war goes on" (57). To which David responds, "So you don't like jokes. What do you like?" and the student replies, "I like sex" (57). With that, they begin a relationship that crosses between Canada and Germany, between reality and imagination.

Up through his time in college, there are family photographs of David. But after coming out he refused to have any photographs taken. Critic Martin Denton comments that

> MacIvor is masterful as he doles out the bits of David's life—to us and
> to his characters—making it clear that whatever the medium, there is
> no way to capture the totality or even a tiny part of another human
> being. David, we are told, developed an aversion to having his picture
> taken—he wanted to remember experiences without artificial aids.

It may also be that photographs, particularly those taken by family or friends, may reveal more about the photographer than it does about the subject. For David, it may well be that the metaphor of dance and the experience of dancing reflected the constantly changing exploration he was feeling at that time in his life.

Instead of the implied stillness of a moment captured in a photograph, David relied upon the ephemeral quality of dancing to convey a sense of free association in which he could be who he wanted when he wanted. This is not unlike his relationships with his family and the structure of the play. He wants to be a different person with each family member. The act of going back and forth telling and retelling his story allows him to be who he wants to be. At the end of the play, after the dying David has died and the family characters disassemble the bed and exit—leaving the stage bare—the memory David enters and begins to spin and then falls. The script informs us,

> *The music continues wildly. David spins again. He falls. He tries to keep spinning. The Student enters the space walking back through it in the opposite direction than he did in the beginning. . . . His presence gives him strength. David spins wildly and spins and spins until he is lit as if he flies into the air and disappears. . . . Silence.* (76)

Many playwrights reference dance as a way by which to bypass the ineffectual rational side of the human experience when trying to relate to others and/or when trying to understand how the inexplicable—God, soul—might feel if it could inhabit one's body. In *The Soldier Dreams* dance becomes a way in which to confront harsh realities with an idealized affirmation and reaffirmation that life—maybe even after death—is worth living, is worth striving for, is worth contesting. The directness that David sees in performing dance as a way in which to express unedited emotion is illustrated in the varied stories each character shares with the audience about their encounter with David when he would insist on dancing as a way to either confront or deny a difficult or challenging problem in his relationships. For David, as for many people, dance is more about suggestion, possibility, hopefulness rather than about proficiency, accomplishment, or artfulness. When playwrights want to move the emotional life of the character into the shared emotional lives of the audience in ways that suggest a kind of hopefulness in the face of adversity, dance can and is often used as a theatrical metaphor—as it is here, as it has been used in a similar way in the recognition dance of Billy Elliot or the tarantella dance of Nora in *A Doll's House*. There is a kind of release in which the character's internal reality and external expression of that reality are finally joined in a kind of exuberant celebration.

To explore this point a little further, it may be helpful to juxtapose MacIvor's 1995 *The Soldier Dreams* with Bill T. Jones's evening-length 1994 dance *Still/Here*. Mira Friedlander, reviewing *The Soldier Dreams* in *Variety* in 1995, succinctly writes,

> The play jumps among three time frames: the death watch, a long-ago chance encounter between David and a young man at an airport, and the memorial service, where the characters attempt awkwardly and often humorously to eulogize the man they have just lost. The funeral speeches are choreographed, both verbally and physically.

It is a play filled with a lot of talk in which dying is a constant backdrop. It is a memory play but the memories here are incomplete. They are being formed, corrected, and created before our eyes. There are moments or shifts of incompleteness—allowing the audience time to participate with their own associations and thoughts. MacIvor conveniently bifurcates the play by creating the two characters of David and David 1. It is theatrical contrivance that allows the audience to split focus on the interior world of David and the external world of the dying David. As the play progresses, the time shifting overlaps and we are led into a space in which time is experienced as more a mind space than a linear experience.

A year before MacIvor's play, American choreography stirred a major controversy when well-known American dance critic Arlene Croce in her *New Yorker* article "Discussing the Undiscussable" characterized Jones's dance as "victim art" and therefore not subject to serious critical artistic commentary (54). The dance, in fact, is a mixed-media danced contemplation based on interviews with people who were suffering life-threatening illnesses. The approach that Jones takes in the choreography is not unlike that of MacIvor in his play. *New York Times* critic Anna Kisselgoff wrote, "*Still/Here* is about nothing but human feelings. But they are expressed through highly formal

structures, including constant intercutting of all the components. The choreography is genuinely abstract, focused on the heightened distillation of gesture
that is Mr. Jones's dance signature." In his autobiography, Jones writes about
the process and construction of the dance. Like MacIvor, he creates a dance
that requires that we use a bifocal lens with which to engage the materials.
The title of the dance itself, *Still/Here*, suggests the sense of the interior aspect
of the experience and the communal aspect of it in the company of others.

Among the many parallels between these two works, it is interesting to
note how they employ the association of dance as identifying the limitation
of our material existence in their final theatrical metaphors. For MacIvor,
we see the play end with David spinning, falling, spinning, falling, spinning,
falling, and he "spins and springs until it is as if he flies into the air and disappears" (76). This idea of falling only to recover is picked up in Kisselgoff's
review of Jones's dance when she writes, "The repeated motif of dancers falling becomes clichéd, but the intricate ways in which they are comforted and
partnered do not."

For Jones, in the epilogue section of *Still/Here*, "The surging and dissolving
groups on stage personify Odetta's pronouncement in the lyrics of the song:

Will I be part of the water?
I'm on a wave being moved.
I'm flying.
I'm still here. (qtd. in Jones 259–60)

For the playwright and the choreographer, dealing with death and dying also means confronting the living—both in the here and now and in the
hereafter. Without committing to a particular interpretation of what that
might mean, each has chosen to use dance as a final act of defiance that will
not give gravity the final say. The theatrical combination of music with the
ethereal quality of the human body aspiring to something beyond the immediacy of illness and mortality by leaping, by flying, strikes an important note
of hopefulness that goes beyond wish fulfillment and suggests something
more substantial in that hope—something that recalls the powerful image

of the Persian poet/choreographer Sufi Rumi spinning, spinning, spinning
until his soul takes flight to Allah.

2-2-TANGO

The use of dance in *2-2-Tango* is quite different from that of *The Soldier
Dreams*. Here the playwright is using dance as a theatrical language and as a
dramaturgical tool in which to convey to the audience his ideas in an imme-
diate and kinesthetic manner. While *The Soldier Dreams* has a clear narrative
structure centred on the dying David, *2-2-Tango* is based on a series of decon-
structed vignettes. In *The Soldier Dreams*, there are clearly drawn characters
who reveal themselves in group and dyadic scenes and in monologues, while
in *2-2-Tango* the characters James and Jim "are attired identically" as if wearing "team costumes," leaving open how realistic this play may or may not be
(*2-2-Tango* 191). Are these two different men? Are they the same man? Are
they representatives of some generic type of man? We may wish to look at
the title to help us unpack its meaning.

It is interesting to note that, in Jorge Luis Borges's often-referenced 1955
essay, "A History of the Tango," he observes that in the Argentina of his youth,
"On the street corners pairs of men would dance, since the women of the
town would not want to take part in such lewd debauchery" (395). In this
essay about the history of the "fighting tango" Borges goes on to describe
"men fighting with each other . . . as a kind of dance" (395). For Borges, sexuality and violence between men combine in tango and are not exclusive to
one gender or the other.

There is no doubt that both of these plays, like many of MacIvor's plays,
are concerned with relationships. *The Soldier Dreams* is more about relationships with lover and family as they help David come to better understand his
own identity. In *2-2-Tango*, the dialogue is stereotypical. The lines can char-
acterize many relationships in the initial stages of attraction, conquest, and
sudden denouement when "the game" is over and the option to really get to
know someone is available. In *The Soldier Dreams*, while there are memory

scenes reminiscent of Tennessee Williams's *The Glass Menagerie*, the style is one of simple realism. In *2-2-Tango*, the dialogue and the movement are contrived, staged, and meticulously choreographed. The author offers us a way into his play in the notes that precede the published script. He writes:

> *2-2-Tango* is written to be performed in a strictly-choreographed style, both visual and verbal. The dances in the play—Tango, Waltz, Hustle, Charleston—are not meant to be authentic but scaled-down, minimalist versions. When the script calls for the performers to "sing" it means make a sound (da, ba, la, etc.) and sing the basic melody of the dance they are doing. Unless directed . . . the performers are speaking to the audience . . . There should be a feeling of vaudeville. (192)

Even props are choreographed. At the top of the show, for example,

> *The men begin to sing a tango off-stage. They tango on from opposite sides. They tango off. They tango on carrying watermelons. They tango off. They tango on without watermelons. They notice one another. They stop. . . . They face the audience. A watermelon rolls on and stops in front of Jim. A moment of unease. Jim rolls it off.* (193)

In addition, the starkness of the set suggests that roles played by each of the characters can extend to location, time period, clothing, props, and so on. In many ways, this play reminds me of the collaboration between director Joe Wright and the modern dance choreographer Sidi Larbi Cherkaoui on their production of the film *Anna Karenina*. As with *2-2-Tango*, everything from sets to props to lights to movement to speech is carefully choreographed. In both, the hyper-attention to physical detail creates a carefully crafted theatricality that is about much, much more than style. Both the playwright MacIvor and the screenwriter for the film, Tom Stoppard, provide the audience with a way into the experience of these commonly recognized characters, not to create a kind of vaudevillian approach for the former or sentimental drama for the latter, but rather to create a theatrical language that invites the audience to participate on many different levels at one time. In Robert Wallace's introduction to *Making, Out: Plays by Gay Men*, he describes what is going on in the staging of this play as a kind of mirror dance—not only between the two male characters but also between the performers and the audience. Because we can recognize and accept the conventions presented to us—here in the form of easily recognizable social dance forms—being performed in a humorous vein, we can open ourselves to a kind of recognition that we might not otherwise. Wallace identifies some of the techniques employed by MacIvor in this play:

> The dance metaphor that MacIvor uses to propel the piece neatly plays with the routine steps of casual encounters, as well as the variety of positions that same-sex partners can assume in and out of bed. It is the recognition of this that makes this piece so funny to an audience. The wit of the writing is that it both precipitates and reflects the visual style of the piece. Offering a verbal dance as elegant and light in its use of repetition, staccato dialogue, and simultaneous speech as the characters' soft-shoe routines, *2-2 Tango* presents gay men with an image of themselves that is both sophisticated and self-conscious. ("Making Out Positions" 33)

The choice of dance styles is interesting in that each suggests additional commentary on the subject of each vignette. For example, the play opens with a tango. Immediately, there is humour injected in seeing not only two men doing the tango together and separately but also introducing the watermelon, which lifts it to the point of absurdity. But its significance is underscored by the fact that this dance is featured in the title of the play and therefore the playwright is asking us to privilege this social dance over the others we will see throughout the play. Art and dance historian Robert Farris Thompson writes in his award winning book, *Tango: The Art History of Love*, that the "Tango is timeless, mixing love and action in the motion of the people" (4).

The tango emerged on the international stage at the same time that ragtime and jazz dance were making their way—that is, the *fin de siècle* period up to the beginning of World War I. Like the cancan before, the tango has its roots in the common experience, in the low life of the times (often associated with brothels), in the sensuality of attraction—often forbidden attraction. These dances relied upon intimacy between performers that often shocked the status quo of their time. There is a sense of abandonment but there is also—at least in the beginning—an "in your face" sense about how these dances were performed. While for many of us today, Vernon and Irene Castle have become "the personification of ragtime, opening the way for the cabarets and nightclubs that will become permanent fixtures in New York and other big cities" (Golden 3), we must remember that in their day, their adaption of Southern African American dance forms was embraced by the younger generations and at the same time shocked the sensibilities of the older generation. They danced too close. They danced in a staccato fashion. They employed hesitations in their movement that created a kind of alluring tease for the viewer. It was, for the time, risqué. It may well be that MacIvor updates this "uncomfortability" with the status quo for this dance of the early twentieth century by moving it into a setting in which the contemporary audience might be asked to confront the homophobia of their times by watching two gay men perform this dance with a kind of "in your face" attitude. These characters have earned the right to be who they are and we are expected to catch up with that acknowledgement.

Each dance colours and shapes the physical execution and gestural suggestions for each scene, while the playwright makes clear that he is looking at the suggestion or minimal hint for each dance that does not minimize the tone that it gives to the scene. The second dance is the waltz. This is a scene that talks about lights on, lights out, and the sexual encounter of "the first time." The choice of the waltz for the dance of initial courtship is most appropriate. Dance historian Mark Knowles points out that the waltz in its day "seemed almost irresistible for those who fell under its spell. The euphoria created by the rapid rotations of the waltz was one of the most viral parts of the thrill—the thrill of losing control. . . . The waltz's real danger was that the vertigo made the dancer fall back into lust" (52–53). Then, in the following scene, they break into the hustle. This dance reached an international audience in the 1970s with the popularity of the Bee Gees and John Travolta in the movie *Saturday Night Fever*. It is easy to imagine the sharp lines and poses from that dance superimposed on the quick repartee of the dialogue in this scene. The hustle then segues into the jitterbug. The individual posing associated with the hustle is now replaced with physical contact in which the characters need to give and take in the sequencing of the typical jitterbug moves, all the while they are talking about independence. The irony would certainly not be lost on the audience. Later, when they talk about the aftermath of that first physical encounter, there is dialogue that is short, sweet, succinct, and to underscore that they are now doing the Charleston, a dance associated with the superficially loud and boisterous 1920s, the era of Fitzgerald's *The Great Gatsby*, but one that often masked the loneliness of its participants. Finally, they return to a tango for an extended scene in which the seduction transforms into a more serious encounter. At first, we are introduced to a highly charged scene of sexual tension and dangerous attraction. But, then, the scene devolves into one of violent confrontation with a dance move that is not so easily defined. The dance moves are more generic and more disjointed. The choice of the tango to explore these contradictory responses by these characters is reinforced by the etymological roots of the word itself. Mark Knowles writes:

> Most historians trace the word directly to African origins and point to its use in various dialects to mean "a closed place," "a reserved place," "a circle," or "any private place to which one must ask permission to enter."
>
> Some suggest that the word is merely onomatopoeic and echoes the beating of a drum. It has also been suggested that perhaps "tango" is a phonetic alteration of the name of the Yoruba god of lightning and thunder, Shango. (105)

Clearly, passion can turn to abuse and violence and then just as quickly back again. The strong, direct, sensual, and unexpected changes in direction we see in the Tango provide a clear theatrical metaphor for the sharp changes in the development of the relationship between these two characters. Borges provides some additional insight that I think can help us to better understand the rich complexity of this play when he writes that "the sexual nature of the tango has often been noted, but not so its violence. Certainly both carry modes or manifestations of the same impulse . . . a fight can be a celebration" (396). The play ends on a question regarding identity and desire as the smile of the boy suggests that there is no resolution—game on! The dance will begin again.

NEVER SWIM ALONE & IN ON IT

There are two other plays I would like to briefly touch on before concluding. First is the 1991 play *Never Swim Alone* and second is the 2001 play *In On It*. The narrative of *Never Swim Alone* is more linear than that of the other three plays discussed here. Rather than engaging in specific dances, the playwright structures the play like a prizefight. There are twelve rounds moderated by a young woman in a blue bathing suit. The two principle characters are childhood friends—Bill and Frank. In manner and background, each of them is hardly distinguishable from the other. This is not unlike *2-2-Tango*. The play starts off with the characters emerging from the audience, engaging in congenial repartee punctuated by short outbursts of nastiness reflecting their ongoing competition. As the play proceeds, each round is characterized by a different tempo reflecting the dramaturgical intent of the scene. We learn pieces of the backstory regarding the girl on the beach and their complicity in what we will eventually discover is her drowning. There is a haunting sense as we move through the play of a kind of Harold Pinter inevitability about to interrupt the proceedings.

We learn that their extreme competitiveness might well have cost the life of a young girl. We learn that years later as grown men there is in a curious way an acceptance of responsibility for their actions. But first there is blame. There is attack. There is a death duel with guns, which we never see resolved. What is interesting here in terms of the staging of this piece is the highly choreographed nature of the arrangement for each scene as a prize-fight. We see the set-up, the action, and the resolution. Each scene builds on the previous one. There may be added intensity. There may be brevity in dialogue. There may be a structured give and take between the performers. As we near the end, there is a cacophony of voices that overlap each other like waves on the ocean's edge. The movement is simple but ferocious—they swim and they swim and they swim. In many ways, the choreography of the piece reminds me of group mime pieces by ensemble companies from the 1970s and 1980s. Vignettes would be set up—not unlike chess matches—and the mimes would go through their movements as if each gesture has been dictated from an unseen source. As you watched these pieces, there was always that sense of the inevitable. In that respect, these performances were not unlike Samuel Beckett's *Act Without Words 1*, a solo piece performed by a silent actor, or mime, or clown; *Never Swim Alone* is like *Act Without Words 1* but with words. It is interesting to note that MacIvor had a production earlier in his career, *Jump*, in which there was only one word spoken in the production and that was the title of the play. Otherwise, physical expression was the theatrical language for its dramaturgy and its performance.

In On It is a play in which Luigi Pirandello meets Italo Calvino in a world that is like a floating Chinese Doll box. Narratives wrap around each other as one informs the next. With the progression of the play, the audience becomes more and more familiar with the theatrical convention the playwright is using and with the characters of That One and This One. By the time we get to the middle of the play, it is clear that no one scene can be taken at face value and that there are multiple realties going on at the same time. To say that the play is about the relationship between life and art is superficial at best. At its heart is an investigation of the creative process as it is lived and understood. We see that being played out on the stage. We, the audience, are implicated in that process. Just as the play within a play within a play structure is being enacted for us on the stage, we too are players on multiple stages in multiple venues creating, confronting, and engaging with metaphors of all kinds. These metaphors, however, while illusory, provide meaning. And meaning is something that the actors, the playwright, and the audience desire and need. As the character of Brian so abruptly reminds us in the last line of the play—"But why are we talking about endings anyway. Some things end. But some things just stop" (199).

There are two prominent dance or dance-like scenes that are contrasted in the play. The first is the throwing of the imaginary ball from Terri and Lloyd in the direction of the audience. The scene is punctuated with the sound effect of the ball as it is caught in the glove of each character. The directness of the travelling ball and the increase in speed as the scene picks up emphasize the rising anxiety and anger in the scene until the character of Terri blurts out, "You've got a good arm but you can't catch for shit" (171).

This is in sharp contrast to the performance of Brad's dance to Leslie Gore's song "Sunshine, Lollipops, & Rainbows" at Kate and Jessica's commitment party towards the end of the play. Initially, there is a sense that we are seeing a kind of non sequitur being performed here. It appears to come from nowhere. And in a way that is true. What the playwright does is invite the audience to abandon a linear rationality in lieu of an invitation to pure exuberance, openness, joy, love expressed for no other reason than that it exists and demands to seek a childlike expression in movement for its own sake. The playwright himself describes the performance of this dance by Brad and Brian as "ridiculous" (175, 195), which suggests a kind of wild abandonment in the manner in which it is performed. It starts off with Brad taking charge and in complete control. He is comfortable in his own skin and he is inviting his partner, Brian, to go public with his feelings for Brad. After some coaxing, Brian accepts and gets caught up in the moment. At the end, the exhilarated Brian is ready to "take a bow" (196), but the now sober Brad brings him and eventually the audience back to the harsh reality of the car crash. The Maria Callas aria comes to a conclusion and Brian drops the jacket, ending the play as it has begun, with the jacket in a spotlight and no one else on stage.

Daniel MacIvor, like many contemporary playwrights, is not satisfied with the linearity often found in realistic plays. His theatrical vocabulary is not limited to a linear narrative that requires performers to play primarily in a Stanislavsky-based psychological realism. Non-linear, imagistic scenes intersect with a kind of realism that *suggests* to the audience's imagination rather than *reassuring* them of an easily accepted conventional interpretation of reality.

MacIvor creates characters that some would describe as outsiders. They wander in and out of simple identity constructions and multiple realities. They are concerned with relationships between characters, between generations, between time past and time present, and between playwrights and audiences. More can be learned about the plays of MacIvor, particularly if we accept the mantle that he throws down to artists gutsy enough to produce and perform his work. In addition to his verbal wit and intelligence, MacIvor invites us to engage kinesthetically with him and with his characters. He does not want the performer nor the audience to be wallflowers. Ideas have consequences. They need to be embodied. If MacIvor had his way, we would all be dancing.

2 MACIVORS:
GAY/QUEER REPRESENTATION AND RADICAL INTIMACY
THOM BRYCE MCQUINN

In Daniel MacIvor's "Man in Scrubs," one of the sections of *I, Animal*, the speaker explains, with an acerbic accuracy, the discursive category of "gay" and why he doesn't include himself in it:

> I mean he was Gay. Gay is a very specific thing. Gay is a white male who likes the outdoors and chopping vegetables on his granite countertop but isn't afraid to dance on the bar once in a while. . . . I am not Gay. And I wouldn't want to be. No offense. (7)

Rather than being capital-G Gay, the man insists he has another identity, at once very specific and remarkably hard to pin down: "I prefer 'Queer,'" he muses, "It sounds like something anyone could be" (11). MacIvor's elegant monologue does much more, however, than merely lambaste contemporary gay culture. It also serves as an illuminating point of entry into MacIvor's own oeuvre, which can be clearly divided into two very different modes of writing.

Rare indeed, of course, is the playwright who does not have thematic elements in his or her work that remain constant over his or her career. Nonetheless, when it comes to sexual representation, MacIvor's plays ultimately skew towards two poles: works that feature lesbian and gay sexualities but present portraits of LGBT characters that border on stereotypes, and works that put forward queer representations that challenge heteronormativity. Unsurprisingly, works from the former category appear to have been more successful commercially. Though MacIvor is now firmly entrenched as one of Canada's top theatre artists, some of his texts are revived much more frequently than others and have proven more popular with audiences. And while every MacIvor play contains his characteristic sly wit and intelligence, theatre patrons have tended to gravitate towards pieces that rely on comedy in order to package LGBT sexualities with easily consumable labels. In this essay I explore MacIvor's experimental, queer theatrical beginnings and contrast them with some of his more canonical later works. I also argue that new pieces such as *Arigato, Tokyo* and *I, Animal* appear to represent a different stage in the author's career, one in which queer modes and sexualities have been brought more to the forefront of his work. As several other scholars and critics, including some in this very volume, have focused upon the author's well-known collaborations with Daniel Brooks (the plays that Robert Wallace has described as MacIvor's Monster Trilogy—*House, Here Lies Henry*, and *Monster* ["Technologies"]—as well as *Cul-de-Sac, This Is What Happens Next*, and so on), and because ensemble pieces by their very nature offer the opportunity to experience eroticized dynamics between characters played by different actors, I have restricted my analysis to multi-performer texts.

The very word that lends its name to queer theory is now one of the most contested in the academy, thanks to its now decades-old critical history. In fact, "queer theory" is an umbrella term that is often used as a signpost for a diverse collection of theories, disciplines, and practices: examples from this group include—but are not limited to—gender theory, cultural theory, sexology, LGBT-oriented studies, sexual diversity studies, and queer intersections with feminist, psychoanalytic, post-colonial, and critical race studies. Nevertheless, my use of queer theory for this explication of MacIvor's work requires that two positions, collated from several major thinkers, be taken as axiomatic. First, I argue for the recognition that heteronormativity is an oftentimes violent, and always insidious, ideology that coats all aspects of culture in twenty-first century North America, despite the enormous and promising advances made by LGBT- and queer-identified persons since the late 1960s. This observation is culled and adapted from Adrienne Rich's groundbreaking essay "Compulsory Heterosexuality and Lesbian Existence," first published in 1980, in which she delineated the concept of compulsory heterosexuality. Rich provocatively argued that heterosexuality needed to be "recognized and studied as a *political institution*" (35; emphasis in original), and suggested that "heterosexuality may not be a 'preference' at all but something that has had to be imposed, managed, organized, propagandized, and maintained by force" (50). Though Rich approached her topic with specific relevance to lesbian erasure in culture, theorists such as Gayle Rubin and Michael Warner have since demonstrated how wide-ranging the damaging effects of compulsory heterosexuality and heteronormativity truly are, Rubin through her now-classic analyses of "hierarchies of sexual value" (150) in "Thinking Sex: Notes for a Radical Theory of the Politics of Sexuality" and Warner in the introduction to his iconic edited collection *Fear of a Queer Planet*.

It is certainly possible that our culture's implicit acceptance and policing of the heteronorm is very gradually beginning to weaken, especially given the rise of same-sex marriage in Canada and many parts of the United States. But the disturbing persistence of homophobic, biphobic, and transphobic violence in both countries tells another narrative. Subjects are still indoctrinated from birth with the idea that a commonly accepted form of "straightness" is expected from them: to express desires that do not conform to this ideology is to immediately classify one's self as the non-normative, or perverse, Other. Subjects who identify as either LGBT or queer (or, in some cases, as members of both categories) are therefore always indirectly, and, more often than not, directly, assured of shared marginal status. This is how it is possible to rebut charges of essentializing spectator identification with onstage representations of desire. Audiences are by their very nature heterogeneous: they are composed of individuals who classify their sexual orientations in many different ways. The repressive apparatuses of heteronormative culture, however, ensure that a heterosexual and masculinist spectator position typically remains a given. Even spectators who consciously work to apply different identifications and reactions to performed works must continuously grapple, in psychic terms, with hegemonic social codes of straightness.

Secondly, while this essay relies upon the acceptance that "gay" and "queer" are concepts that exist on the perverse side of the heteronorm dichotomy, it also seeks to ensure that these ideas are written about in meaningful ways. The two terms, after all, are frequently conflated in the cultural imaginary, and it is here that the Man in Scrub's monologue from MacIvor's *I, Animal* provides valuable interpretive assistance. For while "gay" and "queer" exist together on a spectrum of non-heterosexual desire, they also serve as markers of both cultural identities and political strategies.

I take the words of MacIvor's speaker, then, at face value, and use "gay" to refer to mainstream understandings of sexual desire between two individuals of the same gender (i.e. gay or lesbian sexuality). Bisexual and transgender (and in the case of two of the MacIvor works I discuss, transvestite or drag) sexualities are therefore cleaved off from their typical position in the LGBT acronym, and are placed in the category of queer. With regard to my reading of queerness, I rely upon David Halperin's brilliant summary from his *Saint Foucault*, which states that

> "queer" does not name some natural kind or refer to some determinate object; it acquires its meaning from its oppositional relation to the norm. Queer is by definition *whatever* is at odds with the normal, the legitimate, the dominant. *There is nothing in particular to which it necessarily refers.* It is an identity without an essence. "Queer," then, demarcates not a positivity but a positionality vis-à-vis the normative—a positionality that is not restricted to lesbians and gay men. (62; emphasis in original)

Halperin's explication of the word perfectly suits the erotic representation found in MacIvor's second, queer mode of writing. Plays like *Never Swim Alone* and *Arigato, Tokyo* act as Trojan horses of queer desire: in effect, they turn the dominance of the heteronormative power structure against itself through the radical seduction of all viewers.

PART I. STRANGE BEGINNINGS: THE RHUBARB YEARS

From the very beginning of his impressive career, MacIvor was, to quote fellow playwright Carol Bolt, "a force of theatrical energy" (7). After withdrawing from Dalhousie University in Halifax and moving to Toronto in the early 1980s, MacIvor immediately became involved in the city's vibrant and growing theatre community. He studied at George Brown College, and then quickly began to forge important bonds with Canadian LGBT theatre pioneers. The Rhubarb Festival, originally conceived of by Sky Gilbert, Matt Walsh, Jerry Ciccoritti, and Fabian Boutillier as a festival of new and experimental works (Palmer 11), provided MacIvor (and many other emerging writers, directors, and performers of the era) with invaluable experience in both acting and playwriting.[1] In an email exchange dated 2 November 2014, MacIvor commented upon his participation in the festival in the warmest of terms, reflecting, "Rhubarb was a perfect way to workshop ideas and develop community. I remember it fondly and probably idealize i[t] somewhat." His first involvement with Rhubarb was a role in David Demchuk's controversial *Touch* during the 1986 festival. In terms of overt sexual representation, both gay and queer, the piece is the equivalent of a performer diving into the deep end: two men enter, "*prepare a bed on the stage, remove their clothes . . . climb in together*," and proceed to discuss pornographic magazines (45). MacIvor played the role of Gary opposite Ron Jenkins's Ken; the two characters are lovers and throughout the one-act play debate the place of porn consumption and the function of fantasy narrative in romantic relationships.

In the introduction to his superb collection *Making, Out*, in which the script of *Touch* appears, Wallace notes how the bold sexual content present

---

1   I remain exceptionally grateful to both Buddies in Bad Times Theatre in general and then-Festival Director Laura Nanni in particular for providing me with the position of Research Intern for the 35th Annual Rhubarb Festival from July 2013 to February 2014. My work with Rhubarb helped make this essay possible and provided me with valuable knowledge of queer Canadian theatre history.

in Demchuk's piece masks complex questions about representation and human relationships:

> This is a sex-play with intelligence, titillation with redeeming social
> value. The central irony of this very ironic play is that the charac-
> ters' ideological positions are overshadowed by the actors' physical
> positions in bed. In effect, the actors perform for the audience an
> example of the erotics at issue. ("Making Out" 18)

From the perspective of a contemporary Western culture that is virtually
porn-soaked with XXX imagery, *Touch* appears almost quaint. For example,
in a move to pacify his lover, Gary offers to burn his collection of magazines
in the couples' wok ("Porno dim sum" [54]), while Ken confesses to watching
explicit videos at his friend Paul's, whose largesse has allowed him to pur-
chase "a VCR and . . . a few movies" (50). But one must not underestimate
the subversive political nature of performing in such a piece in mid-1980s
Ontario. Writing eight years after *Touch* premiered, Wallace wryly observes
that "gay characters hardly ever fuck" in Canadian theatre, a statement that
largely holds true even at our present time ("Making Out" 18). Produced by
gay theatre *provocateur par excellence* Gilbert, the production was certainly
daring in its content. Nevertheless, while the story involves a gay couple, it is
Touch's queer seduction of the audience that makes it such an important text,
particularly in the context of MacIvor's own writing. The combination of the
characters' bawdy stories about the porn models, the actors' naked bodies,
and theatre's very nature as voyeuristic forces the spectators to grapple with
their own erotic identifications. In Wallace's superb summary, "Would the
audience watch these two nude men do more than talk? If not, why not?"
("Making Out" 19). Rather than asking the ostensibly straight patrons to distance themselves from different queer desires, Demchuk's clever script tries to
pull them ever closer. The experience must have been formative for MacIvor,
as many of his richest pieces deploy the same strategy.

The following year, MacIvor doubled his Rhubarb exposure, so to speak:
he contributed *The Right One*, with text co-written with Michele M. Jelley, and

performed in Pat Langner's *Something Exotic*. (Like Demchuk's earlier *Touch*, the latter production also contained elements of queer eroticism: MacIvor played a successful businessman "trying to escape boredom" via an extreme and violent role-playing encounter with a male prostitute, a plot point that gave the piece its title [Langner].) And in 1988, the artist achieved acclaim with his hilarious *Theatre Omaha's Production of* The Sound of Music,[2] a one-act so successful it was published in Franco Boni's collection *Rhubarb-o-rama!* and also remounted ten years later in a revival directed by playwright Brad Fraser. Nineteen eighty-nine would see the artist contribute his final piece to the festival with *Yes I Am and Who Are You?* MacIvor then worked as an actor in Ed Roy's *Creatures Like Us* in 1991, which marked his last involvement with the Rhubarb Festival.

Theatre Omaha may be seen as an early, well-crafted amalgam of the two modes of writing that have come to dominate MacIvor's entire body of work. Rather than focus on representations of either gay or queer desire, it mixes them together. A brief piece with a small cast, hilarious one-liners, and much physical comedy, the play is a metatheatrical farce about the titular theatre company's audition process for its production of *The Sound of Music*: an almost maniacal director named Gunther searches for a performer to play Maria von Trapp, "the perfect woman . . . the perfect wife . . . the perfect mother" (128).[3] Four actors (Inez, Bill, Betty, and Wanda) struggle through Gunther's artistic process in order to win the role, enduring his bizarre

---

2   Hereafter cited in the text as *Theatre Omaha*; the same year of its warm reception MacIvor also found time to perform in the festival in Robin Fulford's intriguingly titled *Couch Enigma*.

3   In a twist of fate, the short play's plot would mirror the structure of the reality television show *How Do You Solve a Problem Like Maria?*, in which contestants battled to win the coveted role. The BBC originally produced the show in 2006; it was linked with the Andrew Lloyd Webber/David Ian revival of the Rodgers and Hammerstein musical in the West End. In 2008 a Canadian version of the series was produced by CBC Television for the Lloyd Webber and David Mirvish co-production of *The Sound of Music* in Toronto; Mirvish told *Star* reporter Richard Ouzounian, "It was "thrilling . . . to bring a new star for the people of Canada to discover" (qtd. in "Dark Horse").

questions and demands (e.g. listing what they had for breakfast [128], de-scribing their particular special talent [129], telling him whether they love him more than their own children [133], and so on). Given *Theatre Omaha's* comedic genre and status as a short festival piece, it would be critically un-kind to expect exceedingly rich character development. As a result, the six characters conform to recognizable comic types that can be traced to earli-er backstage farces in the tradition of Michael Frayn's *Noises Off* (1982), or the earlier *Jitters* (1979) by MacIvor's fellow Canadian David French (Crew, "Jitters"): Gunther is the demanding auteur; Trevor, Gunther's assistant, is the meticulous theatre technician; Betty comes across as the over-eager ingenue, and so on. Like the other characters, Bill, a *"man in a colourful shirt reading a script"* (121), can be considered a stereotype; to be blunt, he is the nelly the-atre buff or artistic queen. His colourful shirt marks him as effeminate, and during his initial introduction to the group—a process the director absurd-ly insists on formally listing in the agenda as item "A. [. . .] Identification" (125–27)—the dialogue builds upon this marker of gayness:

> GUNTHER: If you don't mind me asking . . . did you make that
> *chemise* yourself?
> BILL: Sorry?
>
> . . .
>
> GUNTHER: Your shirt? Did you make—
>
> . . .
>
> I don't know why I ask. I seems [*sic*] so perfectly suited to you.
> You seem to "glow out loud," as they say.
> BILL: You find it loud?
> GUNTHER: Oh certainly not, certainly not. It so perfectly projects
> your—though I hardly know you—but you do have a flare, no? A
> flare for style and design, do you not? (126)

Bill's sartorial flare, in other words, ensures he is coded as gay from the very start of the play, and Gunther's lines quickly and comically bring this subtext to the audience's attention. Four pages later the jest gets more explicit as the group perform acting exercises and show one another their special talents: Bill *"performs the last part of Blanche's speech from A* Streetcar Named Desire, *about the boy at the dance"* (130). The character's recitation of Blanche's iconic monologue to her suitor Mitch in Scene Six means he essentially drag-rehearses the most famous of Tennessee Williams's ultra-feminine heroines for the group. And the joke is twofold: not only is MacIvor toying with the audience's knowledge about Williams's biography—he is, after all, one of the best-known gay authors in history—but Bill's performance also riffs on *Streetcar's* plot point that Blanche's husband, Allan Grey, was in the closet. Bill's gayness is a gag, and not an unfunny one at that.

Nevertheless, despite its reliance on gay caricature, *Theatre Omaha* presents to the audience a plethora of queer desires and scenarios. After Bill's *Streetcar* performance, the characters take turns role-playing a scenario in which a wife waits at home for her husband. All three times we see the improvisational sequence the roles are cross-cast, as only one of the competing actors is male. In the first instance Inez is the husband who asks Wanda for a kiss (which the latter flatly refuses), in the second instance Betty replaces Inez, and in the third instance Bill plays the husband to Wanda's wife. Audience members are therefore given faux heterosexual interactions, two of which are seemingly lesbian, and one of which is transvestite. The third pairing even gets swept up in their particular fantasy, with uproarious results:

BILL: Where in the hell have you been? It's four o'clock in the morning!

. . .

WANDA: I was out! I was out getting drunk. Getting pissed out of my mind so I could get up the guts to come home to you, you ugly bitch. You cow. [. . .] *(She starts to break down.)* And if I could find another woman who'd take me I'd be gone so fast . . .
BILL: *(As BILL, comforting her.)* Oh honey—
WANDA: *(Turning on him.)* Don't touch me!

BILL runs from the scene. (131)

The aggression present in Wanda and Bill's scene, though the source of much of the moment's comedy, is actually inconsequential. It is the fact that the actors become emotionally invested in their performative gender-swapping that matters, as it invites audience members to fantasize about their own romantic relationships, and suggests that performance can convincingly alter gender presentation and roles.

The play then concludes with one more queer twist. As a final test before his decision, Gunther forces the actors to attempt to fit into a dress he has chosen to be the costume for Maria's wedding dress. The director immediately dismisses Inez, Bill, and Betty. He considers Wanda, and appears about to declare her the winner, when abruptly Trevor announces he would like to try on the dress. Explaining to the actors that Trevor, being "the other half of Theatre Omaha" (135), has the right to compete for the role of Maria, Gunther then begins to describe their relationship in increasingly erotic terms (e.g. "You never stop surprising me" [135]), while Trevor changes offstage. The play's final moment is a telling parody of Maria and Captain von Trapp's wedding:

> TREVOR *enters proudly in the dress singing a verse of "My Favourite Things."*
>
> GUNTHER: Trevor!
> TREVOR: Oh, sir . . . Oh Gunther . . . *I love you so much I want to be you.*
> GUNTHER: Trevor . . . you . . . are . . . wonderful . . . Trevor. No. I must never call you Trevor again. You are now . . . Maria. Maria. Maria, come to me. [. . .] How could I have thought to look beyond my own right hand. It is a man's best friend. Maria. (135; emphasis added)

The hilarity is then heightened as the two men "*kiss tenderly*" and begin to dance together for the one-act play's last moments (135). Gunther and Trevor's platonic professional relationship therefore rapidly and amusingly morphs into an erotic personal one. The two male characters were never obviously signalled as gay—as the swishy Bill has been—but the power of performance and authentic emotional investment transform them into subjects imbued with queer desire. While the audience is invited to laugh at the men's newly formed sexual relationship, *Theatre Omaha*'s closing tableaux also asks complicated questions about erotic connection. Trevor's line, "I love you so much I want to be you," shrewdly satirizes longstanding, homophobic, Neo-Freudian theories of homosexuality as merely sublimated narcissistic investment. Instead, audience members are forced to question *all* erotic relationships as merely expressions of self-love. Perhaps, the play suggests, each individual is attempting to solve his or her own erotic "problem like Maria" in the same way.[4] In *Theatre Omaha*, the border between straight and queer sexual desire becomes increasingly blurred.

PART II. WATCHING BOYS, WATCHING GIRLS: *NEVER SWIM ALONE*

Overlapping with his Rhubarb experiences in the mid- to late-1980s, MacIvor had already started to receive serious acclaim for his writing. The da da kamera/Buddies co-production of *See Bob Run* (1987)—starring friend and now long-time collaborator Caroline Gillis—had premiered at the Poor Alex Theatre, and the artist himself performed in *Wild Abandon* (1988) at Theatre Passe Muraille. The 1990s, though, ushered in a new level of sustained critical praise: three of MacIvor's pieces, including *Never Swim Alone*, were nominated for the Dora Mavor Moore Award for Best New Play in 1991 alone (Bolt 7). *Never Swim Alone* is structured as a sort of absurdist ultimate male faceoff, what one reviewer deemed a "Battle Royale of vicious undermining

---

4   MacIvor was to return to this point in a darker vein much later in his career. In an interview with the playwright included in the published version of *Arigato, Tokyo*, Joan MacLeod quotes from Brendan Healy's perceptive director's note. He states that "[MacIvor's work] give[s] us space to contemplate what it's like to have a heart. But how do we know that love is not some elaborate trickery, the result of psychological projection or fear of being alone?" (81).

and one-upmanship" (Del Signore), with Frank and Bill jousting against one another in a series of rounds with criteria that initially seem random, such as "Who Falls Dead the Best" (22).[5] Judging the competition is the Referee, an enigmatic young woman dressed in "*a blue bathing suit*" (15). Interspersed between the surrealist rounds are bits of mysterious text, through which a story comes into focus. One summer when Bill and Frank were boys, a young girl named Lisa challenged them to a swimming race across an unnamed bay. The Referee's opening lines plant the seeds of this story:

> She turns her head a little over her shoulder and speaks to the boys
> "Race you to the point?"
> This is the beach.
> Here is the bay.
> There is the point. (16)

This youthful race ultimately has a deadly consequence, however: Lisa is not able to keep up with Frank and Bill. And though "feel[ing] her fall back" (69), the boys, driven on by shared bravado and the need to be "the first man" (72), do not stop to come to her aid. Her death then becomes a linking trauma for the rest of the men's lives.

Given its emphasis on competition amongst straight men, *Never Swim Alone* at first might seem an odd choice to single out for an explication of non-normative desire in MacIvor's body of work. One might indeed point to the equally surreal *2-2-Tango* as a more fitting example, with its central conceit of dance, confessional tone, and explicit references to various forms of gay male intercourse, such as when Jim (originally played by MacIvor in the premiere) tells the audience,

---

5   The comic nature of the play's categories means that *Never Swim Alone* is like *Theatre Omaha* in serving as a sort of theatrical precursor to a popular reality television show. *Kenny Vs. Spenny* pitted best friends Kenny Hotz and Spencer Rice against one another in a series of ludicrous challenges. The show initially aired on CBC in Canada before transferring to Showcase Television; in the United States it was first broadcast on the Game Show Network before being "officially relocated" to Comedy Central ("About").

Well if he's into it I'm into a bit of it.

. . .

I'm a flexible guy, I'm a flexible man, I'm a flexible guy. French, Greek,
B & D, S & M, a water sport now and then, a scattering of humiliation, him hanging from his ankles in the centre of the room with a
snake around his body . . .
I don't mind that. (205)

Nonetheless, *Never Swim Alone* is just as effective as *2-2-Tango* at exploring
the intricacies of queer desires (if not more so) precisely *because* its two characters, A. Francis (Frank) Delorenzo and William (Bill) Wade, are presented
to the audience as heterosexual men. Much like that of *Theatre Omaha*, the
text's representations of desire and intimacy seek to ensnare the spectator via
identification; rather than seal off desire, character relations and symbolism
in the play are used to open it up.

To begin with, MacIvor's Frank, Bill, and Referee present the audience
with a triangle of homosociality that often veers surprisingly close to representations of homosexual eroticism. While the actor who doubles as both
Referee and Lisa is an instrumental aspect to the production—it is, after
all, Lisa's death by drowning that drives the play forward to its conclusion
(73)—the play also seeks to stress the emotional bond between the two men.
Despite being, in the words of *New York Times* critic Jason Zinoman, "Coolly
nonlinear, abstract, and masculine" ("Somewhere"), *Never Swim Alone* makes
clear the men's emotional connection in Round Three, in which the section of
dialogue appears that gives the play its title. After reciting beautiful language
describing "real summers / when you're a kid" (26),[6] the characters explain
to the audience the roots of their relationship:

---

6   This portrait of straight male nostalgia for boyhood summers was to reappear nineteen
years later in Dookie's monologue that opens the second act of *Bingo!*:

Before there were wives and kids and car payments and mortgages and RRSPs
it was only ever summer and we were princes.

. . .

FRANK: And when they said not to swim alone
BILL: this
FRANK: here
FRANK & BILL: this is the guy I swam with!
BILL: I know this guy better than he knows himself. (26)

The characters' manipulative ploys to win the "match" only underscore how correct Bill is in asserting their deep-seated "knowledge" of one another.

At surface level this makes perfect sense: one must know one's "formidable foe" (13) very well indeed in order to vanquish him.[7] (Never her: the only opponents who count to heterosexual men, the play implies, are other men.) But each man's attempt to sever the other's Achilles heel also serves to demonstrate their lengthy and intimate history, such as when Frank wins Round Four ("Friendly Advice Part One" [29]) via a double-pronged attack on Bill's vanity and fear of aging:

BILL: All I'm trying to say here buddy[8] is if you ever need an outside eye, if you ever need a friendly ear, then hey, I'm here.
FRANK: Are you thinner?
BILL: Wha
FRANK: Are you thinner?

Then summers passed and summers passed and in the end the shed became the headquarters for our game. (55–56)

7   One of the terms MacIvor used for Ken McDougall, the play's original director, in his dedication.

8   The word "buddy," which one might initially connect with straight fraternal camaraderie, here has two connotations of same-sex erotic interaction that are particularly satisfying. First, it recalls the famous Gilbert-founded LGBT and queer theatre, which in its various incarnations has always provided a public space for cruising. (See, for example, Buddies in Bad Times Theatre's current space known as "Tallulah's Cabaret," which doubles as a gay dance bar on weekends.) Secondly, men seeking casual sexual encounters with other men frequently use "buddy" as a type of code word. In Terry Goldie's incisive *queersexlife*, he theorizes that the term "assumes . . . a link through sex that goes beyond sex" (203).

BILL: No.

. . .

FRANK: It must just be your hair. (31–32)

This slightly superior ability to press just where it hurts the most eventually aids Frank in being declared the play's first man: he was, after all, first to the point in the race when they were children (73). Yet consider that this skill can also be developed in the context of close, and very often romantic, attachments. In this way *Never Swim Alone* seems more similar to plays detailing marital infernos (e.g. Edward Albee's *Who's Afraid of Virginia Woolf?* or August Strindberg's *The Dance of Death, Part I*) than those centred upon masculine *agons* (e.g. Sam Shepard's *True West*).

The characters' dialogue and movements about the stage also work to emphasize the closeness and intensity of their relationship. Frank and Bill are costumed identically in blue suits, and are nearly the same height: Bill is "almost imperceptibly shorter" than his companion (15). The actors speak a great many of the play's lines in unison, a stylistic effect that reviewers have found both "mesmerizing" (Del Signore) and needlessly "artificial" (Chapman). Regardless of whether this non-realist dialogue suits one's tastes, it has the effect of emphasizing Bill and Frank's sameness. Their simpatico actions and responses easily support a reading of stifled same-sex eroticism. Indeed, the very cover of the published collection *Never Swim Alone & This Is A Play* points towards sexual release: Michael Lo's still from the original production of *Never Swim Alone* depicts Robert Dodds (as Frank) cradling MacIvor (as Bill) in his arms. Dodds wears a subtle smile with his lips slightly apart, while MacIvor's head is thrown back, his mouth open in apparent ecstasy.

Still, sublimated homosexual desire amongst straight male rivals is far from the only method by which *Never Swim Alone* attempts to arouse queer desire in its spectators. Bill and Frank, of course, rely on the Referee to judge their combat, and her presence therefore haunts all of their interactions. Though in one sense the woman acts as a marker of same-sex desire between the men, in another she is knit into symbolic phantasies of voyeurism, incestuous relations, three-way sex, and cuckoldry.[9] The Referee's initial section of dialogue describing Lisa and the boys as adolescents on the beach invokes preconscious eroticism between the three figures onstage: "The boys have been *watching* the girl from a distance but now that the summer is nearly over, from *very close by*. She reminds one boy of *his sister*, she reminds the other of *a picture of a woman he once saw in a magazine*" (15–16; emphasis added). The eroticism of the Referee's portrait of unconscious sexual imaginings and voyeuristic delight amongst the youthful ménage-à-trois that is Frank, Bill, and Lisa is then heightened by the very costuming of the actor's physical form: that "skimpy" blue bathing suit tempts the audience to objectify the female flesh on display (Wagner).[10] Audience members are therefore presented with a multiplicity of desires that can be classified as non-normative. They are able to both mirror the subject positions of the desiring boys in their phantasies about the figure of the woman—one through an incestuous connection to his sister, one through a linkage with a model in a (possibly adult) magazine—and they are also able to identify with fantasies about the three characters sexually interacting in different combinations.

Even the play's most direct metaphors for masculine competition provide the audience with fresh opportunities for queer fantasy. During Round Six, appropriately titled "Members Only," the characters participate in what can only be described as a literal dick measurement: "*FRANK and BILL slowly approach centre. THEY meet and turn to face the REFEREE, their backs to the audience. THEY take out their penises for her inspection. After some deliberation SHE calls a tie*" (38). Similarly, the play's cliffhanger ending relies upon

---

9   The fantasy of the cuckold, in both conscious and unconscious terms, appears in *Never Swim Alone* many times. Besides the suggestion of symbolic cuckoldry in the main triad of Lisa and the two boys, the word appears as one of the insults used in Round Seven, in which the men denigrate one another's fathers (52). It also forms a core tactic used by Bill in the "Business Ties" section: he claims to have witnessed Frank's wife, the unseen Donna, "in the shower" (65) with their mutual colleague Phil.

10   Vit Wagner's review of the original production complimented Gillis on her turn as the "lithe beach goddess," and perceptively described her role in the play as "the referee-puppeteer-sex-object."

a phallic battle. Bill, ominously assuring Frank, "I learned my lesson . . . I won't be second again" (74), removes a gun from his briefcase and aims it at his competitor. After a moment, Frank repeats the action. Finally, after the men have cocked their guns at one another, the Referee eerily informs the audience, "Only One Gun Is Loaded" (75). While this final sequence carries obvious connotations of aggression and combat, the symbolism—aiming a weapon at one's partner, coming "first," shooting one's load, and so on—is larded with sexual double entendres.

Never Swim Alone was undeniably successful; overall the show was a smash with patrons and critics in both Canada and the United States. Zinoman's profile on MacIvor for the Times notes the impact a remount of the play had on New York audiences:

> When it opened at the Fringe in 1999, "Never Swim Alone," which has been brought back for a run in honor of the festival's 10-year anniversary, drew sold-out audiences and became only the second show in the history of the Fringe Festival to transfer (the first was "Last Train to Nibroc"). Before "Urinetown" was moved Off-Broadway, it was arguably the biggest hit in the history of the Fringe. ("Somewhere")

Reviews of different productions of the play read alongside later works from MacIvor's oeuvre, however, strongly suggest that Never Swim Alone succeeded despite its representations of queer desire rather than because of them. Critics, in other words, were more than happy to reward the play for what they saw as its dark satire on a culture of "macho male bravado" (Chapman). No one, it appears, rushed to applaud its carefully constructed proliferation of non-normative, or perverse, desires. Never Swim Alone is therefore an exception to what would become a rule of sorts in MacIvor's later career: successful, mainstream works with easily labelled depictions of straight and gay sexuality. It was able to gain critical popularity and box-office dollars, all the while attempting to seduce audience members with its queer erotics.

PART III. DISGUSTING LIFESTYLES: *BINGO!*

One need not look too far for examples of gay caricature in works from MacIvor's later period. *Bingo!*, a nearly treacle-sweet examination of aging set amongst five Maritimers, works to shore up the heteronorm by inviting audience members to laugh at expressions of sexual desire that deviate from straightness in any form. A well-crafted romantic comedy revolving around a high-school reunion, the play is tailor-made as a crowd-pleaser.[11] After a staged reading at Factory Theatre's CrossCurrents Festival in Toronto in 2010, *Bingo!* enjoyed a successful run at Neptune Theatre in Halifax the following year, before touring Nova Scotia. Winnipeg's Prairie Theatre Exchange produced a version of the show in their 2011 programming. Finally, *Bingo!* closed Factory Theatre's rather turbulent 2013/2014 season.

Though reviews of the different productions of the play had been mostly positive, *Toronto Star* critic Richard Ouzounian gave *Bingo!* a pointedly cool welcome upon its arrival at Factory. In his review, he somewhat archly compared the play to the work of another extremely successful Canadian playwright; proposing a social experiment in which theatre patrons were not given programs, Ouzounian mused, "Would they [audience members] ever guess that the usually quirky Daniel MacIvor had written it? Or would they probably have thought that it was by Norm Foster, Canada's King of Situation Comedy?" ("*Bingo!*"). Though he misinterprets MacIvor's parody of Foster's style as unintentional, Ouzounian correctly gestures towards a flatness of character that permeates *Bingo!*.[12] To some degree, this is because

---

11   MacIvor initially wrote the play in an attempt to please his brother. J. Kelly Nestruck's review of the Toronto production sheds light on MacIvor's intention for *Bingo!* to be highly accessible: "[MacIvor] wrote this nostalgia-suffused lark hoping it would appeal to a sibling who lives in a trailer park in Sydney, Cape Breton, a two-time cancer survivor who likes old westerns and drinking at the Legion but not the theatre."

12   MacIvor explained via email that he purposely wrote *Bingo!* to mirror Foster's aesthetic. In fact, he took his inspiration from a comic dinner discussion he had with Joan MacLeod, Michael Healey, and other playwrights while in residence at the Banff Centre. Observing that "Norm's plays fill theatres," the authors joked that they should collectively

the play's genre dictates stock character types; as *Theatre Omaha*'s farcical qualities required flatter characters, so do situation and/or romantic comedies.[13] Characters exhibiting non-normative sexual desires, however, come off particularly the worse for wear.

The butch Laura "Boots" Boutlier, for example, is frequently mocked as a lesbian by the other characters. The play ultimately leaves Boots's sexuality an open question; we hear that she "liked" (91) the somewhat slovenly Jeff "Heffer" MacInnis before his marriage, and the last time we see the character on stage she is in a bar with him, preparing to dance to a Matt Minglewood song (97). But the play's series of sustained, homophobic innuendos about her possible (or even probable) latent lesbianism are hard to ignore. Her close friendship with the shy Bitsy is clearly under constant scrutiny in the town in which they live, as a discussion amongst the male characters in the first scene makes evident:

> HEFFER: From the looks of it there's quite the opposite of enemies going on there.
> DOOKIE: How do you mean?
> HEFFER: People say what they say.
> DOOKIE: Boots and Bitsy?
> HEFFER: Well you remember Boots, she tried to get on the wrestling team. (15)

Worse still is the play's running gag concerning Boots's strong enthusiasm for the Indigo Girls track "Closer to Fine." Both members of the folk group

---

write a play called "'Norm Foster's Going Bowling' so that people might think i[t] was Norm Foster's 'Going Bowling'" (Wilcox, Message). The published version of *Bingo!* is dedicated to Foster.

13   Though he did not directly address flat characterization or genre constraints, the playwright appeared to gesture towards these points during an email exchange about audience expectations, stating, "I feel like the last six years have been an adventure in exploring the well-made play and the subscriber audience (Tarragon, PTE, the Regionals) and the plays were very much made for those venues and audiences" (MacIvor, Message).

are out lesbians, and their best-known song is therefore used as a crude signifier for Sapphic desire. After she "*groov*[es]" to the song by herself, all four of the play's other characters stop and watch her, and she is forced to deny this unspoken communal suggestion of her lesbianism (65). Boots claims she just likes the song, and Heffer all-too-quickly accepts her lame denial: "No, I know. Just because you listen to . . . you know 'folk' doesn't mean you're a . . . you know, 'folkie'" (65). All of this is meant to be funny, of course, but the subtext is that lesbian desire is inherently disturbing and problematic.

Nonetheless, *Bingo*'s representation of an accepted cultural fear of lesbianism is only matched by its depictions of the heteronorm's obsession and disgust with male sodomy. In one of the play's most distressing moments, a discussion of one of their former classmates prompts Heffer and the loutish Dookie to joyfully partake in a grotesque parody of gay sex:

HEFFER: I'd rather be a fag than Norman Taylor.

DOOKIE comes up behind HEFFER and grabs him, pretending to have sex with him.

DOOKIE: And you got your wish Heffer 'cause you are!
HEFFER: Oh baby oh baby give me that big man-root.

DOOKIE shoves HEFFER away hard, laughing. (19)

This fag bashing is not presented completely uncritically, of course—Dookie, after all, is eventually revealed as the play's chief villain. However, its very inclusion in the play doubtlessly allows some spectators the chance to vicariously revel in homophobic displays. And while there is an argument to be made that Dookie and Heffer's casual homophobia is merely more true to life, reviewer Elissa Barnard of Halifax's *Chronicle Herald* singled the moment out in her otherwise glowing assessment of the original Mulgrave Road Theatre production, declaring, "There is one false note in the first act that may be offensive when Heffer and Dookie use a pejorative term and pretend to be gay" ("*Bingo!*").

Fascinatingly, the straight-identified characters are not immune to this social policing of desires. One of the play's largest surprises occurs towards the end of Act One, Scene Two: during a private conservation in the bar, Bitsy asserts to Boots that she has learned that Heffer and his wife Deb engage in non-monogamous sexual behaviour with other straight couples. Due to Bitsy's natural shyness and embarrassment about the subject matter, the discussion used to reveal this secret is assuredly and absurdly funny (e.g. "BOOTS: Monkeys? They've got monkeys? / BITSY: No. [*whispering unintelligibly*] Swingers" [47]). But the cute dialogue distressingly masks a rigid politics of heteronormativity. In Act Two, Heffer's status as a swinger becomes common knowledge through a forced chain of events involving his naked selfie on Paul "Nurk" Kenney's cellphone, and MacIvor's dialogue serves to transform Heffer into a pathetic figure. Though the play takes pains to stress that he is hardly the brightest bulb—and depicts the character harbouring a grudge against Nurk for gaining admittance to university engineering programs while he could not [12, 25, 27ff]—Heffer himself is well aware that "everybody's laughing at [him]" once they learn of his non-monogamous relationship (87). Dookie promptly refers to his "'lifestyle'" as "just sick" (86), and two pages later he deems it "disgusting" (88). Even Bitsy, by far one of the play's most empathetic characters, decides she feels "sad" for Heffer (49).

Admittedly, Heffer does not seem fulfilled, either sexually or emotionally, by his open relationship with Deb. Not only does the audience learn that he cried while discussing the issue with Bitsy (49), but he also concedes that this openness could be symptomatic of a serious rift in his relationship with his wife:

> I go on that stupid website because Deb wants to. And I go on it tonight because I'm thinking that she went on it on her own, which we're not supposed to do on our own, but she does sometimes, I know she does. We're supposed to only go on it together, not alone, that's the deal. That was supposed to be the deal. (88)

In terms of the retrograde, masculinist sexual politics the play advances, Heffer has lost control of his wife. The offstage Deb has emasculated him as easily as his best friend Dookie. Symbolically, Heffer's "bottoming" for Dookie during the first act's parodic rape turns him into the play's only visible faggot. (We briefly hear of Boots and Bitsy's gay friend Lloyd, who predictably wears eyeliner [35] and hosts late-night Saturday parties [90], but he is never seen on stage.) In its utter rejection of any type of viable queer desire, the play in turn equates the cuckold with the faggot: any sexuality that does not consist of monogamous heterosexuality is quickly placed in the "disgusting" category of gay. In this manner, *Bingo!* allows spectators to easily reinforce and reify the heteronorm by identifying any type of queer desire as pathologically Other. It is therefore no accident that the piece ends with the romantic union of Bitsy and Nurk, the endearing characters with which we are intended to identify; after saying "Bingo" to one another in recognition of their shared desire, the stage directions state "*they kiss again, for real*" (103). Whereas *Never Swim Alone* entices audience members via a radical intimacy that asks them to connect to different queer desires, representations of sexuality in *Bingo!* are strictly controlled and contained.

PART IV. "FLUID ANSWERS": POLYSEXUAL DESIRES AND A DIFFERENT DIRECTION

The generally warm reception that *Bingo!* received from audiences and critics was not destined to be repeated when MacIvor's next major work, *Arigato, Tokyo*, opened at Toronto's Buddies in Bad Times Theatre on 16 March 2013. A dark and glittering tale of a disenchanted writer's trip to Japan, the play sharply divided critics, a point MacIvor himself motioned to during his warm and unguarded interview with Joan MacLeod: "The reviews . . . in Toronto were between 'I have seen God in this play' and 'a weak moment for him.' It's disliking and dismissing, or it's the best thing ever, but somebody apparently said it's another play I've written about love" (80–81).[14] The play most certainly

14   The negative response MacIvor paraphrases is likely a conflation of statements made by Robert Cushman (for *The National Post*) and Martin Morrow (for *The Globe and Mail*);

had its defenders in terms of mainstream media theatre reviewers. For example, in stark contrast to his review of *Bingo!*, Ouzounian gave the production an unequivocal rave review; his comments are the ones MacIvor referenced, as he started his analysis with a congratulatory allusion to Williams's famous line, "Sometimes—there's God—so quickly!" from *Streetcar*, and judged *Arigato, Tokyo* as "one of those unexpectedly unique evenings of theatre that we all hope for" ("Thanks"). Nevertheless, critical adoration such as that from Ouzounian or John Coulbourn (writing for *The Toronto Sun*) ultimately failed to translate into box-office dollars for MacIvor and Buddies in Bad Times. In fact, Brendan Healy, artistic director of Buddies in Bad Times Theatre, took the unprecedented step of addressing the play's lack of financial success in an open letter distributed online (see James Adams). Though he exaggerated in his claim that responses from both audiences and critics had been "overwhelmingly positive," Healy's letter was admirably honest and self-effacing, particularly considering he himself had helmed the play's premiere.[15] Noting that declining theatre audiences are an "industry-wide phenomenon," and that he wasn't "angry at audiences" (qtd. in James Adams), Healy expressed genuine confusion and dismay at the way MacIvor's latest piece had sold:

> [*Arigato, Tokyo*] represents a bold and exciting departure in Daniel's writing and I am deeply honoured that one of our country's greatest living playwrights entrusted us with the responsibility of realizing this latest phase in his oeuvre. . . . Our houses have been disappointingly low. I would even say "shockingly low" for such a critically lauded production by a writer of Daniel's stature. They are low in

---

both reviewers were ultimately unimpressed with the production. Cushman went so far as to describe it as "a low point for MacIvor" ("With Friends") while Morrow decided *Arigato, Tokyo* merely recycled themes the playwright had already explored, writing that "ultimately, this play isn't all that different from MacIvor's other works. Here are his favourite themes of sibling and parent-child tensions, his lyrical bent and his preoccupation with the meaning of love. Only this time he's hidden it all behind a cold, exotic mask" ("*Arigato*").

15   The full text of Healy's open letter was published online in Carly Maga's culture blog posting for *Torontoist*; all quotations unless noted are taken from her article.

such a way that we are scratching our heads and asking some very serious questions.

There can be no debate that the continuing decline of performing arts sales in Canada affects both major arts institutions (the Stratford Festival, the National Arts Centre) and so-called alternative, independent theatre companies (Buddies in Bad Times, Factory, Mulgrave Road). Still, by contrasting the mainstream marketability of the content of *Arigato, Tokyo*—a piece Healy deemed a new "phase" in the author's work—with the financial success of plays such as *Bingo!*, the dismal sales figures for the former piece become less of a head-scratcher. *Arigato, Tokyo* is a text in which each line barely conceals a myriad of beckoning queer desires. In a culture of the heteronormative gaze, a culture that requires all subjects constantly to monitor and discipline their own erotic attachments and identifications, the play's disappointing earnings were a near inevitability.

Arigato, Tokyo features a triangle among three main characters: Carl Dewer, a Canadian author who writes collections of "cynical, personal essay[s]" (qtd. in MacLeod 81) with titles like "*Understanding Everything*" (11), which explore existentialism and the limits of knowledge and feelings; Nushi Toshi, his steely and alluring interpreter/handler during his trip to Japan; and Nushi's brother, Yori, a Noh theatre actor. Woven in and out of this triangle is Etta Waki, who occasionally plays a Tokyo-based drag queen in love with Carl, but who doubles as the "assistant of the story" (3). The play takes as its central premise that desire is hard to pin down—and even harder to resist. Delivered in the original production by the magnetic Tyson James, Etta's opening monologue stresses the themes of Orientalist fantasies and malleable libidinal cathexes that pulse through the text: "I am the laughing room, the crowded table, the angry mob, the cheering throng. / . . . I am Tokyo. / I am your nightmare and your desire" (4). Cycling through book readings by day and buzzing with cocaine and sake by night, Carl begins sleeping with Nushi not long after his arrival in Japan. This sexual relationship is then complicated when Carl becomes entranced by her brother upon meeting him after a performance of the Noh play *Genji Kuyo*: "*YORI sits bare-chested; he is a handsome man. CARL is taken with him*" (20). Yori eventually reveals that Nushi is a woman obsessed with

Carl and his writings; late in the play we learn that she has funded his trip to Japan herself, and she evenly explains "it is a service I am happy to supply" when her deception is revealed (58). But Yori quickly exhibits his own twisted fixation; after manipulating the severing of Carl's relationship with his sister by seducing the writer himself, he cruelly dispatches him back to Canada with icy precision: "Your driver soon will be here. / No regrets" (64).

Though *Never Swim Alone* and *Arigato, Tokyo* are very different texts in terms of aesthetics, they share erotic triangular relationships (both literal and phantastical) that feature men and women at the same time. In the latter play, however, MacIvor pushes the queer subtext even further. Not only does the central three-way relationship feature a man having sexual intercourse with another man and a woman who share direct blood ties, but it also involves the main character sexually objectifying an effeminate man dressed as a woman. Thus *Arigato, Tokyo* presents its spectators with a sort of "polysexual" playground, a term MacIvor has used to describe his protagonist's sexual orientation,[16] stating that

> He [Carl] was polysexual and he had no boundaries. . . . When David Storch stepped into [the role], it became about someone who was not necessarily identified as gay. He was just polysexual. So the tone of it shifted because of the casting, and I think it's a much more interesting story that way. I'm happy about that. (qtd. in MacLeod 79)

MacIvor presents audience members with a number of non-normative desires, and tempts them to identify with any and/or all of them. Nushi and Carl's heterosexual May/December affair, with its Daddy carnalities; the homoerotic behaviour between Carl and Yori, perfectly set at a hot-springs bath to maximize our scopophilic joy in the nude body of the actor playing Yori (35–37); the hallucinatory femme or transgender pleasures Etta Waki provides; Asian

---

16   In response to Nushi's question concerning his sexual partners, Carl answers, "Many women. More men. Several in between" (27). MacIvor has explained that this crucial line was added during previews, after an initial draft of the play was staged in Banff (qtd. in MacLeod 79).

fetishization; unconscious group-sex fantasies, such as when the four characters symbolically parody "*the children's game Kagome, Kagome*" (56): *Arigato,
Tokyo* is a veritable garden of queer delights.

Moreover, Yori's willingness to "ben[d] himself" (39) into a same-sex
union with Carl in order to control Nushi—arguably the play's largest plot
twist—only serves to emphasize the play's privileging of queer representations. In a narrative provocation with an echo of John Ford's '*Tis Pity She's a
Whore*, his dialogue during his final scene with Carl (during which Yori claims
to have become the writer's "master" [63]) strongly implies an unconscious
incestuous desire for his sister. During the original production's showdown
between the two characters, Michael Dufays and David Storch added a chilling intensity to the moment in which Yori tells Carl that

> My sister was of the belief that she could master you.
> She was incorrect.
>
> . . .
>
> You describe many things for this word of love. Of child to parent,
> of husband to wife, of lover to lover. But there is one you omit. *From
> sister to brother and brother to sister.* This was *a sacrifice for me to
> make.* This was *my service to my sister.* (63; emphasis added)

Yori's "sacrifice" for his sister involves him symbolically "servicing" her by
stealing her lover. Hence the main erotic triangle displays psychic components that are for viewers simultaneously disturbing and erotogenic: Carl's
figurative penetration of the consanguine bond between the Toshi siblings
is made both more taboo and more titillating by the suggestion of Yori's unconscious incestuous designs on Nushi.

Therefore representations of erotic desire in the play function only to
breed new and different queer desires, all of which refuse the spectator the
traditional satisfaction of self-definition against the perverse Other. In this
way, *Arigato, Tokyo* can be firmly placed as a MacIvor text written in a mode
quite distinct from plays that feature characters directly labelled as claiming
a gay or lesbian identity. It is impossible to imagine Boots, or Kyle Best from

MacIvor's more recent *The Best Brothers* (2013), sauntering on stage beside Carl, Nushi, Yori, and Etta; the play repeatedly refuses spectator identification via rigid notions of straightness. And as a result, audiences by and large refused to board MacIvor's exquisite "trans-Pacific flight" to queer sexuality (5).

Ultimately, the texts themselves, when read alongside their differing critical and commercial receptions, demonstrate that the playwright's works for multiple performers have moved between two modes: gay and queer. It would be incorrect, however, to point to the radical intimacy forged between spectator and stage in plays such as *Arigato, Tokyo* and *I, Animal* as evidence that MacIvor has entered a completely distinct "new" phase. Rather, early pieces such as *Theatre Omaha* and *Never Swim Alone* demonstrate that the author has long held an interest in queer representation, but that his works that do not challenge the heteronorm have been far more successful with audiences. MacIvor's recent plays suggest that he is at present more comfortable allowing challenging representations of non-normative desire to remain at the forefront of his work. Writing in the aforementioned email of 2 November 2014, MacIvor himself seemed to suggest this. When questioned as to whether we have moved beyond "gay" or "queer" theatre in Canada, the playwright argued for the continuing relevance of queer representation:

> Yes [i.e. we have moved beyond them] to some extent perhaps "Gay" but not "Queer" I don't think. If you look at Brendan [Healy] and his work at Buddies it's very queer—which seems to have little to do with ideas of Gay really, it's more about a radicalization of theatre and thought—pro-sex, poly-sex, polyamorous, far-left politically, so on. I don't think we'll ever move beyond that, there will always be room to investigate—there will always be an "other."

These comments strongly hint that audiences might want to prepare themselves for more performances that radicalize both theatre and thought, more plays featuring fluid and malleable desires that always threaten to spread across the footlights. As the insightful Man in Scrubs from *I, Animal* both warns and promises, "People cross lines all the time" (11).

DANIEL MacIVOR'S *ARIGATO, TOKYO*: CULTURAL PALIMPSESTS IN PERFORMANCE

PETER KULING

One of Daniel MacIvor's more recent shows, *Arigato, Tokyo*, first produced in April 2013 at Buddies in Bad Times Theatre in Toronto, focuses on the hybridized conditions of contemporary culture, language, and sexuality. Brendan Healy, artistic director of Buddies, poignantly reminds audiences of unresolvable paradoxes they may experience during performances of *Arigato, Tokyo*: "It is both the *truth* of love and the *lie* of love that completes our humanity" (*Arigato* 7). MacIvor uses this play to showcase distances between evolving cultural identities in a globalizing world by focusing on a narrative of unanticipated (and unrequited) love between two men from distinctly different cultural backgrounds. *Arigato, Tokyo* allows audiences to witness performances of fractured selves encountering and reacting to their own hybridized personal and cultural realities. Using ideas of mythology, dreams, translation, physical space, and love, MacIvor encourages audiences to speculate on what people lose due to the limits of biographical and cultural translation.

Arigato, Tokyo is a metatheatrical and culturally intertextual play inspired by Daniel MacIvor's experiences travelling through Japan as a writer witnessing the failure of true intercultural communication. This play contains scenes featuring characters explaining the actual meaning of words in translation from Japanese to English and English to Japanese, performances of North American drag and Japanese Noh theatre, as well as recurring motifs of self-authorship and personal agency. MacIvor problematizes many of the countries and communities we call home, the ways we fall in love, and popular concepts of the self in the wake of new and diverse multi-layered personal identities due to globalization. While this play is set in Japan, the text focuses as much on Canadian diasporic experiences as on Japanese ones. Carl, the play's protagonist, introduces Canadian elements—dialogue, phrasing, and social conventions—into almost every scene in an effort to develop layered performances of culture, sexuality, and otherness. The world premiere of *Arigato, Tokyo* at Buddies in Bad Times Theatre in Toronto transported audiences through MacIvor's memories and experiences of different spaces that include Japan and Canada, as well as the queer community.

Arigato, Tokyo tells the story of a Canadian author named Carl Dewer (played by David Storch) and his relationships with three different narrator figures as he completes a reading tour across Japan: Etta (played by Tyson James), a cross-dressing male narrator who exists in Carl's mind; Nushi (played by Cara Gee), a female Japanese interpreter and his official tour guide; and Yori (played by Michael Dufays), Nushi's brother and a Japanese Noh theatre actor. These characters each share differing intimate relationships with Carl and guide him through new cultural, sexual, and historical experiences in Japan. The journey ends with Carl returning to Vancouver confused by his unanticipated affection for Yori as well as by Nushi's attempt to start a relationship with him. The ending emphasizes the inconclusive status of Carl's personal identities in a world of competing cultural and sexual forces. MacIvor encourages audiences to reflect on the paradoxical and hybridized cultural performance elements they have experienced in the play as well as in their own lives. *Arigato, Tokyo* invites audiences into Carl's incomplete reflections on his intertextual and intercultural experiences as a diasporic Canadian in Japan.

Arigato, Tokyo functioned as Daniel MacIvor's "unofficial" return to Buddies with a completely new play since premiere performances of plays like *Yes I Am and Who Are You?* (1989) and *2-2-Tango* (1991). In Buddies's 2006–07 season, MacIvor remounted three of his solo shows (*House, Here Lies Henry*, and *Monster*), and the company produced a fundraising performance of *Cul-de-Sac* in 2008, but none of these were world premieres. Writing much of *Arigato, Tokyo* on retreat in Banff, Alberta, MacIvor transformed his biographical experiences travelling through Japan into a palimpsestic experience for Buddies audiences in Toronto. Many standard MacIvor play elements were purposely excised from the first production: Daniel MacIvor did not appear in the play and neither he nor Daniel Brooks directed it. MacIvor explains that his dramaturg, Iris Turcott, advised him that he should not appear in it or direct it (qtd. in MacLeod 78). These casting and directing elements alone disrupt many audiences' typical expectations of a new theatrical work by MacIvor.

What especially sets *Arigato, Tokyo* apart from many other MacIvor plays is his use of specific cultural elements to create a hybridized palimpsestic theatrical narrative, which transforms this play into multi-layered textual levels of culture and identity all inscribed upon the same structural surface. Palimpsests are manuscripts and/or individual pages with new texts transcribed overtop of original as well as past texts. Past texts remain partially visible on the surface of these newly reconfigured pages. *Arigato, Tokyo* can be read through Gérard Genette's ideas of palimpsestic architextuality, which emphasizes that audiences are textually cued by authors to respond to the various layered cultural intertexts during performance due to "the reader's [or audience's] expectations, and thus their reception of the work" (Genette 5). Carl's expectations of and response to Japanese culture and his identity as a Canadian outsider travelling Japan are central elements of the play's narrative. MacIvor layers cultural representations like race, diction, accents, costumes, setting, and dialogue upon each other to create a new kind of dramatic cultural palimpsest. Since these intertextual elements often present themselves in tandem, characters on stage, as well as audience members off stage, are continually encouraged to misinterpret and respond individually to different multi-layered signs, cues, and cultures in the play. Intertextual palimpsests in *Arigato, Tokyo* consciously echo and evoke many existing public (and often problematic) experiences of contemporary intercultural life.

The palimpsestic structure is inherent in the creation and format of *Arigato, Tokyo*. MacIvor describes how the play began with a trip "to Tokyo to see a production of a play of mine called *You Are Here* that was translated into Japanese by a small company" (qtd. in MacLeod 76). Similarities between MacIvor's personal journey and that of Carl in the play have led many audience members and newspaper critics to read this as an autobiographical play. However, *Arigato, Tokyo* is not so much an autobiographical play in the classical sense, but rather a form of theatrical biography described by Jenn Stephenson as "meta-autobiographies that self-reflexively depict or at least worry at this process of self-creation" (*Performing* 22). In this way biography functions as yet another layer of *Arigato, Tokyo*'s cultural palimpsest—this layer of MacIvor's experience is still present and visible amongst the fictional characters and situations placed over his biography. Many of the personal as well as culturally reflexive elements of *Arigato, Tokyo* are consciously left in troubling states to allow audiences to experience MacIvor's own worries about problematic cultural and identity experiences we sometimes create or encounter: "I would go to a restaurant [in Japan] with four men and a woman and the woman would serve," MacIvor recounts. "So I started thinking about the difference in culture [between Japan and Canada], and I went away and I started playing with different ideas [to write this play]" (qtd. in MacLeod 77–78).

Stephenson goes on to paraphrase Paul John Eakin by further describing the goal of meta-autobiographies as focused on "the experience of catching ourselves in the act of becoming selves" (*Performing* 22). *Arigato, Tokyo* has been similarly written to catch its own characters (and its audiences) in these moments of contributing to their identities becoming something new. Carl begins the play by telling the audience that "'I love you' is a lie" (13) only to later proclaim to Yori, "I love you" (63), as he prepares to leave Japan. Audiences bear witness to Carl's moment of becoming the unrequited lover he did not believe he could become, which he cannot truly reflect upon or understand until he returns home to Canada. Likewise, audiences experience different moments where they personally and collectively are challenged and either accept or resist new definitions, potentially remaining trapped, like Carl, by their current comprehensions of simple and non-hybridized identities in a globalizing world.

Arigato, Tokyo's palimpsest structure ultimately speaks to the many different cultural layers that make up people's unique identities in our globalized world. MacIvor's play highlights the challenge of trying to perform single portions of our diverse personal backgrounds. Cultural palimpsests also allow MacIvor to emphasize his characters' confusing onstage experiences of otherness as we witness them respond and react to culture via their own expectations, as highlighted in Genette's concept of architextuality. Throughout the play, Carl does not appear prepared for different expressions of physical affection and/or intercultural understanding. MacIvor creates several scenes with people directly translating the experiences of others in different languages (e.g. Nushi reading Carl's text aloud in Japanese while Carl reads it in English to the audience) and providing eye-catching onstage performances of notable Noh, Kabuki, and drag figures (e.g. Etta and Yori performing the Noh play *The Tale of Genji* wearing masks, Etta lip-synching Amy Winehouse songs in drag). Hybridized cultural representations exist as palimpsests in this constant state of negotiation and development both on and off the stage in *Arigato, Tokyo*. Characters and audiences must negotiate their comprehension of other cultures during performance, which essentially renders realism and representation as always informed by some form of external cultural and personal impressions already in widespread circulation. Intertextual cultural palimpsests compete throughout the play via various performance styles (Noh theatre, drag performance), literary histories (Nushi's summary of *The Tale of Genji*, Etta's monologues, Carl's reading), locations (Tokyo, Vancouver), and situations (scenes featuring translation, cultural traditions) experienced by Carl in Japan and audiences at Buddies in Toronto.

One of the more complex cultural palimpsests presented in *Arigato, Tokyo* is the production's representation of race. Nina Lee Aquino and Ric Knowles have described how the term "'Asian' is replete with stereotypes, and uninterrogated can participate in discourses and feed representational fields that serve the interest of its inventors [Western culture] rather than its (oppositional) subjects" ("Introduction" viii). Brendan Healy's production of *Arigato, Tokyo* allowed the actors to self-interrogate racial identity as oppositional subjects by using their own personal experiences of racial otherness in their performances. Healy cast Asian Canadian performers—none were Japanese Canadian—as well as one First Nations actress to play all the Japanese characters in MacIvor's play. Performers merged some of their own histories of racial diversity in combination with suggestions by the play's Japanese cultural consultant, choreographer Hiroshi Miyamoto (Healy). Miyamoto worked with Healy to help the cast create realistic performances of Japanese culture. MacIvor's text and Healy's production looked to avoid the fetishization of Japanese and Asian Canadian identities in performance. Healy describes the sensitivity with which he approached language, dialect, and cultural representation: "Buddies audiences were hypersensitive to depictions of culture, to appropriations and cultural representations as well as the framework through which cultures are depicted and experienced." As Healy points out, issues of racial and cultural backgrounds did not emerge uninterrogated by his actors in rehearsal and performance. Tyson James, who identifies as Chinese Canadian, and Michael Dufays, who identifies as Korean Canadian, provided *Arigato, Tokyo* with different hybridized Asian Canadian racial performances during the Buddies run. Cara Gee, who is First Nations Ojibwe, provided a unique performance of otherness as Nushi as not only a Japanese woman but also as the undesired object of Carl's affections, which effectively othered her onstage presence even more. The play's overall representation of racial diaspora therefore emerges as layered with various racial and cultural elements as a performance palimpsest.

While some critics, like Richard Ouzounian, found these Japanese performances to be highly accurate, others, such as Christopher Hoile from *Stage Door* ("*Arigato*"), believed the Japanese performances directed by Healy focused too heavily on linguistic and cultural clichés. Healy believes "authenticity didn't seem to be a value that the play announces" and his direction surrounding cultural and racial performances emphasizes the falsity of believing in concepts of authenticity. Racial and cultural performances were developed as cultural palimpsests replete with dramaturgical input from the racially diverse cast in the Buddies production in combination with many of the problematic and performative qualities of race and culture held by mainstream Western society.

Cara Gee, the First Nations actress who played Nushi, expands racial interrogation further by using Canadian Indigenous experience filtered through an Asian cultural palimpsest in performance. Her appearance as a Japanese

woman in a service position to the Canadian traveller evokes elements of historical and cultural relationships between white and First Nations people in
Canada. Healy's casting choices contribute racially diverse identity palimpsests due to his diverse actors combining their personal cultural experiences
in their characterization. His direction also tried to emphasize the dreamlike
quality of Carl's journey through Japan as a mirror of typical travel experiences by Canadians to foreign places. *Arigato, Tokyo* also echoes other popular
theatre and film narratives containing orientalist themes and elements, such
as *M. Butterfly* and *Lost in Translation*. MacIvor addresses the pitfalls of one
"othered" community assuming immunity to misrepresenting otherness by
foregrounding within Carl's "queer" romance narrative some of the problemat-
ics of exotic orientalism within the queer community. MacIvor interrogates
this material in order to expose many of the problematic layers woven into
different cultural representations (see fig. 1).

Fig. 1. David Storch and Michael Dufays in *Arigato, Tokyo*. Photo by Jeremy Mimnagh
provided courtesy of Buddies in Bad Times Theatre.

Many of the nuances of cultural palimpsests in performance in MacIvor's multi-dimensional play were completely overlooked by critics who only saw one-dimensional depictions, presumably because they expected elements of theatrical realism and cultural authenticity from this performance. Several addressed Asian Canadian and Orientalist representations in the performance. Glenn Sumi from *NOW Magazine* began his review by focusing on the cultural codes of behaviour that distinguish Japanese life on the global stage. Sumi went on to describe this play as "intriguing, if unsatisfying," as it did not quite provide us with the MacIvor experience Canadian audiences have come to expect. He reminded audiences this production did have some realistic elements (e.g. the Japanese accents), but ultimately failed because "what seems passionate on the page needs to smoulder on the stage." But many reviewers could not see past what they described as unrealistic performances and/or stereotypical accents. *Globe and Mail* reviewer Martin Morrow described elements of the play as half-realized and the play itself as "more difficult . . . than it needed to be" ("*Arigato*"). He claimed that MacIvor, who has penned such successful plays as *The Best Brothers*, did not appear to know what he wanted this new play to say to us by the end of the performance. He claimed that the playwright did not meet the genre expectations established by his past theatrical successes. Morrow believed that MacIvor's departure from his standard or conventional approach to writing a play, directing it, and starring in it resulted in an inaccessible script. Morrow's harshest criticism of *Arigato, Tokyo* was its "eagerness to pay homage to a foreign culture" that ultimately led to its downfall as a new and representative MacIvor play. This criticism, however, appears to miss the mark, as MacIvor's play does not so much focus on creating homage to Japan as it tries to implicate its audiences in problematic representations of Japan and Canada on the world stage by highlighting hybridized cultural identities.

One of the least clarified elements in *Arigato, Tokyo* remains Carl's sexual identity. He is queer, but not necessarily gay, yet he does not actively advocate for identifying himself in a conclusive way. Despite Carl coming out and falling in love with another man, MacIvor's play is not the coming-out story of a Canadian man on a journey of sexual discovery who happens to fall in love with a same-sex foreigner. In fact, according to MacIvor, audiences at Buddies were looking for the play to reflect more elements of queer sexuality, if not a distinct and clear homosexuality. *Arigato, Tokyo* showcases how MacIvor, as a self-identified queer playwright, confronts the challenges of writing for new and more broadly diverse Buddies audiences after critically lauded seasons and inclusivity of expanded definitions of queerness since his original experiences with the company in the 1980s. During previews the character of Carl emerged as gay more than bisexual; however, distinct and clear sexual identity was abandoned in order to allow his romantic interests to emerge as more queer or even bisexual than distinctly gay. "He (Carl) was just polysexual," explains MacIvor, "there's a line, she (Nushi) asks him, she says, 'You've been with many women,' and he says, 'Many women, more men, several in between,' and that was really important. That hadn't been there in previews" (qtd. in MacLeod 79). Carl remains open to any kind of physical love and never truly identifies himself via a concrete sexual identity. In this way Carl's polysexuality, similar to the layered structure of MacIvor's play, echoes the culturally palimpsestic experience of *Arigato, Tokyo* as audiences witnessed a stratum of intimate performance through Carl. Ultimately, Carl rejects a clearly defined and contained sexual identity and sees himself as a hybridized individual with a polymorphous sexuality. Healy also believes Buddies audiences seeing *Arigato, Tokyo* "read the play as an investigation of love and the ways love can be expressed and exist across cultures." In the production, all three other characters engaged in intimate acts with Carl at some point, allowing audiences to see him in physical connections with a woman and a man, as well as a trans/drag figure (who may or may not be real). Healy's direction exemplified societal obsessions with reading the language of the body as representative of one's definitive sexual identity, which is another problematic assumption in everyday life.

One particular performance in *Arigato, Tokyo* deserves special interrogation and highlights the numerous layers potentially at play in a cultural palimpsest on stage. Tyson James, in the unrealistic role of Etta, the narrator, remained slightly freer from ideas of "real" and "true," which led to more hybridized performance moments of drag and poetic narration. Etta functioned like a chorus, which itself infused this hybrid text with entirely classical notions of drama and performance (see fig. 2). Speaking directly to the Buddies audiences, Etta performed in drag free from the boundaries of gendered, sexual, and even realistic identity. The opening scene introduced us to Etta in drag as Amy Winehouse behind a scrim, which in itself palimpsestically activated audiences' thoughts of the recently deceased singer (who died in 2011) as well as the artificial gender/body of Etta's drag appearance. Etta lip-synched "Back to Black," which is itself a reflexive song about failed love. Etta re-emerged as different female singers over the course of the performance, appearing later as Nina Simone, until s/he eventually emerged as a geisha in traditional dress for the final scene of the play. There are echoes here of similar drag performances happening nearby on Church Street as well as in the Buddies cabaret room in the same performance building. Drag

Fig. 2. Tyson James portraying the chorus-like narrator, Etta. Photo by Jeremy Mimnagh provided courtesy of Buddies in Bad Times Theatre.

effectively reminds audiences of our status as spectators, as well as our respective agency in contributing to the success or failure of the drag facade.

Some of the most interesting palimpsestic moments in *Arigato, Tokyo* were developed through elements such as dance music, the depiction of drug-induced states, and lighting effects, as well as the physical location of the Buddies theatre itself. Carl has a problem with cocaine abuse throughout the play, which his guide Nushi recognizes and satisfies quickly by supplying him with illegal drugs. Healy added to the drug addiction backstory by creating further suggestions of usage in the Buddies production. For example, Carl snorted lines of cocaine whenever words were used from the contemporary lexicon of drugs and substances. In an early scene Etta described Carl's journey from North America to Asia as "two days in San Francisco, where lines are crossed and limits pushed" (4). Carl appeared and snorted cocaine to coincide with Etta's use of the word "line" and encouraged audiences to stereotype him as nothing more than an addict. MacIvor describes Carl's many addictions: "Carl used sex as much as drugs and alcohol . . . he had no boundaries" (qtd. in MacLeod 79). Carl's addictive personality is something he brings with him during his journey throughout Japan.

Healy did find a unique way to transport Buddies audiences back to the queer village in Toronto from the foreign Japanese setting of MacIvor's play. During one scene Carl is high on cocaine and asks Nushi to take him to a Japanese dance club. MacIvor's stage directions read: "*A dance club. NUSHI has loosened CARL's collar and opened his jacket. They dance in a crowded club. NUSHI produces a pill and places it in CARL's mouth. Music and light become ecstatic then distant. CARL is lost in the moment. His dancing becomes frantic. In time he is alone*" (30). Produced in the main space at Buddies in Bad Times, which itself doubles as a dance club during special events like Toronto Pride, Healy's direction transformed his local audiences' experiences of watching a play set in Japan to seeing the real-world dance space of the theatre itself. The Buddies stage literally became the dance club it is otherwise known as, filled with similar lighting, smoke, and musical effects. No doubt many audience members, myself included, have different personal memories of similarly dancing, getting high, and being lost in the music like Carl in the exact same physical space. This club simultaneously exists in both Tokyo and Toronto, collapsing the real world distance between them and rendering both stages on the same literal surface in a palimpsestic moment. This unique stage transformation remained one of the most impressive transitions in the play as it caused the Buddies audience members unconsciously to break down barriers between performance and their own lives. The extra time taken by David Storch to dance in the flashing lights provided audiences with opportunities to reflect on and/or relive similar experiences in the same real-world space. This may be one of the most metatheatrical moments in the play as well as something completely unique to the production at Buddies in Toronto.

The stage design of *Arigato, Tokyo* at Buddies used elements of lighting, layout, and depth to emphasize classic MacIvor themes of separation and distance between people. For example, the play incorporated minimal stage design and relied on lighting to create barriers between characters. More importantly, the back wall of the set contained a large, slightly reflective piece of metallic material. It was not a true mirror, but rather served to reflect towards the audience, "mirror-like," some of the lights hitting the actors' backs. This reflective design element, a kind of partial mirror, cued audiences to thinking about the self-reflexive elements of the play, but also emphasized the falsity of seeing this production as a truly autobiographical account or realistic portrayal of MacIvor's personal experiences. Other plays similarly employ mirrors as a direct means of implicating audiences by reflecting their image back at them (e.g. Ariel Dorfman's *Death and the Maiden*), yet Healy's "mirror" functioned more as a reminder to audiences that nothing on stage should be seen as a true or realistic reflection of anything else. It also contributed to the depiction of liminal non-geographical spaces inhabited by Carl throughout the narrative. Healy's production of *Arigato, Tokyo* is not an accurate reflection of life and experiences, but rather a reproduction of partial images experienced while travelling in other places far from Toronto and Buddies.

Other mirrors emerged in unexpected places, such as when Carl was doing lines of cocaine before leaving Japan: *"Carl leans down and snorts a line of cocaine from the bedside table"* (51). Buddies did not have a bed or a table on the stage, but used instead a small vanity mirror for Carl to look into as he snorted and got high. Themes of reflection featured prominently as these characters came to understand themselves as well as the people they believed they were falling in love with throughout the performance. Lighting helped to isolate fifteen squares of interaction along the wooden stage used in various combinations throughout the show. These traversable boundaries functioned to create distance between characters at different points and rows of hallway movements across the stage. Ultimately these lighting configurations created permeable boundaries that characters had trouble crossing throughout the performance.

As in other MacIvor plays, language functions largely as a performance boundary between characters as well as audiences during dialogue exchanges and monologues. There were numerous levels of narrative and language in the performance, most often seen when Carl read to the audience while Nushi stood behind him, speaking his words in Japanese. Etta functioned as a linguistic guide throughout the piece and emphasized the hybridized languages of the voice and body through impeccable transformations of the self during costume changes. MacIvor knowingly uses clichéd and stereotypical language to have us focus on how the limits of translation block explanations of true experiences and emotions. Much of the dialogue about language focuses on the misrepresentations held by Canadians and Westerners about the Japanese language in particular cultural contexts.

Nushi and Carl have a long debate about how the word "arigato" does not actually mean "thank you," and that there is no Japanese equivalent for expressing thanks. Completely different definitions and understandings exist in Japanese and in English, which brings us back to the palimpsestic experience of reading words (and their conflicting definitions) in the same exact time and place. MacIvor hopes audiences will struggle with comprehension in these moments and experience two hybridized language systems effectively becoming one. Nushi explains, "Even 'arigato' does not translate to 'thank you' like you would know it in English. 'Arigato' would say exactly 'this is difficult,' 'suimasen' would be more 'I have shame'" (15). She describes "arigato" as a slightly more poetic word used incorrectly by foreigners. Carl expresses bewilderment at the differences he has discovered in the words "suimasen" and "arigato." The scenes when Carl reads from his publications begin with Nushi delivering his writing aloud in Japanese (see fig. 3). While Hoile explains in his review that he often heard stereotypical English translations of Japanese poetry in Etta and Yori's dialogue, audiences were left wondering, if they did not speak Japanese, what Nushi's translations of Carl's writings sounded like in Japanese. Are her words just as riddled with stereotypical cadences as MacIvor's English translations of Japanese dialogue?

As with most journey narratives, the main character eventually returns home after completing his travels. In these moments MacIvor has the opportunity to use the proper names overheard during international travel that contain resonances for audience members of the places and spaces they have journeyed through. Carl leaves Tokyo through Narita Airport on his way to Vancouver: "And it is here in the airport of Narita / Where the servant becomes a fool to passion" (67). The words "Tokyo" and "Japan" are not spoken

Fig. 3. David Storch as Carl reads from his book as Cara Gee's Nushi simultaneously translates his words into Japanese. Photo by Jeremy Mimnagh provided courtesy of Buddies in Bad Times Theatre.

during Etta's closing phone conversation with Carl before he boards his flight home. While Carl does refer to Vancouver several times, neither Nushi nor Yori ever say the words "Tokyo" or "Japan." Japanese characters are never concerned with saying the specific name of their city or country; the words "Tokyo" and "Japan" remain Western terms (and obsessions) in *Arigato, Tokyo*. Carl repeats both constantly.

MacIvor transports audiences back to a Canadian space in Vancouver just before Buddies audiences re-emerge onto the streets of Toronto after experiencing his dreamlike play. This moment of combining Vancouver and Toronto into the same physical space is yet another of the seductive hybridized palimpsestic qualities of this play. During his final monologue to audiences at his reading in Vancouver, Carl describes himself via a series of fantastical metaphorical relationships to other famous literary figures. "I have been had by the unhaveable and been hoist by my own petard. I am Byron ordering his final glass of ouzo. I am Dorothy back in Kansas but dreaming of Oz" (70). This is another example of MacIvor's palimpsestic approach to cultural inter-texts in this play. References to Hamlet, Byron, and Dorothy function to bring to mind different literary canons and genres featuring characters struggling with their in-betweenness in foreign places. Hamlet's reference to the petard only emerges after returning from his travels to England sailing the North Sea. Byron's last glass of ouzo refers to his autobiographical accounts of travelling throughout Greece as an English foreigner. Dorothy refers to Judy Garland's iconic performance in *The Wizard of Oz* (1939), which ends with her desire to return to the dream world of Oz rather than live in Kansas. These references to characters in different lands across diverse film, theatre, and literary texts all involve characters like Carl in liminal states in-between cultures. With this final reference to Dorothy from *The Wizard of Oz*, MacIvor not only draws Carl closer to the queer community but also finds an opportunity to invert the standard representative phrase she evokes: "There's no place like home." We are left wondering if any of us are ever truly home.

Arigato, Tokyo uses hybridized performance to highlight the transfor-mative nature of our personal and cultural identities in the contemporary globalizing world. MacIvor has achieved notoriety and status as a key Canadian (and global) playwright by this point in his career. This play showcases his return to Buddies and Toronto by way of deeply reflexive and intertextual playwriting. By not appearing in the play or directing it, he has participated in the key component of personal transformation required by arts, particularly Buddhist art in Japan. As Richard Pilgrim describes in *Buddhism and the Arts in Japan*, "Most Buddhist art is 'performing' art" (21). Pilgrim emphasizes how Buddhist art aims to transform both the viewer and the artist through the formlessness developed by diverse styles: "Art is used and 'performed' rather than merely appreciated or understood for its expressive value, and its 'performance' is a means to religious transformation" (21). *Arigato, Tokyo* follows the traditions of Buddhist art by exploring similar transformative experiences of culture, performance, and identity. MacIvor has been a practicing Buddhist at different points in his life. *Arigato, Tokyo* allows Carl the opportunity to experience performances of his writing and to perform his interculturalism. It also allows Canadian actors of different Asian Canadian and Indigenous backgrounds to perform versions of otherness in hybridized ways for Canadian audiences at Buddies.

Yori reminds Carl about the individual power he holds to choose to see the global world in different ways. The play contains several lengthy, reflective monologues by Carl about his childhood desire to want to know absolutely everything: "I'd lie there and stare up into the sky and I'd want to know everything. How the world worked. What my future would be. What eternity looked like" (43). Carl follows this statement by singing a song about a bear going over the mountain to see what he could see; this moment emphasizes human agency to see the world in unique ways. We have seen much at Buddies in this particular production but we cannot be completely sure of what we have seen. The crux of Carl's monologue at the middle point of the play comes back to the paradox of love, focusing on the mantra "accept change" (44). Carl does not want to accept change; he claims he would prefer to return to a time before he was the boy looking at the stars. Yori leaves the play with a final statement to Carl (and the audience) about their capability to self-author the future: "Genji reflected back on all his misdeeds and became a good man. He discovered his regrets and became a man of truth. You can do this too in time" (63). When *Arigato, Tokyo* ends Carl has returned to Canada and, in a unique meta-autobiographical moment, speaks to Canadians from where his journey began as a cultural palimpsest by appearing simultaneously in Vancouver (in the play text) and Toronto (in the first production at Buddies).

SOMEWHERE I HAVE NEVER TRAVELLED: DANIEL MACIVOR'S GAY HOMETOWN PLAY

CHRISTOPHER GRIGNARD

"OUR [HOME]TOWN"

> More and more of us are choosing to live wherever it suits us. This
> is a free country, no? As one gay man in northern Ontario said, "It's
> my goddamn country too."
> —Michael Riordon, *Out Our Way: Gay and Lesbian Life in the
> Country*

Daniel MacIvor has often mentioned Thornton Wilder's *Our Town* as having a significant influence on his career.[1] Wilder's play has been heralded as a classic of small-town Americana, the "most fastidiously humble of plays" (Gardner), and "the great American drama" (Stephens 258).[2] These accolades are testament to its "continuing popularity . . . as evidenced in performances, mainly in college and community theatres, and by discussion in critical and academic circles" (258). What is it about this landmark play that makes it so readily embraced? Is it the idea of unity suggested by the title's use of the possessive pronoun? Is it, as George D. Stephens adds, the play's "nostalgic haze evoked by memories (or illusions) of 'the good old days in the old

---

1   See Jennie Punter's article, "Daniel's Town," in which MacIvor states, "My whole understanding of theatre started with that play, and it was life-changing" (17).

2   Arthur H. Ballet is quoted as making this widely held claim in George D. Stephens's article, *"Our Town*—Great American Tragedy?"

home town'" (262)? Is it the simplistic arrangement of the three acts: "Daily Life," "Love and Marriage," and what Min Shen calls "Death and Rebirth"?[3]

As much as *Our Town* has been celebrated for its inclusion, others have critiqued the play for its observance of exclusion, and therefore have found ways in which they can belong; by doing so, they can make the play their own. For instance, playwright Susan Miller recognizes the absence of gay and lesbian representation in Grover's Corners. Her play *It's Our Town, Too!* (1992) retells Wilder's story with gay and lesbian characters in order to ensure that queer folk are included amongst the town's populace.

Like Miller in her response to absence, and her desire for belonging and visibility, I want here to create and re-map "our gay hometown" into existence. My analysis of MacIvor's *Somewhere I Have Never Travelled* begins to address another blank: an absence of a visible study of the representation of the gay male playwright's hometown in Canadian drama. As is the case with Wilder's title, my use of the possessive pronoun suggests a common narrative, a common shared experience. Essentially, the hometown patterns and characteristics observed in *Somewhere* reflect an alternative perspective on the idea of the hometown. MacIvor's personal accounts of his hometown offer a significant narrative that documents a specific time for the closeted male and, ultimately, gives voice to the gay male experience.

---

3   The third act is never named in the play, as the previous two are; however, considering what the third act presents as its focus (Emily's death) and where the act is set (the town's graveyard), calling the act "Death" seems appropriate. In her article "'Quite a Moon!': The Archetypal Feminine in *Our Town*," Min Shen calls the act "Death and Rebirth."

CREATING COMMUNITY, NEW WORLDS, AND GAY THEATRE

> Gay and lesbian communities, however, have not always existed. As with all communities, they are historical creations, imagined in the process of speaking, writing, and communicating publicly.
> —Jeffrey Escoffier, "Intellectuals, Identity Politics, and the Closets for Cultural Authority"

Wilder's Stage Manager is concerned with preservation, and the preservation has to do with playmaking. The concern for preservation is similar to David Allan King's concern for the preservation of Canadian gay theatre in his article "Cultivating Queer: The Invisibility of the Canadian Gay Play." King concludes his article by stating, "The key to [gay theatre's] preservation may well rest in balancing the strengths of its historic invisibility with its commitment to maintaining visibility" (268). Many have emphasized the benefits of retaining the term *gay*, especially when the slippery and equally problematic category *queer* emerged in the 1990s as an all-encompassing term. Thus, the choice to use gay—in lieu of queer—has been a long-held strategy, particularly in studies that focus exclusively on gay males; citing Terry Goldie's "Queer Nation?," André Grace and Kris Wells remark, "Gay remains a more specific term to refer to male homosexuality."[4]

There is a subversive strategy in the use of the term gay when demarcating space. As Sherrie Inness urges in "Lost in Space: Queer Geography and the Politics of Location," "Scholars need to construct a new queer geography" (257). She states:

> When a space is labeled gay, it becomes part of a common language and enters into the gay discourse. Places that do not receive the label

---

4   My thanks to André Grace and Kristopher Wells for reminding me of this comment in their article, "Gay and Bisexual Male Youth as Educator Activists and Cultural Workers: The Queer Critical Praxis of Three Canadian High-School Students."

do not become part of the "lens." They are not used in the process of creating a standard against which gay and lesbian experiences are measured. (269)

My analysis of *Somewhere* enables new gay worlds to be both created and considered. Through this lens the confluence of MacIvor's hometown and his sexuality is uncovered and recognized, which in turn exposes how the combination of the two inform this play and all of MacIvor's work. We need to remember Sky Gilbert's enjoinder to resuscitate gay culture because, if we do not, our work may not be preserved and will remain invisible: "Queers are the only ones who really cared about queer culture in the first place—when they stop caring, it will disappear" ("Writing Gay" 263). I want to ensure that MacIvor's play, one that is based on, or inspired by, the Canadian gay male playwright's hometown, is made visible (otherwise it will remain invisible); as well, I want to ensure that the creative work that has been done on "our gay hometowns" will be preserved (otherwise it will disappear).

Inness notes, "Lesbians and gays need not only to create a new, inclusive geography but also to analyze the dominant, exclusive geography around them" (256). In the attempt to locate further meaning in the gay play, it is crucial to recognize that definitions are always building or working from pre-existing models and categories. In his book *Gay and After* (1998), Alan Sinfield makes this point; he recognizes that when one conducts critical work on gay subject matter (what he calls "subcultural work"), that work is both working and building from the consequences of our history.

Writers such as Eve Sedgwick have remarked that writing or reading gay representation validates gay individuals in places where they may not necessarily have been represented, such as literature, history, landscape, or, for the sake of this project, the hometown.[5] Thus, gay writing serves not only as a corrective to the past (a response to a notable absence), but also as a means for inclusion.

---

5   For Sedgwick, it is the queer adult who has survived his/her childhood, and who, since that time, having acquired the necessary agency, can now insert his or her desire for queer visibility into spaces and places that, at an earlier point, did not and could not exist for them in childhood:

Critical attention has also been paid to writers who have rewritten regions into existence. In other words, an imagined space that is created in either art or literature becomes real. Certainly, the process around the recreation of space—*how* and *why* the space is redefined—is significant not only for the purposes of drama/theatre, but also for the purposes of larger society. Examples of gay spaces that have intervened in dominant ones are: the gay neighbourhood, gay ghetto, gay community, and gay village. I set up this critical context so that one can recognize how and why the gay hometown is an important addition to spatial discourse. Alternative demarcations of space strategically provoke reinterpretations of dominant ones. Gilbert, in the introduction to his anthology *Perfectly Abnormal: Seven Gay Plays*, talks about the creation of gay worlds:

> The first requirement for the plays in this collection was that they create their own gay worlds . . . All of the plays in this collection are perfectly abnormal, some, both in form *and* content. Theodor Adorno suggested that art need not reflect daily life in all its detail, but should instead create perfect worlds that operate by their own rules. . . . We may make connections between a work of art and our own reality (which is where some interesting issues of reception are raised). For by juxtaposing these worlds against our own we can learn about who we are. (ix)

In addition to the world created by the play, my study of MacIvor's work creates its "own gay worlds," reimagining the setting of this particular play as being a gay hometown.

I think many adults (and I am among them) are trying, in our work, to keep faith with vividly remembered promises made to ourselves in childhood: promises to make invisible possibilities and desires visible; to make the tacit things explicit; to smuggle queer representation in where it must be smuggled and, with the relative freedom of adulthood, to challenge queer eradicating impulses where they are to be so challenged. (3)

I wanted to know how MacIvor as a gay male playwright imagined his own hometown and whether he had consciously represented this site in his plays. I wondered whether his experiences growing up in a particular time and place had influenced his representations not only of home, but also of the violence and death often associated with gay theatre and indeed with the gay experience. MacIvor's response confirms my sense that the hometown—the gay hometown—is of vital importance to a reconsideration of *Somewhere I Have Never Travelled*.

THE GAY EXPERIENCE—MACIVOR AND SYDNEY, NOVA SCOTIA

MacIvor remained closeted the whole time he was living in his hometown of Sydney, Cape Breton, Nova Scotia. MacIvor, in an interview, speaks about living "an interior double life"[6] from the time he was around ten—when he credits his complete acknowledgement of being gay—to the time he was seventeen, when he moved to Halifax to attend university. In Sydney, he was "terrified . . . of being found out." These closeted years, he admits, took their toll on his personality:

> I just needed to get out of Sydney. I had to get out of high school and get out of Sydney in one piece, and I was gonna be okay . . . I guess Sydney represents . . . being forced into a closet.

Further, MacIvor acknowledges that he "still carr[ies] a little resentment," that the difficulties he experienced in Sydney—ones he identifies as "self-esteem issues" and "emotional security issues"—have not affected him positively. As he states,

---

6 The following quotations from MacIvor are taken from my personal interview of him conducted in 2007, unless otherwise noted.

I wouldn't consider [them] positive to some of my personal relationships and I think it has a lot to do with the fact that growing up in
a place where you felt that you couldn't really be who you were, you
couldn't articulate who that was, and then you were sort of stuck
with an identity crisis of some sort or another.

MacIvor developed a form of self-hatred that affected his involvement (or lack
of it) in drama as an extracurricular activity while living in Sydney. However, in
a familial context, drama was there: "My home life was incredibly dramatic, and
so I guess I had enough of drama in my life that I didn't really need the drama
club." As well, homosexuality "kept me from joining the drama club . . . because
that's what the fags did" (unlike his openly gay friend Bryden MacDonald,
one year his senior, whom he admired at the time for his openness with his
sexuality). As much as MacIvor wanted to join, and be an out-gay person like
MacDonald, he did not want to be, as he put it, a "target." MacDonald, of course,
would also become a successful playwright, writing a number of plays, such as
the successful gay/AIDS play, *Whale Riding Weather* (1991).

BE-LONGING FOR/IN THE PAST

Much of gay drama is an expression of what might be called "the
historical impulse" in gay literature—the impulse to depict and define the collective past of gay men to affirm a sense of identity and
solidarity and to educate the dominant culture about the brutal effects of its heterosexism.
—John Clum, *Acting Gay: Male Homosexuality in Modern Drama*

My interest in the relationship between MacIvor and concepts of his hometown
is similar to that of John Preston's prose collection of stories by twenty-eight
gay male writers (one of whom is Canadian[7]), *Hometowns: Gay Men Write*

---

7   Robin Metcalf's piece is entitled "Halifax, Nova Scotia."

About Where they Belong (1991). In the introduction, Preston foregrounds the premise to his investigation:

> The overstatement that was the first cry of gay liberation, the neces-
> sary embellishment of a tribe just coming into being, has mellowed
> enough that many people are going back to the place where they
> were born, if not physically, at least enough to examine from where
> they came and how it affects who they are today. (xiii)

It is crucial to recognize both the time of Preston's study and the time to which he refers here: the beginning of the 1990s. The "overstatement" to which Preston refers is the AIDS epidemic—the haunting "embellishment" that not only exposed the gay community to incredible loss, but also pulled the community tighter because of it. Nonetheless, Preston recognizes that, over the last three decades, in the face of gay activism—and in the face of massive death—choices for gay men to assess, evaluate, and discuss their lives openly and artistically have increased. Edmund White poignantly summarizes and regards these past decades for the gay community as contributing to an urgency to acknowledge, and thus write, what he refers to as a "cultural moment":

> To have been oppressed in the 1950s, freed in the 1960s, exalted in
> the 1970s, and wiped out in the 1980s is a quick itinerary for a whole
> culture to follow. For we are witnessing not just the death of individ-
> uals but a menace to an entire culture. All the more reason to bear
> witness to the cultural moment. ("Esthetics" 215)[8]

---

8   Edmund White has been regarded as a spokesperson for gay men, having written on gay male culture based on his own lived experiences for more than four decades. He writes about being "oppressed in the 1950s," remarking how homosexuality at that time was "routinely labeled disquieting or tragic at best" (*My Lives* 119). In his memoir, he recalls a play which he had written and starred in as a young boy at summer camp (his version of *Boris Godunov*). He recounts the dramaturgy of the play and how it reflected the period in which he wrote it: "The formula emerges: I wanted to be a king, but I also needed to die, go mad or undergo humiliation for my arrogance, a scenario that resembled the plots of

Preston's collection is testament to the license and the urgency the authors had to write, share, and publish how their gay identities intersected with their understandings (and redefinitions) of the hometown.

Furthermore, Preston's methodology for gathering the various stories for his collection played with the various understandings of the hometown by asking "gay writers to approach their hometowns, either their birthplace or the place where they've chosen to live as adults," and having them "describe their context and how they react to their place in the world" (xiii). In his observation of those descriptions and those reactions found in their stories, he notes that the gay man is either captivated by his new experience, or horrified by the changes he must undergo to make his new world work for him (xiii). Additionally, "Many [of the stories] are about the places that have been left behind, the exile of the beloved son. Others are about the place that is discovered" (xiii). In view of the latter, many of the narratives in Preston's collection feature the "exiled" gay man discovering a new world. This new world refers to new families or new communities that have necessarily been formed. MacIvor speaks to this idea of the "new world" in his two-tiered definition of hometown:

> The hometown is two things . . . The hometown . . . is the place where you were raised. . . . Then there's the hometown—it's the place where you choose to live. You know, it's sort of the same as family and family. You see, it's the family that you were born into, and then there's the family that you choose.

It is this kind of retrospective evaluation of varying families found in both old and new hometowns that is at the heart of not only Preston's collection, but also other gay-related creations, such as the gay hometown.

---

queer novels of the 1950s" (5). Similarly, in his 1979 memoir *Wild Man* Tobias Schneebaum observes how "the post-war homosexual novel could be published and reviewed only in newspapers and periodical journals only if the protagonists (always pathetically unhappy, utterly at a loss, alcoholic and happen worse) were seen to come to criminal peculation and a dread end" (qtd. in McCourt 11).

It is essential to create these new worlds, as John D'Emilio argues in addressing the plight of the gay man: "Because of our oppression, our desire for 'home' and 'family' is so strong that we become deeply, desperately attached to the homes and fictive families that we are able to create for ourselves" (171). On this note, the sort of gay plays that were created and produced at Toronto's Buddies in Bad Times Theatre in the 1980s, according to then Artistic Director Sky Gilbert, "were about the new kind of families that queer people make for themselves—with their lovers, friends, and community" (*Ejaculations* 100). These plays, as Gilbert sees it, differed from the gay plays that were being done at Toronto's Tarragon Theatre, which were "usually about middle-class gay men going home to their small-town families" (100).[9] One of the plays to which Gilbert is referring is Daniel MacIvor's *Somewhere I Have Never Travelled*.

This discussion of the different kinds of venue—Tarragon and Buddies—in which these new worlds were being created is vital. In the interview, MacIvor addresses the various elements that create the production of a dramatic work, including audiences as one of them. He passionately emphasizes that the dramatic text is only one of six elements that he recognizes as the production:

Well, I'm very specific when I'm writing. . . . You know this is the theatre and theatre is . . . there are five elements. There's six actually:

---

9   In relation to Gilbert's note about the kind of gay plays that were being created and produced at Buddies in the 1980s, Alec Scott observes: "[Gilbert's] theatre, the influential Buddies, would avoid AIDS plays, throughout the crisis, and the subject matter, so central to contemporary gay drama south of the 49th parallel, seldom gets a theatrical airing in Canada—except in American imports, like *Angels in America* and *The Normal Heart*." Gilbert has noted, however, that he steered away from producing AIDS plays because of the risk of their sentimentality. Similarly, Daniel Harris addresses how prominent gay writers avoided writing AIDS fiction for that very reason:

[They] conscientiously refrain from indulging in tearful bedside farewells and shocking expulsions of ailing children by heartless parents, all of the schmaltzy, yet appetizing tidbits that the American public finds so alluring. The fear of sentimentality haunts fiction about AIDS, serving as a constant break that keeps writers from slipping into self-pity, from striving to be poignant yet falling into bathos. (232)

the performance, the direction, the design, the *text*, the marketing, and the audience. . . . These six are equal elements in creating what is called a production. The text is just an element.

Adding to MacIvor's list, a seventh element that merits attention is venue.

I recognize the importance of not overlooking *how* a production, as MacIvor sees it with its six elements, is ultimately associated with what the theatre, as an artistic form, has long been associated with: its ability to create community, its potential to mobilize an audience, its ongoing commitment to being in the here and now (its immediacy), its reliance on ritual, and its capacity for transformation, among others. Hence, an awareness of these attributes, which are interrelated with the elements MacIvor outlined, provides a critical framework that can assist one when facing a question that runs throughout my inquiry. It is a question concerned with the link between the medium of theatre and gayness: what is the role theatre has played and continues to play for gay men?

There is always a risk when applying a particular definition or model to a pre-existing concept or term that is—and continues to be—heavily contested, such as the Canadian gay play, or even the term gay itself, in the added attempt to imbue the concept or term with further critical significance. The newly created concept of the gay hometown attempts to add just such significance.

What is occurring in MacIvor's representative gay hometown space?

SOMEWHERE I HAVE NEVER TRAVELLED[10]— MAPPING THE IMAGINATIVE GAY HOMETOWN AND ITS GAY LANDSCAPE

> Here we go again. Another small play about small-town Canada.
> —Robert Crew, "High Quality Work On Mediocre Play"[11]

Two gay hometown plays opened Toronto's 1988–1989 theatre season. While Sky Gilbert was returning to his hometown in *Lola Starr Builds Her Dream Home* at Buddies in Bad Times Theatre through "poetic/hopeful fantasy, or cheery musical comedy, or outrageous satire" (*Ejaculations* 50), Daniel MacIvor was returning to his hometown in *Somewhere I Have Never Travelled* at Tarragon Theatre through sombre naturalism.

I first became familiar with *Somewhere I Have Never Travelled* by reading Gilbert's memoir, *Ejaculations from the Charm Factory*. To date, there has been no critical work done on it, and it remains unpublished. Gilbert refers to MacIvor's play a few times in his memoir primarily to illustrate the difference in theatre styles (Tarragon versus Buddies) and to show a distinction between the kind of gay plays that were being done at Buddies and the kind of gay-themed plays that he saw happening at Tarragon at the same time.

By speaking of MacIvor at this particular point in his career, Gilbert also wants to show how "a tug-of-war developed between Buddies and Tarragon for MacIvor's soul" (138). Gilbert writes,

---

10   I obtained the tenth draft of the play from Tarragon Theatre.

11   This was the first line of Robert Crew's review of Raymond Storey's *The Last Bus* (1989)—another gay hometown play, set in a small town in Ontario (Orillia), that premiered within the same Tarragon season as MacIvor's ("High"). As well, Ken Garnhum's *Beuys, Buoys, Boys* (1989)—a gay hometown play evoking Charlottetown, PEI—preceded Storey's play in the 1988–89 Tarragon season. Clearly, Crew draws a connection between Storey's play and both MacIvor's critically panned season opener and Garnhum's play. It should be no surprise that Storey's play would be received this way. This subsection shows MacIvor's response to the negative reception he received for his play.

[MacIvor's] work was undergoing some very interesting developments, and wavering between two contrasting styles. For the
Tarragon Theatre, he was working on a naturalistic play, *Somewhere
I Have Never Travelled*, about a young man who visits his home in
the Maritimes and almost incidentally confronts his family with his
homosexuality. For Rhubarb!,[12] however, Daniel was experimenting with something different. . . . I thought Daniel's Rhubarb! work
was much better than the naturalistic pap the Tarragon required of
him. In fact, it seemed to me he was selling out and rejecting a truer, more profound style in order to get a mainstage production at
Tarragon. (137–38)

Buddies, in many ways, operates as a hometown for Canadian queer playwrights, in that it continues to be a place where experimental queer work can
be developed and presented. In the same way, Tarragon Theatre continues
to be a crucial home for Canadian theatre; it has served as a starting point
for the careers of a number of prominent Canadian playwrights. It has also
been the place where a number of English productions of Michel Tremblay's
work have received their premiere. And so, it is possible to understand what
Gilbert is saying in his memoir about the tug-of-war between the two companies for MacIvor's soul. It is also possible to understand how MacIvor would
want to leave a smaller, marginal company, like Buddies, and move into a
more mainstream theatre like Tarragon. In 1987, MacIvor was invited to join
the Playwrights Unit at Tarragon Theatre, where he developed *Somewhere*;
the play was then produced the following year as Tarragon's season opener.

Tarragon is the place where David French's *Leaving Home* had its premiere
in 1972—a quintessentially naturalistic play often regarded as a classic piece
of Canadian theatre. It contributed to the theatre's reputation of the kind of

---

12   This annual queer festival at Buddies (started in 1977) has been a place where many
queer playwrights got their start. In his memoir, Gilbert recalls MacIvor's experimental
work for the 1986 festival.

plays they would produce in the years to come. As Urjo Kareda writes in his famous introduction to the play:[13]

> Toronto audiences were profoundly affected by these plays [produced
> in the 1971–1972 season], which were political only in the crucial
> sense that they explored the relationships of men, and nationalistic
> only in the sense that they sprung from, and now have returned to,
> a specifically Canadian experience. In *Leaving Home*, David French
> handles the form with great maturity, confidence and *honesty*; nothing
> is generalized, everything is specific, and yet from a personal reminis-
> cence comes a universal—dare I say national?—experience. Because
> he doesn't lie, David French has found a way to speak to us all. (ix)

The late Kareda was deeply influential in the creation of *Somewhere*. In his recollection of writing *Somewhere* under Kareda at Tarragon, MacIvor states:

> Urjo was always there all the time . . . Urjo was always there. He was
> always there. . . . He had his hand on your forearm as you wrote. . . .
> You really, really felt like you were trying to please Urjo. That's what
> you were doing at Tarragon, at that time. You were trying to make
> Urjo happy.[14]

---

13   Ric Knowles makes mention of the popularity of this introduction (how it is "famous") in his discussion of forms of naturalism in his book, *The Theatre of Form and the
Production of Meaning: Contemporary Canadian Dramaturgies* (25).

14   Furthermore, MacIvor recalls how he and Don Hannah were writing to please Kareda:

> We were writing for him in both ways: we were writing for him like he wished
> he could be writing these plays, and we were writing for him because we were
> writing to please him. . . . If he didn't like something, you wouldn't write it. . . .
> The writing that he liked, you would continue with that. . . . He really liked the
> poetic stuff. And he really liked . . . the current gothic stuff.

Yet *Somewhere*, one of MacIvor's most personal and most autobiographical works, surprisingly remains to date his least successful. For MacIvor, "It was *totally* devastating, because it was so *badly* received." How could a play, released by an emerging and promising young Canadian playwright from the Maritimes, and produced in a city (the same theatre house, even) that embraced plays like *Leaving Home*, have done so poorly? In terms of successful models of drama, *Somewhere* exhibits many of the characteristics that Kareda praised in *Leaving Home* and other naturalist plays produced around that time. One of these plays was David Freeman's *Creeps*, a play MacIvor acknowledges as being "very important" to him. What happened? It becomes necessary to look at the play closely, particularly its development.

As Gilbert recognized in his memoir, part of the reason the show did not do well had to do with the form of the play. There was also a conflict of styles happening within the play. MacIvor states,

> There was a timing thing . . . with my play. . . . [The critics] were really attacking Tarragon, and they used my play as a way to attack Tarragon. Because they thought Tarragon was doing too many of these plays and it needed to move forward. . . . You know, Urjo Kareda had described my play as a cross between Judith Thompson and David French. . . . And that's not what my play was. But that's what he wanted it to be. That's what the theatre needed.

Like *Leaving Home*, *Somewhere* focuses largely on the relationships of a male protagonist and springs from a specific Canadian male experience. In the play, Joey returns home to Cape Breton for his father's funeral. *Somewhere* operates as a memory play; characters are both trying to forget and trying to remember. Characters are running away to flee the past, yet coming back to revisit it. The play continuously flashes back and forth between the past and present to illustrate the abuse Joey, the play's protagonist, received from his father Buck, thus illustrating the cycle of abuse Buck brought to his family. As MacIvor explains, "It's a difficult play to do. . . . 'Cause it needs an understanding of how you flip between time." Through flashbacks, we learn that

Joey had to endure an abusive climate with his family; especially, he had to witness the pain his father brought to his mother. At one point, Joey has a decisive moment with his family: "I'm not livin here anymore" (32). However, by the play's end, after the funeral has occurred (and following a drunken domestic dispute regarding the past), Joey reaches an understanding that his father did have some good qualities to him.

MacIvor identifies Sydney as his hometown in the "traditional, *growin' up* kinda sense of hometown." He locates Sydney in *Somewhere*, and he does so by indicating how integral the people of Sydney were to this particular play—especially their relationship to the land and their history in getting there. He addresses the history of Sydney and how very small it was for him (dropping below 30,000 recently, he noted) and how it had become a regional municipality[15] by amalgamating with other towns:

> In a place like Cape Breton, you have people who come in—are raised in the country, as it were, which is thick in the woods . . . it's like I say, it's like the Ozarks or something, and they come into . . . a very small city like Sydney . . . from the billows of their country into these tiny cities . . . which were really just towns. . . . Then there'd be people who would leave and go to the mainland and then return. And there were these three levels: there were the people who didn't leave the country; there were people who went to the city, being the town; and then there were the people who went to the real city. . . . That's kind of represented in *Somewhere I Have Never Travelled*, which was . . . a very specific experience of Sydney for me.

Indeed—following the form in which Kareda describes naturalist theatre—in *Somewhere* "nothing is generalized, everything is specific" and the play is chock full of "personal reminiscence." According to MacIvor, Cape Bretoners are "a passionate group . . . geographically passionate." Thus, it's not surprising when MacIvor admits, "I'm very specific when I'm writing." Like his description

---

15   Cape Breton Regional Municipality (1995).

about the various "levels" of people in Sydney, characters in his play speak of the surrounding country, to the town, and make several references "to the city." They speak of how their sunrise is unlike anywhere else. There are landscape references to the nearby frozen lakes, the beach, open spaces and fields. Specific places are mentioned: Cutler's barn, Devil's Hill, Roy Vicker's Store, St. Stephen's Hall. And there is discussion of its nearby neighbour to the south, "the States," as Buck's sister, Agnes, moved there to get away from their abusive father.

MacIvor admits to being "discouraged at Tarragon from making [Joey] a gay character." He acknowledges that in the *many* rewrites of the play, "There were actually versions where he talked about his son." He also admits that the time of the play's premiere was a factor in why Joey did not end up being an openly gay character (as MacIvor would like to make him, if he were to rewrite the play now):

> But I was discouraged at Tarragon by Urjo from going in that direction . . . Yeah, it was '89, '88. . . . So, it was different then. Things were different then. . . . It would have meant that the play was going to be for a very specific audience, and it would have been quite political if he was gay.

Because it was already so autobiographical, and he was attempting to be "honest" in representing his family, MacIvor acknowledges the difficulty of having to compromise part of his own identity. As he sees it, the artistic compromise was another form of closeting. For him, "Urjo was my Sydney."

For MacIvor to compare Urjo Kareda to such a place is significant and telling. This takes me back to Gilbert's poignant metaphor of the "tug-of-war for MacIvor's soul." After the run of *Somewhere*, Gilbert wrote MacIvor a letter: "In it I urged him to continue writing gay work. Later, he told me that he really cherished those words. But the proof is in the pudding—the experimental style that Daniel developed at Buddies became his signature and the gateway to his success" (*Ejaculations* 138). In his eighteen-year tenure at Buddies as artistic director, Gilbert notes, MacIvor is "my biggest success story—if you measure success by how famous a person gets. I was instrumental in his career" (249).

DEATH AND VIOLENCE IN *SOMEWHERE I HAVE NEVER TRAVELLED*

A playwright's decision to bring death into a play as a means to have the protagonist come home is of importance; this was the case in MacIvor's *Somewhere*, with Joey returning home for his father's funeral. As for his other plays, MacIvor states,

> If there's a death, it's really the star of those plays . . . without death, there'd be no play. . . . Without death, there's no reason to come home. And death is what causes people to start considering their lives. So I suppose the role that death plays is the *lead role* . . . and violence is the villain.

As much as the tools of the craft need to be taken into account, one cannot overlook how this subject matter has been associated not only with gay theatre history, but also with gay male identity. Much critical work has observed death, violence, and plain misery as being inextricably bound up in the history of gay male theatre. For instance, Nicholas de Jongh, looking at the period of 1925–58 when "homosexuality is reckoned the archetype of evil," notes, "Suicide, alcoholism, murder, mental breakdown, death, imprisonment, ostracism, blackmail or mere misery are the ends to which homosexuals are brought at a play's lysis" (3). The protagonists of these plays, as de Jongh explains, are victims of the times in which they were written; thus, a play's "lysis," or resolve, what de Jongh regards as the "triumphalism of the Christian ethic," is not necessarily the conflict of a play, but rather the gay male character himself; in other words, he gets what is coming to him. Robert Wallace observes in his study of gay theatre that "the gay person is invariably sick and/or sad, more often a victim of self-doubt and deception than social pressure and ostracism" ("Image" 29).

Other critically acclaimed—and mostly commercial—Canadian gay plays produced in the same period by other notable gay playwrights reveal this morbid and morose fascination. The protagonists are in despair, and death and violence serve as the dominant theme in many, including René-Daniel

Dubois's *Being at Home with Claude* (1985), Robin Fulford's *Steel Kiss* (1987), Kent Stetson's *Warm Wind in China* (1988), Raymond Storey's *The Last Bus* (1989), Ken Garnhum's *Beuys, Buoys, Boys* (1989), Bryden MacDonald's *Whale Riding Weather* (1991), and Colin Thomas's *Flesh and Blood* (1991).

The history of gay male theatre has shown us that death and violence are also inescapable contexts when looking at representations of gay men in drama. Death and violence have been associated with gay men long before the AIDS plays of the 1980s; these factors have also reconstituted gay men.

SOMEWHERE TO SINK THE HURT

Journey through the Maritimes, trek through the Prairies, and you'd be hard put to find a drearier example of Canadian kitchen-sink drama than *Somewhere I Have Never Travelled*. . . . Why doesn't someone quietly tell playwrights to stop parading their uninteresting personal demons in front of an innocent audience.
—Robert Crew, "Not a Family You'd Ever Spend Any Time With"

So there's a darkness . . . about a place like Sydney and Cape Breton . . . there's something melancholic and depressing. . . . And an economic depression that I think probably influences what people see as a darkness in my work. . . . The subject matter can be incredibly dark and *death* is often very much at the centre of it. . . . And the death thing . . . that's sort of island life. I think that those of us who live, or grow up on islands, I think we understand that . . . because of the finite nature of the land . . . you just have a sort of innate understanding of the *ends* of things: that things do end, and things are finite.
—Daniel MacIvor, Interview

MacIvor's hometown of Sydney, Cape Breton, and his experience growing up there have major bearing on the death and violence found not only in *Somewhere I Have Never Travelled*, but also in his other plays. *Somewhere* remains one of MacIvor's most personal works, drawing heavily from his own family drama. "Obviously where I'm from affects my writing," he states in an interview with R.M. Vaughan. Furthermore, when discussing a childhood related to "anger, indecision, and abuse suffered," MacIvor responds, "It's in my work, maybe not directly, but it's in there. I'm conflicted" (Vaughan). Vaughan is then quick to point out that the one play MacIvor has written "directly" about Cape Breton is *Somewhere I Have Never Travelled*.[16]

Bev Brett, a Cape Bretoner who directed *Somewhere* soon after its premiere at Tarragon, finds the play to be "a very true depiction of Cape Breton experience."[17] She emphasizes how crucially linked the landscape of Cape Breton is to the play's violence and its characters. She particularly empathizes with the play's subject matter of alcoholism and abuse. She selected it because she knew that the subject "would resonate strongly in our community."[18]

> People would talk after the production about how abuse was passed from one generation to another—the repercussions. They would talk about how affected they were by the play. Because they accept the setting and the people without question—as a given, they are more likely to react to the emotional content.

---

16   This interview was conducted in 1995, so it was long before *Marion Bridge*, which was largely successful, unlike *Somewhere*. *Marion Bridge* has been published, produced often, and adapted into a film.

17   Brett quickly (and generously) replied to my email inquiry regarding the play (sent 19 Feb. 2008) in a few emails over the course of the next two days; in the interests of time, she provided an ongoing response under the same email subject line. Thus, all references from her are cited under the date 20–21 Feb. 2008.

18   Brett notes,

> One of the great things about doing community theatre in my community and why I love it so much is that ultimately I choose plays for my audience. We know the people in the audience. We know who had lives like the people in the play. You are interested in their reactions—not as critics but as people. . . . They aren't trying to figure out what Cape Bretoners are—or matching the story to their own preconceptions.

Of course, this kind of reception did not happen in Toronto. Ray Conlogue opens his review: "The Tarragon Theatre's season opener is yet another tormentedly artistic look at a set of tormentedly banal lives." Robert Crew concludes his review, "It's the sort of piece that makes you wonder if theatre isn't, in fact, just an expensive form of therapy for a fortunate few" ("Not a Family"). In a play largely about burying abuse, literally and metaphorically, certainly, "torment" and "therapy" will come into conversation.

MacIvor understands how central death is to the play's life. For him, death is "the star of the play"; without death, plays like *Somewhere* and *Marion Bridge* would not exist. For both these plays, death is the reason characters come home and start considering not only their lives, but also the life of the deceased. The only reason why Joey comes home from Toronto is the death of his father, Buck MacLean. MacIvor empathizes with Joey's reluctance to return home:

> Imagining myself in the same situation, I would certainly say, *at that time*—things are different now—but, *at that time* . . . it would be the only way that I would be able to return and bring my full self to returning would be in and around an idea of a death or something like that.

As much as MacIvor was reluctant to go back home at the time, whether on an actual visit or an imaginative one, via his writing, he saw "a necessity in returning." He makes it clear as to why the hometown experience was a painful one: "Sydney represents . . . being forced into a closet"; "I always felt that I was not really welcomed there . . . for who I was." However, despite the discomfort and alienation, MacIvor continuously comes home through his writing. As Vaughan observes, "Though MacIvor hasn't lived in Cape Breton for years, he finds himself returning, again and again, to the dramas of his youth." The large number of his plays that feature characters from his hometown shows how the painful voyage home has been essential. MacIvor admits,

> There's always going to be a character that in my mind is from Sydney . . . There's always somebody from Sydney, and they're usually

trying to hide that . . . these are people who are pretending they're not from Sydney . . . the hometown is in all of them somewhere, even if it's not articulated.

He used several of his plays—*House, In On It, Cul-de-Sac, You Are Here*—to illustrate such characters, all of whom, incidentally, are associated with death and violence. In many of these plays, the characters are actually dead, supporting his assertion that death is the star of his plays.

If death is the star, MacIvor conceptualizes violence as being the villain in *Somewhere*:

> It creates the tension that creates the schism between the people that are the loved ones . . . what gets in the way of the love is the violence. It's what stops the love . . . it's handed down through generations—it's generational. Even though the violence . . . doesn't manifest itself . . . in this generation . . . it's the residue of the violence that . . . disconnects the love of this family.

Thus, Buck represents both death and violence; he is both the star and the villain of the play. The play shows how Buck's family members (those in mourning and those who have been abused) are trying to process both the death and the abuse. As Brett notes, Joey tries to understand his father, now that he has grown, because "growing up you just react." On a macro level, *Somewhere* is structured in a way for an audience member to get an overall understanding of both the villain and "the residue of the violence that . . . disconnects the love of this family"—largely through Buck's extensive monologues, where he talks about his relationship with his abusive father. On a micro level, audience members see some of the family members attempt to understand Buck and deal with their fragmented relations with one other (what MacIvor identifies as the residual effects of abuse); unlike the audience members, the family is not able to witness Buck's monologues and thereby take in the bigger picture. In any case, critic Robert Crew was unimpressed with the presentation of both the macro and micro:

All in all, it's not a family that you'd want to spend much time with. But we are forced to sit through seemingly interminable flashbacks so that some incident from the past can be dredged up and picked over . . . the characters are so off-putting that by the time we've sorted everyone out, we've long since ceased to care. ("Not a Family")

MacIvor is aware that, typically, the way to process violence in the past involves reliance on memory; therefore, the play flashes back and forth between past and present.[19] In these flashbacks, MacIvor shows not only Buck's abuse of his family, but also the abuse Buck received. In order to write Buck's abuse, MacIvor pulled from his memory: "I used stories my father had told us many times about how he was raised in a tragically abusive home by a rum-runner and his frightened and obedient wife" (Pupo 54). Buck recounts instances of his father's abuse:

Beat me so bad one night and I got away. Ran down the road two miles . . . maybe more. All bloody and bustin in the door of this house. Americans, hardly knew them summer people. They're the ones who called the law. Law comes in a car takes me up to the house. Took one look at the old fella all drunked up and me black and blue, no questions asked they took him. (26)

---

19 The play was renamed *Present Time* after the Tarragon production. Brett mentioned that MacIvor was thinking of renaming it after she had expressed interest in it. At the time, she thought the new name was more sellable, but now she likes the old one better. Moreover, both MacIvor and Brett spoke about how tricky the staging of this play is; that is, all the flipping back and forth between past and present time. MacIvor added that a director would need to have a strong understanding of how time is staged in order for this play to work. Conlogue found these flashbacks as a setback: "The play jumps back and forth in time so frequently that it doesn't really have a temporal headquarters." Even Crew in his review of the opening night stated, "This series of fragments takes the audience on a lurching roller coaster of a ride through time that has you reaching for your travel pills" ("Not a Family").

For Brett, "Buck's father sounds brutal and ignorant—one generation of bad alcoholism can destroy and dissolve all the inheritance of a culture." Joey's inner torment that stems from his painful past is similar to how Buck's abusive relationship with his father has stayed with him. For instance, the death of Buck's father offers him no resolution, as he mourns, "Ashes to ashes and dust to dust . . . But where does all that hurt go?" (95).

Buck's inquiry about where all the hurt goes is an important one, providing a key to the play's title; for anyone subject to abuse and a hostile environment, the desired escape route is often, as the saying goes, *anywhere but here*. Agnes, Buck's rebellious sister, takes her share of hurt from their father's abuse and leaves Cape Breton for the United States. We learn that she has travelled all over. In the same way, Joey takes his hurt and leaves for Toronto. Both go somewhere they had never travelled in order to get away from the abuse. However, the past catches up and collides into their present time.

An example of this collision—death and violence coming together—occurs right after Buck's funeral, as Joey confronts his family: "We're remembering Buck. Who's going to start?" (127). He brings up unpleasant memories that cause further disconnection within the family, especially Joey's relationship with his mother and his sister, Dolly. Joey accuses his sister of continuing the cycle of abuse: "You must have loved it, you went out and married an asshole just like him" (128). Joey then recalls the fighting between his parents and the infidelity. He confronts his mother, saying, "He hurt you, every goddamn day . . . you can't just forget that" (129), after which she slaps him. Sitting in the audience on opening night in Toronto, MacIvor's mother and his two sisters (Dolly and Ann) realized the play "lifted its material from their lives" (Pupo 54). According to MacIvor, they did not mind; as Dolly states, "There are parts of all of us in a lot of what he does. And there's a lot of exaggeration as well" (qtd. in Pupo 54).

Crew's criticism of *Somewhere* as a self-serving therapeutic endeavour is not altogether incorrect, for MacIvor is exorcising his family demons and drawing from his personal experiences growing up. Indeed, the play features a son returning to his hometown and facing the painful memories of a broken family and a damaged home that he managed to escape. Both Joey and

Buck attempt to place their past into perspective. Although Joey has found the strength to leave his family and his hometown, the play reveals how memories of abuse and family never left his side. Even Buck, who left his family, recalls how he was not able to rid himself of the memory of his father:

> Things that happened and you carry them forever like a slab of iron on your shoulders, like a concrete block on your back. And you can travel this whole world over and no matter where you go: there it is still pushin you closer and closer to the ground. And maybe it's not so heavy if you just forget . . . if you just forget that it's there. (70)

Indeed, violent memories pursue Buck and Joey even as they continue to pursue MacIvor. In order to extinguish the torment in his psyche, Joey tries to kill the memory of his father the same way that Buck's father had tried to kill him. Buck tells the story to Joey of the time his father had him walk over a section on a frozen lake,[20] knowing that the ice was thin enough for his son to fall through. In hindsight, Joey admits his ongoing desire to rid himself of the memory of his father in a similar way: "I walked him over every piece of thin ice I could see but he wouldn't go down" (150). For Brett, this chilling confession served as the impetus for her to direct the play; coming from an abusive background herself, she understood Joey's—and MacIvor's—need to deal with a painful past in Cape Breton, and to sink that hurt. In the same way, Aunt Agnes admits, after her brother's funeral, the need to sink the hurt: "Buck gave burying that hate a good shot. Now it's my turn. Finish it off. Time to bury old Charlie [her father]" (149). "Daniel's dad must have been one charming likeable tortured alcoholic," Brett wrote, after she had re-read the play for the purposes of our discussion, still finding it "painful and bittersweet." She continued, "Such a hard story to tell and Daniel did it with so much love."

---

20   Brett informs me that this lake would have to be a lake between Washabuck and Baddeck. There are a number of lakes, but she figures it probably is Bras d'Or; however, the representation of this particular lake in the play is smaller than its original size. Buck's story takes place in Washabuck (hence, *Buck*).

One factor to suggest that MacIvor was unable to exorcise his father through this play—to have him fall through that ice—is the dramatic representation of Buck MacLean. As reflected in his review's title, "Clever but Unconvincing," Conlogue astutely observes: "The writer has not managed to get the Buck MacLean of his imagination onto the stage." Conlogue found the character of Buck unconvincing; he also found the actor playing Buck not entirely convinced of his character. Similarly, after MacIvor had watched Brett's production in Cape Breton, he informed her that he had not found his Buck yet—suggesting the Buck in Toronto did not convince him. In any event, MacIvor told Brett that she could do whatever she wished with the play, as he was done with it. It may be a burden for MacIvor to have to carry this unresolved feeling. However, MacIvor's artistic career *depends* on carrying the burden, and how his line of work pulls from that pain. As he has stated, "I carry the romantic idea of the tortured artist. I laugh at it, but I think we all have that in us somewhere" (Vaughan 10). Death and violence have proven to be necessary ingredients of so many of his plays, and of so many of his characters, who are all, in his mind, from Sydney.

CONCLUSION

Jill Dolan proclaims, "Our theater is our historiography; it encompasses our past, present, and future; our practice writes our history. . . . Theatre is our cultural memory" (6). This investigation into MacIvor's hometown is an act of preservation of MacIvor's cultural memory, as a gay male playwright, and his history. *Somewhere I Have Never Travelled*, which to the general public has either been defined as MacIvor's biggest critical flop or as unmemorable to the point of non-existence, occupies a space for the gay male and his past, present, and future. The recognition of "our gay hometown" is an integral step in reclaiming the unpublished text and making visible narratives and personhoods that have been too easily dismissed.

TENNESSEE WILLIAMS, DANIEL MACIVOR, AND BIODRAMA IN CANADA

JOHN S. BAK

Tell all the Truth but tell it slant—
Success in Circuit lies
—Emily Dickinson, "1128"

His Greatness (2007), Daniel MacIvor's biodrama about Tennessee Williams, is not, nor was ever meant to be, a historically accurate portrait of the playwright's brief tenure as writer-in-residence at the University of British Columbia (UBC) in the fall of 1980. Instead, the Canadian playwright captures what *could* have happened in a Vancouver hotel room in the hours preceding and following the premiere of Williams's "new" play, *The Red Devil Battery Sign*. Anecdotal bordering on spurious, the stories about Williams's hijinks in Vancouver, on which MacIvor founded his play, are anything but flattering for the American playwright, but they were not entirely uncommon either. Americans were largely familiar with Broadway's *enfant terrible* following the publication of his confessional *Memoirs* in 1975, or even as early as 1972, when various unsavoury features on Williams began appearing in major magazines, such as Tom Buckley's piece in *The Atlantic Monthly*. That such a portrait of Williams should emerge over three decades later in Canada raises the questions "Why Williams?" and "Why now?"

Setting, to be sure, plays a central role in MacIvor's play. Had it been set in a hotel room in New York City—where, in all likelihood, similar stories about Williams *had* regularly played out—few Americans, gay and straight alike, would have batted an eye. There was a reason why the Hotel Elysée, where Williams spent much of his last years when staying in New York, was

notoriously dubbed the Hotel "Easy Lay." Why such stories should have created a brouhaha in Vancouver back in 1980, and why they should have kept
reappearing in Canadian theatre circles over the next thirty years, then, point
not just to the differences between American and Canadian theatre, but also
between their gay communities, something Dirk Gindt recently demonstrated
in his essay on MacIvor's play and fellow Canadian Sky Gilbert's *My Night With
Tennessee*, an earlier one-act based on the same Vancouver gossip ("Sky").[1]

What MacIvor, or Gilbert for that matter, claims to have found enter-
taining in the stories about Williams in Vancouver was not their prurience
(though that no doubt helped) but rather their moxie: the defiant playwright,
unflagging in the face of those who had opposed him in the theatre—critics,
audiences, producers, and interviewers alike. It was *this* Williams, a character
taken straight from one of his own plays—the Blanche Williams, the Alma
Williams, the Princess Williams—that steeled Vancouver's gay community,
most of whom were not yet as *out* as were many of their brothers and sisters below the forty-ninth parallel. If Williams appears broken in both plays,

---

I would like to thank Sky Gilbert for giving me his version of the Williams gossip in
Vancouver and for allowing me to cite from his emails to me. Thanks also go to Dirk Gindt,
for sharing with me his knowledge of the Vancouver gossip and for reading an early draft
of this essay, and to John Tofanelli of Columbia University Library for tracking down a
few important sources in the Williams collection there. Finally, I would like to thank the
Tennessee Williams Estate and the University of the South for allowing me to quote from
Williams's unpublished manuscript "Twenty Years of It" and letter to *PRISM International*.
Copyright © 2015 The University of the South. All previously unpublished materials were
all reprinted by permission of Georges Borchardt, Inc., on behalf of the University of the
South, Estate of Tennessee Williams. All rights reserved.

1   As Gindt notes,

>   Gilbert first heard the anecdote about Williams in 1983, but did not produce *My
>   Night With Tennessee* until 1992. After that it would be another fifteen years be-
>   fore MacIvor wrote *His Greatness*. The story about Williams's visit to Vancouver
>   has thus been circulating in Canadian theatre communities for decades; in some
>   ways, it has served both as an entertaining cautionary tale and as a means to
>   create bonds between performing artists. ("Sky" 192)

especially in *His Greatness*, it is a *felix culpa* that allows MacIvor's Playwright to rise above his naysayers and, by extension, elevate the gay community with him. A Christ figure of sorts, at least in the Miltonic tradition. *His Greatness* is thus meant to celebrate Williams's decline, or "brokenness" as MacIvor prefers to call it (Foreword i), as Christians celebrate the Passion:[2]

> How the plays were broken, was how I was broken, was how we are broken. Suddenly I felt a deep connection with Williams, and I remembered that Vancouver story. . . . *His Greatness* is, in its deepest, most flawed and weakest heart, a play about me. And if you are anything like me at all, it is a play about you. (ii–iii)

His Greatness is ultimately about Williams's—and no doubt MacIvor's—post-lapsarian ascension, although on first reading/viewing, one might not get that impression.[3]

Gindt argues that the triumph of which MacIvor speaks is not disingenuous reverence or churlish mockery of Williams's decline in the theatre, American or otherwise. Despite recent favourable reappraisals of some of his late *maudites* plays—*The Red Devil Battery Sign* included—it was clear to everyone (most of all Williams) that his theatrical offerings from the mid-sixties onwards pleased few critics and even fewer audiences. Gindt instead "reflect[s] on how the gossip surrounding the playwright's visit to Vancouver

---

2 Perhaps not coincidentally, Easter often figures in the temporal setting of several Williams plays, such as *Battle of Angels* and *Sweet Bird of Youth*.

3 Even with the cover of the printed version, the final "s" of *Greatness* is depicted as falling off the word, suggestive of Williams's tarnished image. In January 2010, J. Paul Halferty wrote that he did "not see the human condition in *His Greatness* as tragic because its characters, particularly the Assistant, exhibit a hope for redemption" (105), but a year later Martin Morrow still felt the sense that the play is an unflattering portrait of Williams: "But I don't think Williams, who died in 1983, is rolling in his grave over this unflattering portrait of his twilight years. After all, he set the standard for biographical candour—especially in sexual matters—with his 1975 *Memoirs*. If anything, his corpse might sit up and applaud this play for its honesty" ("*His Greatness*").

has influenced the narratives of gay communities and, in so doing, contributed to queer theatre history in Canada" ("Sky" 188). Drawing upon Joseph Roach's assertion that "gossip, like myth, brings secrets into the public light, charming audiences with the socially cohesive pleasures of other people's pain" (297), Gindt posits that gossip functions in the play "as a structuring narratological facet as much as a repertoire of easily recognizable characters" (191). Williams's story in *His Greatness* becomes a parable for all gay Canadian men, Gindt concludes, with "gossip prov[ing] to be a useful tool in the process of rediscovering and preserving a sense of history and thereby help[ing] to foster community narrative" (205).

Gindt's article is indisputably groundbreaking for Canadian theatre studies, and I do not wish to take issue here with its cogent arguments. Gossip of the kind that has kept the stories of Williams's stay in Vancouver alive invariably mixes fact with fiction, and no one mastered the art of anecdotal self-promotion better than Williams himself. The closet requires fiction, and opportunities for gay men to emerge from it on the cusp of the AIDS epidemic varied from city to city, with sexual plurality being largely more visible in New York in 1980 than in Vancouver.[4] For that reason alone, one does not need to know what really happened in Vancouver, because what *really* happened is only important in how it served the greater cause of community-building gossip.

---

4   See, for instance, David Rayside's *Queer Inclusions, Continental Divisions: Public Recognition of Sexual Diversity in Canada and the United States*, where he explains how differences in political, legal, and religious issues in cities such as New York, Toronto, and Vancouver account for the disparities in the ways their gay communities have developed over time. If indeed the New York of 1980 was ahead of Vancouver in recognizing gay rights, Rayside posits, by the mid-1990s the trend had reversed its course:

> Change to existing patterns of regulating sexual diversity extends rapidly beyond just one or two specific policies or practices, and spreads rapidly across regions [of Canada, . . . and] the loosening or elimination of official barriers to parenting for Canadian lesbian and gay couples achieved a form of take-off from 1995 to 2001. In the United States positive change was spreading, but very slowly and unevenly across policy areas. (5)

What I do wish to challenge, however, is the idea that MacIvor contributed to that community gossip with *His Greatness*, as Gindt claims, by adding additional layers to the Williams myth, like some queer napoleon cake. Gossip, despite its intention to cling, if even precariously, to the truth, is based on a fictional imperative that serves the transmitter's desire to shock and the audience's need to be titillated, even if the truth behind that fact is misunderstood, misrepresented, or ignored all together. And in *His Greatness* there is certainly an admixture of fact and fiction surrounding Williams's stay in Vancouver, a disclaimer MacIvor proffers in his foreword to the published edition:

> *His Greatness* is not a play about Tennessee Williams. Reading or viewing this play will not give one insight into the man who was born Thomas Lanier Williams and became the great playwright who called himself Tennessee. It will not shed light on his relationship to his family or the reasons for his work. It will not have you closing the book or leaving the theatre saying: "Oh, so that explains why he. . . . " (ii–iii)

I beg to differ. Undeniably, there are traces of gossip here, information about events that MacIvor himself had only heard second-hand at a party. Yet what Gindt and others who have read or analyzed the play fail to mention, which undercuts this "gossip" thesis, is that MacIvor was fairly accurate in his portrayal of Williams in the play, from the poetic language to the literary allusions, from the southern mannerisms to the fear of encroaching madness, from the dislike of vulgarities to the bipolar behaviour. Even Williams's signature line "En avant!" or "Right on!" finds its way into the play (*His Greatness* 74). Accuracy like this is not obtained through the spread of gossip alone. MacIvor did his homework and is himself deceiving us when he says that "viewing this play will not give one insight into the man who was born Thomas Lanier Williams and became the great playwright who called himself Tennessee" (iii). Of course it does, and does it well. Why MacIvor should say otherwise is a curiosity, a theatrical conundrum to which perhaps he alone knows the answer.

As an overview of various sources on Williams's stay in Vancouver—interviews, letters, memoirs, and biographies—will reveal, MacIvor does indeed "shed light" on what made Williams tick, and how that personal drive and artistic integrity kept him sane and productive in the face of mounting hostility. If gossip celebrates the here and now, the scintillating and the scandalous, it cares little about the backstory. Yet *His Greatness* is as much about the backstory to Williams's misadventures in Vancouver as it is about his brokenness. Simply put, "fact" is fiction, and "fiction" fact in *His Greatness*, and MacIvor moves beyond the intertextuality that several critics like Gindt have recognized ("Sky" 193, 199, 200) and instead pays homage to the American playwright. The Williams that appears in *His Greatness* is thus not the patsy of a scandalous story involving a young man reading poetry in his underwear, but rather the protagonist of his autobiographic Künstlerroman in the autumn of his life. Examining where facts concerning Williams's escapades in Vancouver merge with fiction will thus demonstrate how MacIvor slants gossip into truth, where his biodrama celebrates the historical value not of what *was* but what *should* have been and *can* now actually be.

THE "FACTITIOUS ANAMNESIS": TOWARDS A DEFINITION OF BIODRAMA

While the writing of biographies and autobiographies dates back millennia, the ancestry of auto/biographical studies, or life-writing per its current moniker, is much harder to fix because its history is an amalgam of "celebrated ambiguity and disciplinary iconoclasm" (Jolly ix). Having said that, the *study* of biographical fiction—that is, the creative representation of a real person's life—is a recent trend in academe. Biofiction, as the hybrid form is often referred to today, is a French neologism coined by Alain Buisine in the early 1990s to describe the auto/biographical works that recount truthful stories in narrative- and dialogue-driven formats; in short, tweaking fact with fiction to make emotional sense of a life. A postmodern genre that combines "à la fois une reconfiguration de territoire du roman moderne et une révision de

l'histoire littéraire" (Gefen 305), biofiction fills the spectrum between fictionalized biographies and biographical novels, or, as Anne-Marie Monluçon and
Agathe Salha note, between "biographies imaginaires de personnages réels"
and "un récit de vie d'un personnage fictif, reprenant la forme, les conventions du genre biographique" (8).[5] Monica Latham defines the "portmanteau
word" in these terms:

> [Biofiction] encompasses the transfers that are operated from biog-
> raphy to fiction and the cross-over genre which fuses two opposed
> poles when narrating the imaginary lives of people who really exist-
> ed. This life-writing transgeneric literary product offers the reader
> a simulacrum of a real life: the writer-biographer's subjective rep-
> resentation of his/her subject's life. This phenomenon is part of the
> current postmodern cultural and literary practice that manipulates
> the real and plays with different layers of truths and pluralism of
> realities. (355–56)

Biofiction functions as a narrative historiography that reconstitutes, reorders,
or reconstructs what Roland Barthes has described in the preface to his *Sade,
Fourier, Loyola* (1971) as the *biographèmes* of a person's life, those individual moments or photographic impressions that represent discrete fragments
of a larger truth, such as one's date of birth or high-school senior portrait:

> Were I a writer, and dead, how I would love it if my life, through the
> pains of some friendly and detached biographer, were to reduce itself
> to a few details, a few preferences, a few inflections, let us say: to "bi-
> ographemes" whose distinction and mobility might go beyond any
> fate and come to touch, like Epicurean atoms, against some future
> body, destined to the same dispersion. (9)

---

5   Gefen describes it as "fictions littéraires de forme biographique (vie d'un personnage
imaginaire ou vie imaginaire d'un personnage réel)" (305).

Largely unintelligible in isolation, like phonemes to sounds or morphemes to words, biographemes elicit meaning only when they are structurally combined to produce biographical knowledge, where the gaps between the recorded events are as important as the events themselves. A biographer, like a film editor, cuts the story of a person's life into manageable scenes and, leaving some clips on the cutting-room floor, stitches together into a compelling narrative what he or she deems to be the best fragments. These fragments, however, are highly subjective and context dependent, though most audiences would agree that selective highlights of a person's life make for a more compelling spectacle than exhaustive narration. Biographemes, then, and the manner in which they are combined, have as much to say about the biographer as they do about the subject him- or herself, a phenomenon that led Barthes to conclude that all biography is essentially fiction.

Unlike historical biography, biofiction celebrates the gaps between biographemes and reproduces not "the *what*" of a given life but rather "the *what could have been*." The concept follows the phenomenological precept that all history, including biography, is based on a personal narrative and thus contingent upon subjective determinism. The closest that we can get to objective history is one that is agreed upon by the majority, though actual facts may be misinterpreted, misconstrued, or ignored all together. Jean-François Lyotard later called this process of truth-conferral "paralogy," whereby biographical certainty is bound by the perspective lenses of an era that produced it, necessitating subsequent paralogical assessments with each new generation (60–67). In terms of Williams's life, biographies written about him in the pre-Stonewall, post-Stonewall, and homophobic Reagan years unavoidably reveal a different man simply because the biographer's era has influenced his perception of Williams and the open secret of his homosexuality. Perhaps biofiction is the inevitable result of the closet since it requires a queer slant on the truth, and many gay writers in Williams's in-again/out-again inner circle of literary friends (such as Truman Capote, Christopher Isherwood, Donald Windham, and Gore Vidal) repeatedly infused their factual writings with fiction.

To a great extent, Tennessee Williams's autobiography and the many biographies written about him (unavoidably based in part on his *Memoirs*) are all examples of auto/biofiction because each tends to rewrite more than recount Williams's life. And if anyone is guilty of tainting the biographemes of his own life, it is Williams himself, who failed, even in his non-fiction (letters, essays, memoirs), to get the facts straight. As Gindt rightly notes, "Biographical information, dramatic fiction, anecdote, and gossip are conflated not only in Gilbert's and MacIvor's plays, but also in the general reception and perception of Williams" ("Sky" 203). For instance, like MacIvor's Playwright, who refuses to "write about my life" (7), Williams repeatedly said that he would never write an autobiography because he felt the plays spoke for him. When his agent Audrey Wood asked him as early as 1960 to start writing his autobiography, he was insulted, believing she meant that his career was now over, and he responded to her directly in an unpublished essay entitled "Twenty Years of It" (c. 1965):

> I thought my agent should know that my biggest and last indiscretion would be to come out with the sort of autobiography that I would write if I wrote one. I would have to write it in the psycho-analytical style of free-association, and if I did write it, which I am not about to do, now or ever. (1)

A half-dozen years later, history would prove him wrong: he did indeed write that autobiography but held true to his claim that it would be written in "the psycho-analytical style of free-association" that he had practised with Dr. Lawrence Kubie back in 1957.

Williams's free-association recollections in his *Memoirs* helped consolidate a gay community for it spoke to and for gay men and boys, closeted or not, at a time when the sexual cold war was thawing in the US, even if full sexual liberation had not yet been obtained. What is important here in Williams's *Memoirs* is that the queer gossip that emerged from it was supplied by the playwright himself. "Truth is the bird we hope to catch in 'this thing,'" Williams writes midway through *Memoirs*, and "truth" for him was something "better approached through [his] life story than an account of [his] career" (173).[6] Readers were thus forced to decode the autobiographemes of his sexual exploits to uncover his commentaries about art and the theatre, a point MacIvor makes clear in the foreword to *His Greatness*:

> The story was vivid and shocking and the archetypal portrait of a broken man. Such a heartbreaking and darkly poetic tale. . . . [I]t was a story I continued to hear in different forms and from many people for years. It was the theatre practitioner's cautionary tale. Just the way we like it, sordid and beautiful. (ii)

Unlike Oscar Wilde, who spoke his queerness through his art, Williams used his queerness to speak about his art, but only those in the know about all things Williamsian would have recognized the playwright's legerdemain. Williams's sexting was a diversion, a way for him to disguise his true thoughts and feelings, which were alone channelled through the creative process of playwriting.

We encounter Williams's sex-for-art's sake credo frequently in *His Greatness*, which attests to MacIvor's intimate understanding of the later Williams. When MacIvor's Young Man begins stripping for the Playwright at the end of Act One, for example, the Playwright stops him from taking off his underwear. "Leave that. As you are," the Playwright tells him. "You're beautiful" (48). Instead of having the Young Man read from the ubiquitous Gideon's Bible placed in a drawer of the bedside table, the Playwright asks him to read poetry, *his* poetry: "*The Playwright hands THE YOUNG MAN the book from the bedside table. It's a special night. Read one of mine*" (48). While the audience interprets the scene as being representative of Williams's unorthodox "sex" habits, MacIvor culls it for its "creativity" message, employing Williams's own method of achieving poetic truth. "Why do I resist

---

6   I have explored elsewhere Williams's relation to "truth" in his essays and autobiographical writings. See my biography *Tennessee Williams: A Literary Life* and "*Where I 'Love*': Tennessee Williams's Indiscrete Truths."

writing about my plays?" Williams asks himself provocatively in the *Memoirs*. "The truth is," he responds,

> I feel that the plays speak for themselves. And that my life hasn't and that it has been remarkable enough, in its continual contest with madness, to be worth setting upon paper. And my habits of work are so much more private than my daily and nightly existence. (193)[7]

To Williams, there was a difference between historical truth and poetic truth, with the latter being significantly more trustworthy precisely because it was not bound by historical imperatives. Poetic truth can be half-truths or even lies that, when collected, capture the truth of a life more accurately than the reconstruction of historical facts (recall Blanche's explanation to Mitch here about her having never lied in her heart, and how her life in Laurel could never have been faithfully reconstituted by Stanley's inquisition).

Whether or not the real young man present in Williams's hotel suite—whom Sky Gilbert identifies in his own memoirs as Daniel Allman (*Ejaculations* 49)—read from the Bible, as the Vancouver gossip reveals, or from Williams's poetry matters little here, least of all to MacIvor. The biographeme that MacIvor dramatizes in this central scene is truer than truth

---

7   As Williams writes in *Memoirs*, "Of course, I could devote this whole book to a discussion of the art of drama, but wouldn't that be a bore?" (181). Then later, as if almost apologetically, he adds:

> Well, now, about plays, what about them? Plays are written and then, if they are lucky, they are performed, and if their luck still holds, which is not too frequently the case, their performance is so successful that both audience and critics at the first night are aware that they are being offered a dramatic work which is both honest and entertaining and also somehow capable of engaging their aesthetic appreciation. I have never liked to talk about the professional side of my life. (212)

itself, if only because it is faithful to Williams himself.[8] In my afterword to
Williams's *New Selected Essays: Where I Live*, I explain this phenomenon thus:

> In many ways, the essays collected here form individual chapters
> of Williams's shadow memoirs that when read in parallel with the
> *Memoirs* demonstrate how his non-fiction prose constituted for him
> singular pieces of a complex mosaic: by themselves, the essays capture
> those significant moments in Williams's personal and professional
> life, to which he referred time and time again; reconstituted as a

---

8   Sky Gilbert offers his version of the Williams Vancouver gossip in his memoirs,
Ejaculations from the Charm Factory (2000):

> About Tennessee Williams, I happen to know two boys he tried to pick up. One
> is an ex-boyfriend, Shaun, and the other is Daniel Allman, who performed in
> my play *Pasolini/Pelosi*. These two encounters inspired a play I wrote in the mid-
> '80s called *My Night with Tennessee*.
>   Shaun was just a 15-year-old boy living in a Vancouver hotel with his mom
> back in 1979. Williams was staying there during a production of *The Red Devil
> Battery Sign*. He saw my lithe and lovely future boyfriend and slipped him his
> card, inviting Shaun to "come up and see him sometime." Shaun was too shy and
> didn't take him up on the request. He's cursed himself ever since. Daniel Allman
> was also propositioned by Tennessee in Vancouver. He invited the small, dark
> pretty boy to visit his hotel room and read poetry. There was one hitch—Daniel
> had to read in his underwear. Well, Daniel agreed. He said that Tennessee was
> pretty stoned and that nothing sexual happened. (49)

In a personal email from Gilbert, he had this to add:

> In terms of MacIvor's play I would have to say that I was surprised that he wrote
> it. Of course we have very different takes on the incident in question, but I
> couldn't help feeling my play about the incident wasn't good enough—so there
> had to be another! Of course the plays reflect our different sensibilities—my
> play celebrates Tennessee Williams's life, really trying hard not to censure him
> for being a promiscuous old alcoholic (being one now, I think that was a wise
> decision!). Daniel's play is a very different type of play, looking at Williams's
> "lifestyle" with perhaps a more critical or distanced eye.

whole, they display the splendor of Williams's lifelong pursuit of the truth, personal and artistic alike. (260)[9]

If sex was Williams's obsession, truth was surely his mantra. In his life as in his plays, you needed the one to achieve the other, and MacIvor reproduces that equation to the nearest decimal.

His Greatness is more than biofiction, however; it is also biodrama. As Anne-Marie Monluçon and Agathe Salha write, "La fiction biographique investit en effet plusieurs genres et plusieurs formes—romans, nouvelles, essai, voire poésie ou théâtre" (16). Like biofiction, biodramas are plays based "on real authors' lives and imagin[e] a world which they might have lived in and created," where the fictional elements become truth the more accurate the biographemes used. In this sense, Shakespeare's histories, such as *Henry V*, are historiopoetic, that is, dramatized studies of real figures for essentially literary ends (even if the history is accurate); biodrama, on the other hand, concerns "les rapports entre creation et créateur" (Monluçon and Salha 24). Edward Bond's play *Bingo*, about Shakespeare's shady dealing during the Welcombe enclosure, is biodrama not just because Shakespeare is the protagonist but also because the play uses Shakespeare's life to comment upon the creative process.

To a large extent, Williams's plays were themselves autobiodrama, so closely linked as they were to his life, a fact MacIvor makes clear in the metatheatrical prologue (and final soliloquy) to the play, as well as in his overall aesthetic. "There you are, still and silent," the Playwright says in the opening line of *His Greatness* (3). "Believing that I will have something to say. All I have to offer now is my life, or what's left of it" (3). MacIvor's Playwright

---

9   The narrator of Williams's second novel, *Moise and the World of Reason*, written simultaneously alongside *Memoirs*, comments once about the looseness of the novel's structure in words that echo what Williams had said himself about the rather unorthodox organization of his thoughts and recollections in *Memoirs*:

> It's seldom my practice to observe sequence. When I try to, my thoughts blur and my fingers shake. . . . Now I have got to discontinue this *thing* for a while, even though I never ignore the possibility that some inadvertence, a sudden subway of sorts, may stop it permanently in its tracks. . . . (38–39; emphasis added)

is not only Williams here but also Tom Wingfield (an avatar of Williams) in the opening of *The Glass Menagerie*:

> TOM: Yes, I have tricks in my pocket, I have things up my sleeve. But I am the opposite of a stage magician. He gives you illusion that has the appearance of truth. I give you truth in the pleasant disguise of illusion.
>
> To begin with, I turn back time. (135)

MacIvor's Playwright is also, perhaps more so, the Writer in Williams's *Vieux Carré*, the post-*Menagerie* Tom, or what we could have imagined happened to him after he left the Wingfield apartment in St. Louis and, like Williams himself, drifted about the cities "like dead leaves" (237):

> THE WRITER: Once this house was alive, it was occupied once. In my recollection it still is but by shadowy occupants like ghosts. (5)[10]

MacIvor clearly grasped the relationship between Williams's life and his creative process, how one was intimately tied to the other. But MacIvor does not simply recount that fact in the plot of *His Greatness*. Instead, he uses that knowledge of Williams to construct his own play's dramatic framework. For example, in the opening of *His Greatness*, the fourth wall is lowered à la *Glass Menagerie* or *Vieux Carré*, and the Playwright addresses the audience directly: the stage is "dark," the voices "silent," and the hotel room empty because the Playwright's "river" of creativity has run "dry" (3). What seems like defeat here, as the Playwright can no longer pull things out of his sleeves as Tom does to give to eager audiences, is cleverly inverted by the play's end, when

---

10   MacIvor's Playwright even recalls Williams's Playwright in *I Never Get Dressed Till After Dark on Sundays*, a one-act metadrama that eventually merged with another short play to become *Vieux Carré*.

the stage is bare yet again, and we have returned to where the play began, only something is different now.

With the Young Man and the Assistant now "shadowy occupants like ghosts" long parted, the Playwright returns to the present time and addresses the audience, just as he had in the play's prologue. But the Playwright is now addressing the audience (or himself) in the present tense: "There is a door stage right," "The king-size bed takes up the centre of the room," "On the left wall is . . . " (79). Gone is the prologue's use of the conditional or past tense, as in "the words would come" or "that was the beginning and now we are in a place that must be near the end" (3), suggesting the Playwright's nostalgia for a muse who has long since left him. We are witnessing the Playwright's creative process *in medias res*, demonstrating that he is anything but "broken" since he is using his life's experiences, even failures, to reproduce art afresh.

Moreover, MacIvor turns the opening scene's italicized stage directions that set the Vancouver hotel stage (if only for the reading public) into the Playwright's direct dialogue. Thus the read line, "*We are in the bedroom of a hotel suite in Vancouver, Canada, November of 1980*" (4), becomes the spoken line, "The bedroom of a hotel suite in Vancouver, Canada, 1980" (79). Made to think that we are witnessing the Playwright's curtain call, the audience in fact partakes in his next creative endeavour. The Playwright begins reciting, nearly word for word, the same play that the audience has just witnessed acted out in real life on stage. Therefore, the concluding words of the prologue, "The stage is dark" (3), do not define the end of the Playwright's career; rather, when repeated at the end of play, they announce the beginning of his next play: "The stage is dark. It begins" (80). From the very beginning of *His Greatness*, the audience had been inside the Playwright's head, not at the dark hour of depressive recollection but at the actual moment of composition.

What the audience has just witnessed were not the events that actually took place in Vancouver, reconstructed like some gossipy biography, but the Playwright's "factitious anamnesis" of his own life's story, which he turns into art, and the audience participates in the creative recovery process. Defeat at the beginning becomes triumph in the end because life's tragedy has produced art. *That* is Tennessee Williams par excellence, especially the later Williams who turned his repeated struggles with critics and audiences into poems, stories, and plays that bear testament to the fact that Williams bent but did not break.

Like the Assistant's "Rise and shine" (4) wake-up call, or the various references to angels throughout the play, which Gindt rightly notes are intertextual references to *The Glass Menagerie* and *Vieux Carré* ("Sky" 193, 199, 200), the opening and the closing lines not only reproduce biographemes of Williams's characters' lives, but also autobiographemes of his own life, since both references worked into his plays were in fact based on real-life events. The biodrama that is produced in the end captures Williams the man, Williams the rising playwright, and Williams the embattled playwright all at the same time. Even if the various "facts" are wrong or "slant," the larger portrait of the playwright is true and honest. As Monluçon and Salha put it, "La fiction biographique échappe à l'alternative du vrai et du faux, mais constitue bien souvent un détour pour aboutir à une forme de savoir ou de vérité" (23–24). Gossip, it would seem, has given over to historiography or, at least, biodrama where *His Greatness* is concerned.

The stories, particularly the "underwear" incident at the heart of MacIvor's and Gilbert's plays, are many,[11] and if gossip favours oral history, there are also sources on paper (or computer screen) that have documented Williams's time in Vancouver. Individually, the sources vary in accuracy, but viewed collectively like the discrete biographemes of Williams's essays or his *Memoirs*, they help to establish the poetic truth of Williams's tenure there. To begin

---

11   Marsha Lederman adds these pieces of gossip: "The stories of his stay paint a picture of a man in decline: Williams at a party, drunk, singing *Don't Cry for Me, Argentina* repeatedly all night; Williams going out for dinner and leaving a single sock behind at the restaurant; Williams falling asleep at a preview of his own play" (R1). And this: "The tale that stayed with MacIvor is not a pretty one. A professor friend of MacIvor's, who used to be a hustler in Vancouver, recalls being recruited by Williams's personal assistant to find other young men to come to Williams's hotel room, strip to their underwear and read to the playwright from the Bible. Williams would then insult their reading abilities" (R1). One of the final recollections of Williams's time in Vancouver comes from Kenneth J. Emberly. An aspiring playwright at the time, Emberly recalls how Williams took the time to read his play and even wrote a letter of praise to the young man on 19 October 1980, just before he left for Chicago.

with, there was not one trip to Vancouver, but *at least three*, and one wonders how much of the stories are a conflation of what actually took place over the span of a year.

Williams "packed up and went off to Vancouver" (Douglas, 27'05"), arriving at UBC in October 1980. During his stay, Williams lived in a suite at the inn at Denman Place at 1733 Comox Street. It is in this hotel that MacIvor sets his play. Though MacIvor gives his Playwright a room overlooking "*an unseen parking lot*" (4), Williams's actual suite was on the twenty-seventh floor of the inn and had a "magnificent" view overlooking the Pacific coast "studded with mountainous little islands" and the harbour full of the "little sailing boats" (*Five O'Clock* 381). Historically inaccurate, MacIvor's fictional setting for *His Greatness* is nonetheless visually poetic, intending to illustrate how far Williams had "come terribly down in the world" (*His Greatness* 15).

Though all of the details differ slightly, the general story of Williams's arrival in Vancouver, his initial dissatisfaction, and his eventual departure and return are fairly accurate. MacIvor's diversions from fact transform historic truth into poetic truth. Just as the Young Man questions the theatre critics' birthright to defining literary excellence, MacIvor seemingly inquires of these historical sources on Williams, "But why do they get to be right?" (*His Greatness* 60). His Playwright's response was also Williams's: "I only speak the truth I see" (10).

"I HELPED CREATE THE MODERN WORLD": GLEANING THE PUBLISHED VANCOUVER SOURCES

Once he was settled in Vancouver, Williams divided his day between his teaching, his rehearsal work with director Roger Hodgman, and his free time. Per each activity, there exists various testimonies, some of which merely fill out the backstory to Williams's time in Vancouver, while others speak directly to *His Greatness*. In all likelihood, MacIvor did not know about some of these sources, but certain similarities between Williams's interviews for and texts about *The Red Devil Battery Sign* and *His Greatness* suggest that MacIvor did indeed consult a few before writing the play. And what the similarities demonstrate is that MacIvor chose to remain historically accurate in his fictive representation of Williams's struggle with his critics..

When the Assistant suggests to the Playwright that he is no longer writing because he is "allergic to words," the Playwright retorts: "I'm not writing because I am busy with my teaching" (10–11). Williams was contractually obliged to teach courses on writing and theatre at UBC, and there is an online source that captures a little bit of what he did during one of his university classes. A former student, known today as blogger Father Theo, was in one of Williams's creative-writing seminars back in 1980 and describes how the lesson included the collective writing of a short story in the vein of a Surrealist *collage*:

> I remember the students in the creative writing department were presented to him in an expanded classroom, more than one class brought together in that room. He entered with a faculty entourage, and quietly entering with him, saying not a word the whole time and sitting on [a] chair behind the eminent author while the proceedings went on, was a very pretty young man who nobody bothered to introduce or refer to. Tennessee's date [*sic*].
>
> I suspect that young man felt a little lost.
>
> . . . Tennessee sat at one end of the table and wrote the first paragraph of about 100 words. The person next to him wrote the second paragraph based on what Tennessee had written. So on for the next person. The story progressed around the table from Tennessee Williams to me, each person only aware of the paragraph before and of what they themselves had written. After we each had done—I forget exactly how long we were given to complete our parts—we each read out our paragraphs in sequence.
>
> Williams began the story. I ended it. It must have been 2000 words produced by 20 hands in less than an hour, and it actually was not that bad a story. Although I can't recall a single detail, a single

word, or the slightest notion of what it was about, I remember being impressed and surprised by how well it held together.

But it was pure ephemera. The story only had one reading.

Albeit about one specific class, this recollection does offer a sampling of what the pedagogical Williams actually did during his lessons. When MacIvor's Playwright suggests that a lot of his time was spent in the classroom, then, the exaggeration seems intended to justify his current lack of creative inspiration or output.

Never the pedagogue, Williams was primarily interested in getting another crack at *The Red Devil Battery Sign*, which was now as "tight as a fist," cut down to eighty pages or "about twenty less than it was in England" back in 1977 (*Five O'Clock* 381). *Red Devil* was to open at the Vancouver Playhouse on 18 October, and, on 14 October, Williams confided to Maria St. Just that "the definitive production of *Red Devil Battery Sign* [was] being staged by a brilliant director," Roger Hodgman (*Five O'Clock* 381). In *His Greatness*, MacIvor chose not to draw much attention to the director, making only one reference about how the Playwright tried to seduce him, believing that he was gay: "Oh, please, the only pussy he ever had would have been furry and purring in his lap" (10). Ironically, this anecdote was in real life made in reference to a minor actor in Williams's play. During rehearsals for *Red Devil* back in 1980, David Marr, who later performed the role of the Assistant in the premiere of *His Greatness*, had a small role in the chorus and confided to journalist Marsha Lederman some of his recollections about working with Williams:

> Marr's memories of Williams the artist . . . are largely positive. "He was great in rehearsal," he remembers, "very funny and charming." He was also productive, as Marr remembers it. "He was there as a writer and would try to fix things that needed fixing."

However, Marr also recalls a Williams a little less charming:

"[He was] going off the rails," being "lubricated" and at times inappropriate. Marr was late for notes one day, and as he came running down the stairs of the theatre, he remembers Williams saying: "Well, if it isn't the gay one." Marr (who is not gay) was speechless. "I stopped. And everyone laughed and I had nothing to say. I must have gone beet red and I thought, 'Maybe he just thinks I'm happy.'" (Lederman R2)

In reality, Williams had a lot of respect for Hodgman, and there is plenty of evidence of their convivial relationship in the interviews they conducted together, as well as in the letters Williams wrote to him. One particular interview has a central place in *His Greatness*. In Act One, the Assistant arranges a telephone interview with a local radio station: "Get yourself together—they'll be calling for the interview in a few minutes" (11). The interview that takes place on the speakerphone, ending with an irate Playwright hanging up on the ingenue reporter, Julie, is similar to an actual interview that Williams and Hodgman gave to St. John Simmons and Joe Martin, student editors of UBC's literary magazine, *Prism International*, which was later printed in the magazine along with the version of *The Red Devil Battery Sign* that premiered at the Playhouse Theatre.[12] MacIvor was clearly referring to this interview in his play since Julie's naïveté about the Playwright's place in modern theatre

---

12   According to Veronique West, the magazine debated whether or not to print the play: "Williams produced *The Red Devil Battery Sign* while he was Writer in Residence in Theatre & Creative Writing at UBC. He was a fan of PRISM, and he suggested that the magazine print his play." *PRISM*'s board was hesitant about printing the play, given its recent critical panning in Vancouver:

UBC Faculty emeritus George McWhirter told Andrea Bennett about the debate, describing it as a battle between PRISM editors St. John Simmons and Joe Martin. According to McWhirter, Martin wanted to publish the play, and Simmons did not. Eventually, after the editorial board had a chance to see a dress rehearsal of *The Red Devil Battery Sign*, the decision came down to a vote at an editorial board meeting. The first question Simmons posed to the editorial board: Did you like the play? Eight or nine people voted *No*, while three (which MacIvor later echoes in his interview with Colin Thomas ["MacIvor Explores"[13]]) is reflected in the questions Williams was asked by the two student editors.

Though the tone of Williams's voice is not present in the published transcript of the interview, given the curtness of some of his responses, he seems as annoyed with the interviewers as MacIvor's Playwright is with Julie in *His Greatness* in response to her question about his efforts to "enter the modern world": "It wasn't this play. This is a new play. And I don't need to enter the 'modern' world, I am in the modern world. I helped create the modern world" (18). In the *PRISM* interview, Williams's reply is strikingly similar:

PI: What is your view of the role of the artist in society?
TW: I think he has to be a visionary to a certain extent. There are several kinds. A soothsayer, perhaps. He feels, he is solipsistic [*sic*], that's what makes him so difficult and unattractive, the solipsism, the self-absorption, but he needs that to defend himself and to contain

---

voted *Yes*. Second question: Should PRISM publish the play? All hands went up for *Yes*. (West)

In a handwritten letter in the Harvard archives addressed to the "Editors of Prism International" (and more than likely not mailed), Williams attacks the theatre critic Wayne Edmundson for his scathing review of Williams's play. Williams concludes the letter, "May I spark such a suggested appraisal of Wayne Edmundson with the question: 'Is sadism acceptable as a highly pronounced element in the character of a man who serves as a theatre critic?'" (Letter to *PRISM International* 2).

13   Thomas interviewed MacIvor in October 2007 for *The Georgia Straight*, just prior to the opening of *His Greatness*. In the interview for the Vancouver online news source, MacIvor "attributes Williams's failure at least partly to the deceased playwright's desire to please. 'It feels like Williams was trying to be modern,' MacIvor explains, referring to his later work. 'You look at something like *The Red Devil Battery Sign* and it's just a steaming mass of. . . . It just doesn't connect. It seems like he was making such an effort to do something other than the thing he was born to do.'" In a similar pre-opening interview with Marsha Lederman, MacIvor admits to having read—and disliked—*Red Devil*, calling it "almost impenetrable" and "unfortunate" (R2). Both interviews suggest that MacIvor was familiar with the *PRISM International* material on Williams.

his world from which he looks out and interprets reality as he sees
it. He has a role in society, I think society considers him at their service to entertain, but he doesn't see it that way, he sees the need for
entertainment and excitement but what he's at is something else, he
wants to make some meaning out of his life and he's selected the role
of artist to attempt to make some meaning and to make an order out
of chaos. I think an artist ceases to be what the society he lives in—
he doesn't limit himself to what the society he lives in, wants him to
be. He explodes from that because it's too limiting for him, he has
to express himself.

PI: Do you see him as "the unacknowledged legislator of the world"?

TW: No. That becomes paranoia, it becomes madness. I think you'll
find the best answer to this in "Fear and Misunderstandings in the
Artist's Revolt." ("Interview" 50)

MacIvor has fun with the passage in *His Greatness*, where Williams fails entirely to respond to Julie in like kind about what defines the "modern theatre"
and his role in it:

JULIE: *(voice over)* When you premiered this version in London last
year the critics said . . . that the play was an attempt for you to enter
the modern world but in essence it was an old-fashioned play. How
do you respond to that? . . .

PLAYWRIGHT: It wasn't this play. This is a new play. And I don't
need to "enter" the modern world, I am in the modern world. I
helped create the modern world. What is "modern"? Tell me that.
The human heart is not modern anymore? Longing, love, loss? No?
What's a "modern play"? (18)

In the Playhouse's *Program Magazine* from October 1980, MacIvor could
also have encountered a similar diatribe by Williams about his contribution
to the modern theatre, very likely motivated by this interview with *PRISM*:

*I confess to you without shame, without apology that this is melodra-
ma, not classically pure tragedy. . . .*

*Of course I know that in Greek drama there were tragedies and there
were comedies and the two were very distinct from each other. But in
modern theatre many conditions have changed—the masks have been
discarded and also the stilt-like elevations on which the actors walked
to give them a super-human aspect.*

*My kind of serious theatre is to somehow combine humor and terror
and sensuality and heart-break.* ("Playwright's Preface")

Williams finishes the "Preface" by half-scolding his spectators, predicting
that they would not "get" his play: *"To have great theatre we must have great
audiences too."*

"Getting" the play, and its new ending, was something important to
Williams and Hodgman, and MacIvor makes this clear in *His Greatness*. In
the *PRISM* interview, for example, Williams and Hodgman discuss the play's
ending and how it had changed since the previous versions of the play and
how it will need to be "pull[ed] off" for this audience if the play were ever to
be a success. We find traces of that new ending here in this interview (which
also gives us insight into the number of daily revisions that were made to
the script, most of these manuscripts eventually filling up several files in the
Harvard Theatre Collection):

TW: If we can pull off the ending then we've got it made. But there's
a big question mark there.

[A discussion ensues over which version we have read and it becomes apparent that considerable changes have been made since
rehearsals began.]

PI: Did you put forward suggestions, Roger?

RH: I certainly had some ideas. It's always a collaborative effort. . . .

PI: At what point do you have the finished play?

TW: We don't. We don't have it now. We don't know if the ending is going to work. . . .

RH: It's a very positive ending. It's easy to see that ending as negative or sad or tragic. It's a very positive ending.

TW: Dynamically positive.

RH: That's what people are going to find hard to accept, because what's positive about it is really uncomfortable. ("Interview" 51–53)

This discussion is partly dramatized in the ending of Act One of *His Greatness*, where, returning to the hotel after opening night, the Young Man says that the audience really "got" the play's ending:

I mean, first it all seemed a bit kind of fake, but then I really got into it. I, like, really believed them and everything. . . . And no, but, like, and at the end, and everybody's all freaking out and that guy's howling and they're all jumping off the stage. It was amazing. And people were like watching it like: *(makes a face of jaw-dropping amazement)* They were, I looked at them, they were like: *(makes a face of jaw-dropping amazement).* (40–41)

MacIvor's intertextuality here, as elsewhere in the play, is not pastiche. *His Greatness* transcends the playful allusions to Williams's prior work, such as *The Glass Menagerie* and *Vieux Carré*, and recycles previous material on Williams's stay in Vancouver to provide a rounded characterization of the American playwright at an extremely low point of his career. In constructing his play around these two significant scenes (the radio interview and *Red Devil*'s ending), both seemingly drawn straight from the pages of *PRISM International*, MacIvor is balancing the biographemes of a few weeks spent in Vancouver with the poetic truth of Williams's lifelong struggle to survive as an artist in a world hostile, or at least indifferent, to what he has to say about the human condition.

"I ONLY SPEAK THE TRUTH I SEE": CONCLUSION

"His Greatness is not about Tennessee Williams," MacIvor claims in his foreword (ii). It is instead about "three lost men who have forgotten their dream of
a life, and as a result of the events of two days come to remember, if not their
dreams, at least that they had once had a dream" (iii). But this was Canada,
more specifically Vancouver, and Williams had brought with him an aura as
a playwright and as an openly homosexual man to a city that was internationally renowned for neither. He brought cachet to two communities—artistic
and gay alike—and his actions left traces (some would say scars) on both.
What took place during the few weeks in Vancouver was so significant that
Canadians are still talking about it, even in a day where celebrity scandals are
daily fodder for the press. Why that should be the case is important both to
the theatre world and to the gay communities in Canada, as evidenced by the
number of plays or diaries or other recollections that have since circulated
there like currency, from one generation to the next.

For that reason, MacIvor's recounting of the stories surrounding Williams's
stays in Vancouver should be seen not as an attempt to bring shame upon
Williams, but rather to expose the cruelties of a theatre world towards an aging artist, any artist, by forcing him to accept its literary aesthetics, and of a
homophobic world towards the gay communities by repeatedly shoving them
back into the closet. Williams, of course, refused to genuflect to the great-
god critic, or homophobe (often, in America at least, they were one in the
same), and was consequently reduced to being a broken man from which he
would emerge the following morning steeled by his resolve to complete his life's
work and to continue writing plays that the critics would hate and the public
would not understand. Resilience was Williams's middle name, as he declared
in one Vancouver interview: "I have a favorite line in the play [*The Notebook
of Trigorin*]. The character, Trigorin, is a writer and he talks about critics. He
says, 'If the critics like my work, I am happy. If they don't, I'm depressed for
a couple of days, and then I continue to write.' I'm much like Trigorin" (P.C.).

There is gossip, plenty of it, in *His Greatness*, but there is a lot more.
While gossip celebrates the community that shares the stories between them,

biodrama celebrates the sources of those stories. *His Greatness* is as much about those sources as it is about the stories they have perpetuated, and at the heart of both of them was Tennessee Williams. Whether he was liked, admired, or even loathed, Williams commanded attention in Canada, arguably more than he did in New York during the final years of his life. Perhaps it was because visits from internationally known playwrights were a novelty in Vancouver theatre at that time; perhaps it was because American celebrities in general were rarely seen walking on the city's streets. In Williams you had both, and that alone suggests why the stories about Tennessee Williams circulated among the city's gay and theatre communities for years before spreading across the entire country. It mattered little, then, which Williams play was performed in Vancouver in the opening years of the 1980s—any would be both a failure and a success, simply because its author was.

WORKS CITED

"About." *Kenny Vs. Spenny*. Kenny Vs. Spenny, 2013. Web.

"About WorldPride 2014." *Pride Toronto*. Pride Toronto, n.d. Web.

A Beautiful View. By Daniel MacIvor. Dir. Ross Manson. Perf. Becky Johnson and Amy Rutherford. Volcano/BeMe Theatre. Baby Grand Studio, Kingston, ON. 12 Mar. 2014. Performance.

A Beautiful View. By Daniel MacIvor. Dir. Ross Manson. Perf. Becky Johnson and Amy Rutherford. Volcano/BeMe Theatre. Einstein Kulturzentrum, Munich, Germany. 27 Oct. 2012. Performance.

Adams, James. "'Shockingly Low' Attendance: Buddies in Bad Times Theatre Really Is in Bad Times." *The Globe and Mail*. The Globe and Mail Inc., 5 Apr. 2013. Web.

Adams, Tim. "The Interview: Robert Pirsig." *The Observer*. Guardian News, 19 Nov. 2006. Web.

Ahmed, Sara. "'She'll Wake Up One of These Days and Find She's Turned into a Nigger': Passing through Hybridity." *Performativity & Belonging*. Ed. Vikki Bell. London: Sage, 1999. 87–106. Print.

Aitken, Robert, trans. *The Gateless Barrier: The Wu-men Kuan (Mumomkan)*. By Wumen Huikai. San Franciso: North Point, 1990. Print.

Allen, Nancy K. *Bequest and Betrayal: Memoirs of a Parent's Death*. Bloomington: Indiana UP, 2000. Print.

Anna Karenina. Dir. Joe Wright. Screenplay by Tom Stoppard. Universal Pictures, 2012. Film.

Appiah, Kwame Anthony. *The Ethics of Identity*. Princeton, NJ: Princeton UP, 2005. Print.

Aquino, Nina Lee, and Ric Knowles. "Introduction to *Asian Canadian Theatre.*" Introduction. *Asian Canadian Theatre.* Ed. Aquino and Knowles. Toronto: Playwrights Canada, 2001. vii–xvi. Print.

Arigato, Tokyo. Toronto: Buddies in Bad Times, 2013. Print.

Austin, J.L. *How to Do Things With Words.* Ed. J.O. Urmson and Marina Sbisa. 2nd ed. Oxford: Clarendon, 1975. Print.

Bacalzo, Dan. "Reviews: The Soldier Dreams." *Theatermania.* Theatermania, 29 Mar. 2011. Web.

Bak, John S. Afterword. *New Selected Essays: Where I Live.* Ed. Bak. New York: New Directions, 2009. 259–68. Print.

---. *Tennessee Williams: A Literary Life.* New York: Palgrave Macmillan, 2013. Print.

---. "*Where I 'Love':* Tennessee Williams's Indiscrete Truths." *A Streetcar Named Desire: Play & Film.* Exp. ed. Ed. Marie Liénard-Yeterian and Aliki Diaz-Kostakis. Paris: Les Éditions de l'École Polytechnique, 2012. 97–113. Print.

---. "'White Paper' and 'Cahiers Noirs': Williams's many ur-*Memoirs.*" *Études Anglaises* 64.1 (2011): 7–20. Print.

Barnard, Elissa. "*Bingo!* is a Wonderful Present from MacIvor." Rev. of *Bingo!,* by Daniel MacIvor. Neptune Theatre, Halifax. *Chronicle Herald* (Halifax). The Chronicle Herald, 21 Oct. 2012. Web.

---. "MacIvor Dazzles in One-Man Vision of Inner Space." *Chronicle Herald* (Halifax). The Chronicle Herald, 22 Nov. 2012. Web.

Barthes, Roland. *Sade, Fourier, Loyola.* 1971. Trans. Richard Miller. Berkeley: U of California P, 1976. Print.

Beckett, Samuel. *Endgame & Act Without Words 1.* New York: Grove, 2009. Print.

Bénard, Johanne. "'Stand Up' or 'Sit Down': Daniel MacIvor's *House.*" Trans. Jenn Stephenson. *Solo Performance.* Ed. Stephenson. Toronto: Playwrights Canada, 2010. 29–35. Print.

"*Bingo!*" *Celtic Life International.* Celtic Life International, 2014. Web.

Bolt, Carol. Introduction. *Never Swim Alone & This Is A Play.* By Daniel MacIvor. Toronto: Playwrights Canada, 1993. 7–9. Print.

Boni, Franco, ed. *Rhubarb-o-rama!: Plays and Playwrights from the Rhubarb! Festival.* Winnipeg: Blizzard, 1998. Print.

Borges, Jorge Luis. "A History of the Tango." *Jorge Luis Borges: Selected Non-Fictions*. Ed. Eliot Weinberger. New York: Viking, 1999. 394–404. Print.

Brett, Bev. "Re: Somewhere I Have Never Travelled / Present Time." Message to Christopher Grignard. 20–21 Feb. 2008. Email.

Brooks, Daniel. Foreword. *Cul-de-Sac*. By Daniel MacIvor. Vancouver: Talonbooks, 2005. 1–15. Print.

---. "Some Thoughts about Directing *Here Lies Henry*." *Canadian Theatre Review* 92 (1997): 42–45. Print.

Buckley, Tom. "Tennessee Williams Survives." *Atlantic Monthly* (Nov. 1970): 98–109. Print.

Burroughs, William S. *The Adding Machine: Selected Essays*. New York: Arcade, 1986. Print.

Butler, Judith. *Gender Trouble: Feminism and the Subversion of Identity*. New York: Routledge, 1990. Print.

Calhoun, Craig. "Social Theory and the Politics of Identity." *Social Theory and the Politics of Identity*. Ed. Calhoun. Oxford: Blackwell, 1994. 9–36. Print.

Castiglia, Christopher, and Christopher Reed. *If Memory Serves: Gay Men, AIDS, and the Promise of the Queer Past*. Minneapolis: U of Minnesota P, 2012. Print.

Chapman, Geoff. "Furious Word-Duels Convey Male Idiocy." Rev. of *Never Swim Alone*, by Daniel MacIvor. Dir. Ken McDougall. *Toronto Star* 21 Jan. 1994: D12. Print.

Claycomb, Ryan. *Lives in Play: Autobiography and Biography on the Feminist Stage*. Ann Arbor, MI: U of Michigan P, 2012. Print.

Clum, John M. *Acting Gay: Male Homosexuality in Modern Drama*. New York: Columbia UP, 1992. Print.

Coleman, Rebecca. "An Interview with Daniel MacIvor." *Rebecca Coleman*. 2 Nov. 2009. Web.

Conlogue, Ray. "Tarragon Opener Clever, but Unconvincing." Rev. of *Somewhere I Have Never Travelled*, by Daniel MacIvor. *The Globe and Mail* 5 Oct. 1988: C8. Print.

Coulbourn, John. "Thank you, Arigato." *The Toronto Sun*. Sun Media, 25 Mar. 2013. Web.

Crew, Robert. "High Quality Work On Mediocre Play." Rev. of *The Last Bus*, by Raymond Storey. Tarragon Theatre, Toronto. *Toronto Star* 22 Feb. 1989: C1. Print.

---. "*Jitters*: Hilarious Love Letter to Canadian Actors." Rev. of *Jitters*, by David French. Soulpepper Theatre Company, Young Centre, Toronto. *Toronto Star*. Star Media Group, 1 Jul. 2010. Web.

---. "Not a Family You'd Ever Spend Any Time With." Rev. of *Somewhere I Have Never Travelled*, by Daniel MacIvor. *Toronto Star* 5 Oct. 1988: F1. Print.

Croce, Alrene. "A Critic At Bay: Discussing the Undiscussable." *The New Yorker* (26 Dec. 1995): 54–60. Web.

Cushman, Robert. "Soldier Comes off Vague and Arid." Rev. of *The Soldier Dreams*, by Daniel MacIvor. Canadian Stage Company, Toronto. *The Globe and Mail* 29 Mar. 1997: C10. Print

---. "With Friends Like These . . . Melissa James Gibson's *This* Debuts in Toronto." Rev. of *This*, by Melissa James Gibson, and *Arigato, Tokyo*, by Daniel MacIvor. *National Post*. Postmedia Network, 30 Mar. 2013. Web.

de Jongh, Nicholas. *Not in Front of the Audience: Homosexuality on Stage*. London: Routledge, 1992. Print.

Del Signore, John. "*Never Swim Alone*." Rev. of *Never Swim Alone*, by Daniel MacIvor. The Lion Theater, New York. *Gothamist*. Gothamist LLC, 17 Sep. 2006. Web.

Demchuk, David. *Touch: A Play for Two*. Wallace, *Making, Out* 41–57.

D'Emilio, John. "Gay and Lesbian Studies: New Kid on the Block?" *Making Trouble: Essays on Gay History, Politics, and the University*. New York: Routledge, 1992. 160–76. Print.

Denton, Martin. "The Soldier Dreams." *Nytheatre*. New York Theatre Experience, 7 May 2005. Web.

Dickinson, Emily. "1128." *Collected Poems*. Ed. Thomas H. Johnson. London: Faber, 1970. 506. Print.

Derrida, Jacques. *Of Grammatology*. Trans. Gayatri Chakravorty Spivak. Baltimore: Johns Hopkins UP, 1998. Print.

---. "Signature, Event, Context." *Limited Inc*. Trans. Samuel Weber. Chicago: Chicago UP, 1988. 1–23. Print.

Dolan, Jill. "Introduction: Building a Theatrical Vernacular: Responsibility, Community, Ambivalence, and Queer Theater." Introduction. *The Queerest Art: Essays on Lesbian and Gay Theater*. Ed. Alisa Solomon and Framji Minwalla. New York: New York UP, 2002. 1–8. Print.

Douglas, Mitch. "Coffee with Mitch Douglas: Part I." Interview by Thomas Keith. Provincetown Tennessee Williams Theater Festival, 20–23 Sep. 2013. *Vimeo*. Vimeo, 3 Oct. 2012. Web.

Egan, Susanna. *Burdens of Proof: Faith, Doubt, and Identity in Autobiography*. Waterloo, ON: Wilfrid Laurier UP, 2011. Print.

Escoffier, Jeffrey. "Intellectuals, Identity Politics, and the Closets for Cultural Authority." *American Homo: Community and Perversity*. Berkeley: U of California P, 1998. 142–57. Print.

Father Theo. "How I Wrote a Story With Tennessee Williams." *Father Theo's Blog*. Father Theo, 2 Jul. 2012. Web.

Folkerth, Wes. "Recent Canadian Drama." *Canadian Literature* 195 (2007): 123–25. Print.

Foucault, Michel. *The History of Sexuality*. London: Penguin, 1981. Print.

Freud, Sigmund. "The Material and Sources of Dreams." *The Interpretation of Dreams*. 1900. Trans. James Strachey with Anna Freud. Rpt. *The Standard Edition of the Complete Psychological Works of Sigmund Freud*. Vol. 4. London: Hogarth, 1953. 261–66. Print.

Friedlander, Mira. "Review: The Soldier Dreams." *Variety*. Penske Business Media, 3 Dec. 1995. Web.

Gardner, Elysa. "'Our Town' Right at Home On Broadway." *USA Today* 4 Dec. 2002: 4D. Print.

Gefen, Alexandre. "Le Genre des noms: la biofiction dans la littérature française contemporaine." *Le roman français au tournant du XXIe siècle*. Ed. Bruno Blanckeman, Aline Mura-Brunel, and Marc Dambre. Paris: Presses Sorbonne Nouvelle, 2004. 305–19. Print.

Genette, Gérard. *Palimpsests: Literature in the Second Degree*. Trans. Channa Newman and Claude Doubinsky. Lincoln, NE: U of Nebraska P, 1997. Print.

Gilbert, Sky. *Ejaculations from the Charm Factory: A Memoir*. Toronto: ECW, 2000. Print.

---. Introduction. *Perfectly Abnormal: Seven Gay Plays*. Ed. Gilbert. Toronto: Playwrights Canada, 2006. iii–xix. Print.

---. *Lola Starr Builds Her Dream Home*. *Canadian Theatre Review* 59 (1989): 60–76. Print.

---. Messages to John S. Bak. 13–14 Sep. 2013. Email.

---. *My Night with Tennessee*. *This Unknown Flesh: A Selection of Plays*. Toronto: Coach House, 1995. 145–71. Print.

---. "Writing Gay, Is it Still Possible." Kerr 256–64.

Gindt, Dirk. "Queer Embodied Absence: HIV/AIDS and the Creation of Cultural Memory in Gordon Armstrong's *Blue Dragons* and Daniel MacIvor's *The Soldier Dreams*." *Journal of Canadian Studies/Revue d'études canadiennes* 48.2 (2014): 122–45. Print.

---. "Sky Gilbert, Daniel MacIvor, and the Man in the Vancouver Hotel Room: Queer Gossip, Community Narrative, and Theatre History." *Theatre Research in Canada/ Recherches théâtrales au Canada* 34.2 (2013): 187–215. Print.

Golden, Eve. *Vernon and Irene Castle's Ragtime Revolution*. Lexington: UP of Kentucky, 2007. Print.

Goldfarb, Martin, and Howard Aster. *Affinity: Beyond Branding*. Toronto: MacArthur, 2010. Print.

Goldie, Terry. *queersexlife: Autobiographical Notes on Sexuality, Gender & Identity*. Vancouver: Arsenal, 2008. Print.

Grace, André, and Kris Wells. "Gay and Bisexual Male Youth as Educator Activists and Cultural Workers: The Queer Critical Praxis of Three Canadian High-School Students." *International Journal of Inclusive Education* (2007): 1–22. Web.

Grace, Sherrill. "Theatre and the AutoBiographical Pact: An Introduction." Introduction. *Theatre and AutoBiography*. Ed. Grace and Jerry Wasserman. Vancouver: Talonbooks, 2006. 13–29. Print.

Halferty, J. Paul. "Defying Tragedy: Hope in *His Greatness*." *Canadian Theatre Review* 141 (2010): 104–06. Print.

Halperin, David. *Saint Foucault: Towards a Gay Hagiography*. New York: Oxford UP, 1995. Print.

Harris, Daniel. *The Rise and Fall of Gay Culture*. New York: Hyperion, 1997. Print.

Hawkins, Erick. *Here and Now With Watchers: Erick Hawkins*. New York: M.L. Norton, 1997. Print.

He, Sheng. "Bistable Perception." *Encyclopedia of Perception*. Ed. E. Bruce Goldstein. Sage Publications, 16 Dec. 2009. Web.

Healy, Brendan. Personal interview with Peter Kuling. Buddies in Bad Times Theatre, Toronto. 7 Aug. 2014.

Heddon, Deirdre. *Autobiography and Performance*. Houndmills, Basingstoke: Palgrave Macmillan, 2008. Print.

Hofstadter, Douglas R. *Gödel, Escher, Bach: An Eternal Golden Braid*. New York: Vintage, 1980. Print.

Hoile, Christopher. "*Arigato, Tokyo*." Rev. of *Arigato, Tokyo*, by Daniel MacIvor. Buddies in Bad Times Theatre, Toronto. *Stage Door*. Stage Door Archives, 24 Mar. 2013. Web.

---. "Reviews 2003: *Cul-de-sac*." *Stage Door*. Stage Door Archives, 29 May 2003. Web.

Huyssen, Andreas. *Twilight Memories: Marking Time in a Culture of Amnesia*. New York: Routledge, 1995. Print.

Inness, Sherrie A. "Lost in Space: Queer Geography and the Politics of Location." *Queer Cultures*. Ed. Deborah Carlin and Jennifer DiGrazia. New Jersey: Pearson Prentice Hall, 2004. 254–77. Print.

"Interview: Tennessee Williams." *PRISM International* 19.3 (1981): 49–55. Print.

Jolly, Margaretta. Editor's Note. *Encyclopedia of Life Writing: Autobiographical and Biographical Forms*. Ed. Jolly. London: Routledge, 2001. ix–x. Print.

Jones, Bill T. *Last Night on Earth*. New York: Pantheon Books, 1995. Print.

Kareda, Urjo. Introduction. *Leaving Home*. By David French. Toronto: Stoddart, 1985. v–ix. Print.

Keown, Damien. "Mu." *A Dictionary of Buddhism*. Oxford UP, 2004. Web.

Kerr, Rosalind, ed. *Queer Theatre in Canada*. Toronto: Playwrights Canada, 2007. Print.

King, David Allan. "Cultivating Queer: The Invisibility of the Canadian Gay Play." Kerr 265–70.

Kisselgoff, Anna. "Dance Review: Bill T. Jones's Lyrical Look at Survivors." *New York Times*. The New York Times Company, 2 Dec. 1994. Web.

Knowles, Mark. *The Wicked Waltz and Other Scandalous Dances: Outrage at Couple Dancing in the 19th and Early 20th Centuries*. Jefferson, NC: McFarland & Company, 2009. Print.

Knowles, Ric. *The Theatre of Form and the Production of Meaning: Contemporary Canadian Dramaturgies*. Toronto: ECW, 1999. Print.

Langner, Pat. Message to Thom Bryce McQuinn. 1 Nov. 2014. Email.

Latham, Monica. "'Serv[ing] Under Two Masters': Virginia Woolf's Afterlives in Contemporary Biofictions.'" *a/b: Auto/Biography Studies* 27.2 (2012): 354–73.

Lederman, Marsha. "Remembering Vancouver's Tennessee Waltz." *The Globe and Mail* 17 Oct. 2007: R1, R2. Print.

Lejeune, Philippe. "The Autobiographical Pact." *On Autobiography*. Ed. Paul John Eakin. Trans. Katherine Leavy. Minneapolis: U of Minnesota P, 1989. 3–30. Print.

Levidow, Les. "Witches and Seducers: Moral Panics for Our Time." *Crises of The Self: Further Essays on Psychoanalysis and Politics*. Ed. Barry Richards. London: Free Association Books, 1989. 181–215. Print.

Lyotard, Jean-François. *The Postmodern Condition: A Report on Knowledge*. 1979. Trans. Geoff Bennington and Brian Massumi. Minneapolis: U of Minnesota P, 1984. Print.

MacDonald, Bryden. *Whale Riding Weather*. *Canadian Theatre Review* 71 (1992): 57–80. Print.

MacIvor, Daniel. *2-2-Tango*. Wallace, *Making, Out* 189–217.

---. *Arigato, Tokyo*. Toronto: Playwrights Canada, 2013. Print.

---. *A Beautiful View*. MacIvor, *I Still Love You* 200–44.

---. *The Best Brothers*. Toronto: Playwrights Canada, 2013. Print.

---. *Bingo!* Toronto: Playwrights Canada, 2011. Print.

---. *Cul-de-Sac*. Vancouver: Talonbooks, 2005. Print.

---. "Daniel MacIvor Speech." *Siminovitch Prize*. 28 Oct. 2008. Web.

---. "The End Is the Beginning." Preface. MacIvor, *I Still Love You* iii–vii.

---. Foreword. *His Greatness*. By MacIvor. Toronto: Playwrights Canada, 2007. i–iii. Print.

---. "The Heart of the Actor." Preface. *See Bob Run & Wild Abandon*. By MacIvor. Toronto: Playwrights Canada, 2012. vii–x. Print.

---. *His Greatness*. Toronto: Playwrights Canada, 2007. Print.

---. *House/Humans*. Toronto: Playwrights Canada, 1997. Print.

---. *I, Animal*. N.d. TS.

---. *In On It*. MacIvor, *I Still Love You* 149–99.

---. *In On It*. Winnipeg: Scirocco, 2001. Print.

---. *I Still Love You*. Toronto: Playwrights Canada, 2007. Print.

---. *Marion Bridge*. Vancouver: Talonbooks, 1999. Print.

---. Message to Thom Bryce McQuinn. 2 Nov. 2014. Email.

---. *Never Swim Alone & This Is A Play*. Toronto: Playwrights Canada, 1993. Print.

---. Personal interview with Christopher Grignard. 9 Dec. 2007.

---. *See Bob Run & Wild Abandon*. 1990. Toronto: Playwrights Canada, 2012. Print.

---. *The Soldier Dreams*. Winnipeg: Scirocco, 1997. Print.

---. *Somewhere I Have Never Travelled*. N.d. TS.

---. *Theatre Omaha's Production of* The Sound of Music. Boni 121–35.

---. "This Is An Article." *Theatrum* 30 (1992): 15–17. Print.

---. *This is What Happens Next*. Toronto: Playwrights Canada, 2014. Print.

---. *Was Spring*. N.d. TS.

MacIvor, Daniel, and Daniel Brooks. *Here Lies Henry: A Play*. Toronto: Playwrights Canada, 1996. Print.

---. *Monster*. Winnipeg: Scirocco, 1999. Print.

MacLeod, Joan. "Interview with the Playwright." Daniel MacIvor, *Arigato, Tokyo*. Playwrights Canada, 2013. 75–83. Print.

Maga, Carly. "Buddies in Bad Times Theatre's Brendan Healy Writes an Open Letter to Theatregoers (Or the Lack Thereof)." *Torontoist*. Ink Truck Media, 4 Apr. 2013. Web.

McCourt, Frank. *Queer Street: Rise and Fall of an American Culture, 1947–1985: Excursions in the Mind of the Life*. New York: Norton, 2005. Print.

Metcalf, Robin. "Halifax, Nova Scotia." Preston 311–20.

Monluçon, Anne-Marie, and Agathe Salha, eds. *Fictions biographiques, XIXe-XXIe siècles*. Toulouse: Presses Universitaires du Mirail, 2007. Print.

Moore, Linda. Foreword. MacIvor, *I Still Love You* ix–xi.

Morrow, Martin. "*Arigato, Tokyo*: An Odd, Unsatisfying Excursion to the Inscrutable East." Rev. of *Arigato, Tokyo*, by Daniel MacIvor. Buddies in Bad Times Theatre, Toronto. *The Globe and Mail*. The Globe and Mail Inc., 23 Mar. 2013. Web.

---. "*His Greatness*: Channelling Tennessee Williams." Rev. of *His Greatness*, by Daniel MacIvor. Factory Theatre, Toronto. *The Globe and Mail*. The Globe and Mail Inc., 23 Sep. 2011. Web.

---. "MacIvor's Lively Ghosts." *Books in Canada* 35.9 (2006): 45–46. Print.

---. "Writing With Purpose: Daniel MacIvor Returns with Philosophical Plays and a Rock 'n' Roll Film." *CBC News Arts & Entertainment*. Canadian Broadcasting Corporation, 3 Mar. 2010. Web.

Muise, D.A. "Cape Breton Island." *The Canadian Encylcopedia*. Historica Foundation, 7 Feb. 2006. Web.

Nemetz, Andrea. "MacIvor Seeks Shades of Gray." *The Chronicle Herald* (Halifax). The Chronicle Herald, 23 June 2014. Web.

Nestruck, J. Kelly. "*Bingo!*: A Brother-pleasing Comedy." Rev. of *Bingo!*, by Daniel MacIvor. Factory Theatre, Toronto. *The Globe and Mail*. The Globe and Mail Inc., 9 May 2014. Web.

New International Version Bible. Colarado Springs: Biblica, 2011. Web.

Nolen, Stephanie. "The Art of the Positive." *The Globe and Mail* 1 Aug. 2000: R1. Print.

Ouzounian, Richard. "*Bingo!* Not So Winning." Rev. of *Bingo!*, by Daniel MacIvor. Factory Theatre, Toronto. *Toronto Star*. Star Media Group, 9 May 2014. Web.

---. "Buddies in Bad Times Theatre Company Cancels March Show as Cash Crunch Hits." *Toronto Star*. Star Media Group, 5 Feb. 2009. Web.

---. "'Dark Horse' Wins Maria Role." *Toronto Star*. Star Media Group, 29 Jul. 2008. Web.

---. "Review: 'Cul-de-Sac.'" *Variety*. Penske Business Media, 24 Oct. 2004. Web.

---. "Thanks to a Wonderful Cast the Riches of *Arigato, Tokyo* Are Unlocked." Rev. of *Arigato, Tokyo*, by Daniel MacIvor. Buddies in Bad Times Theatre, Toronto. *Toronto Star*. Star Media Group, 21 Mar. 2013. Web.

---. "This is What Happens Next: Addictive Play that Keeps Us Guessing." *Toronto Star*. Star Media Group, 15 Apr. 2010. Web.

"Overview: A Beautiful View." *Volcano Theatre*. Volcano Theatre, n.d. Web.

Palmer, John. "An Interview with Franco Boni." Boni 11–14.

P.C. "From *Streetcar* to *Seagull*." *The Globe and Mail* 9 Sep. 1981: 20. Print.

Pilgrim, Robert. *Buddhism and the Arts of Japan*. Chambersburg, PA: Anima, 1981. Print.

"Pink Noise." *Wikipedia*. Wikimedia Foundation, 15 May 2014. Web.

Pitman, Teresa. "The Play's the Thing: *Canadian Theatre Is Entering New Stage of Confidence, Says Award-winning Playwright*." *At Guelph* 53.2. University of Guelph, 28 Jan. 2009. Web.

Playing Shakespeare. Dir. John Carlaw and Peter Walker. Perf: John Barton, Judi Dench, and Patrick Stewart. 1982. eOneFilms, 2009. DVD.

Preston, John, ed. *Hometowns: Gay Men Write About Where They Belong*. New York: Dutton, 1991. Print.

Priestly, Mel. "Back in Black." *Vue Weekly*. Aberdeen Publishing, 17 Nov. 2011. Web.

Punter, Jennie. "Daniel's Town." *Canplay* 21.1 (2004): 16–17. Print.

Pupo, Mark. "Acting Out." *Toronto Life* 40.5 (May 2006): 52–55. Print.

Radstone, Susannah. *The Sexual Politics of Time: Confession, Nostalgia, Memory*. London: Routledge, 2007. Print.

Rawson, James. "Why Are Gay Characters at the Top of Hollywood's Kill List?" *The Guardian*. Guardian Media Group, 11 June 2013. Web.

Rayside, David. *Queer Inclusions, Continental Divisions: Public Recognition of Sexual Diversity in Canada and the United States*. Toronto: U of Toronto P, 2008. Print.

Rich, Adrienne. "Compulsory Heterosexuality and Lesbian Existence." *Blood, Bread, and Poetry: Selected Prose 1979–1985*. New York: Norton, 1986. 23–75. Print.

Riordon, Michael. *Out Our Way: Gay and Lesbian Life in the Country*. Toronto: Between the Lines, 1998. Print.

Roach, Joseph. "Gossip Girls: Lady Teazle, Nora Helmer, and Invisible-Hand Drama." *Modern Drama* 53.3 (2010): 297–310. Print.

Rubin, Gayle S. "Thinking Sex: Notes for a Radical Theory of the Politics of Sexuality." *Deviations: A Gayle Rubin Reader*. Durham, NC: Duke UP, 2011. 137–81. Print.

Sasha. "Let Go of My Ego, Daniel MacIvor." *Nomorepotlucks* 3 (2009): n. pag. Web.

Scott, Alec. "Out There: Gay Theatre Artists Move Beyond the Coming-Out Drama." *CBC*. Canadian Broadcasting Corporation, 20 Jan. 2005. Web.

Sedgwick, Eve. *Tendencies*. Durham, NC: Duke UP, 1993. Print.

Segneri, Giordana. "Iron Crow Theatre's *The Soldier Dreams* Wages War on Death Through Joy and Dancing." *Broadway World Baltimore*. Wisdom Digital Media, 16 Apr. 2012. Web.

Shakespeare, William. *Hamlet*. Ed. Robert Hapgood. Cambridge: Cambridge UP, 1999. Print.

Shen, Min. "'Quite a Moon!': The Archetypal Feminine in *Our Town*." *American Drama* 16.2 (2007): 1–14. Print.

Sinfield, Alan. *Gay and After*. London: Serpent's Tail, 1998. Print.

Stephens, George D. "*Our Town*—Great American Tragedy?" *Modern Drama* 1.4 (1958): 258–64. Print.

Stephenson, Jenn. Introduction. *Solo Performance*. Ed. Stephenson. Toronto: Playwrights Canada, 2011. vii–xiv. Print.

---. *Performing Autobiography: Contemporary Canadian Drama*. Toronto: U of Toronto P, 2013. Print.

Sumi, Glenn. "Theatre Review: *Arigato, Tokyo*." Rev. of *Arigato, Tokyo*, by Daniel MacIvor. Buddies in Bad Times Theatre, Toronto. *NOW Magazine*. NOW Communications Inc., 28 Mar. 2013. Web.

Taylor, Kate. "How Caroline Gillis Became an Unlikely Theatre Muse." *The Globe and Mail*. The Globe and Mail Inc., 2 April 2012. Web.

"This Is What Happens Next." *One Yellow Rabbit*. One Yellow Rabbit, n.d. Web.

Thomas, Colin. "MacIvor Explores Tennessee." *The Georgia Straight*. Vancouver Free Press, 3 Oct. 2007. Web.

---. "The Soldier Dreams." *The Georgia Straight*. Vancouver Free Press, 30 Mar. 2006. Web.

Thompson, Robert Farris. *Tango: The Art History of Love*. New York: Vintage, 2005. Print.

Vaughan, R.M. "A Gay Man's Everyhomo: RM Vaughan Tracks Down Daniel MacIvor." *Books in Canada* 24.9 (Dec. 1995): n. pag. Web.

Wagner, Vit. "MacIvor Dives Deep Into Stylish Oneupmanship." Rev. of *Never Swim Alone*, by Daniel MacIvor. *Toronto Star* 1 Mar. 1991: D9. Print.

Walker, Craig. "Daniel MacIvor." *The Canadian Encyclopedia*. Historica Foundation, 10 May 2011. Web.

Wallace, Robert. "Image and Label: Notes for a Sense of Self." *Canadian Theatre Review* 12 (1976): 27–33. Print.

---, ed. *Making, Out: Plays by Gay Men*. Toronto: Coach House, 1992. Print.

---. "Making Out Positions." Introduction. Wallace, *Making, Out* 11–40.

---. "Technologies of the Monstrous: Notes on the Daniels's *Monster* Trilogy." *Canadian Theatre Review* 120 (2004): 12–18. Print.

Warner, Michael. Introduction. *Fear of a Queer Planet: Queer Politics and Social Theory*. Ed. Warner. Minneapolis: U of Minnesota P, 1994. vii–xxxi. Print.

West, Veronique. "PRISM Decides Whether or Not To Publish Tennessee Williams." *PRISM International.* University of British Columbia, 29 Nov. 2011. Web.

White, Edmund. "Esthetics and Loss." *The Burning Man Library: Writings on Arts, Politics and Sexuality. 1969–1993.* Ed. David Bergman. London: Chatto and Windus, 1994. 211–17. Print.

---. *My Lives: A Memoir.* New York: Harper Perennial, 2007. Print.

"Who Killed Spalding Gray?" *Magnetic North Theatre Festival.* Magnetic North, n.d. Web.

Wilcox, Richie. "Daniel MacIvor is Dying." Canadian Association of Theatre Research Conference. Waterloo, Ontario. 2 June 2012. Lecture.

---. Message to Thom Bryce McQuinn. 24 Nov. 2014. Email.

Wilder, Thornton. *Our Town.* New York: Harper Collins, 2003. Print.

Williams, Tennessee. *Five O'Clock Angel: Letters of Tennessee Williams to Maria St. Just, 1948–1982.* Ed. Maria St. Just. New York: Alfred A. Knopf, 1990. Print.

---. *The Glass Menagerie. The Theatre of Tennessee Williams.* Vol. 1. New York: New Directions, 1971. 143–237. Print.

---. Letter to *PRISM International.* Tennessee Williams Papers (MS Thr 397). Folder 1324: P- through Q-. Correspondence with Tennessee Williams, 1963–1983 and undated. Houghton Theatre Collection, Houghton Library, Harvard University, n.d. Print.

---. *Memoirs.* 1975. New York: New Directions, 2006. Print.

---. *Moise and the World of Reason.* New York: Simon and Shuster, 1975. Print.

---. *New Selected Essays: Where I Live.* Ed. John S. Bak. New York: New Directions, 2009. Print.

---. *Notebooks.* Ed. Margaret Bradham Thornton. New Haven and London: Yale UP, 2006. Print.

---. "Playwright's Preface." *Vancouver Playhouse Program Magazine* 8.2 (Oct. 1980): 17. Print.

---. "Twenty Years of It." Fragment of an essay [c. 1965]. Tennessee Williams Papers (MS Thr 397). Folder 780. Harvard Theatre Collection, Houghton Library, Harvard University, n.d. Print.

---. *Vieux Carré. The Theatre of Tennessee Williams.* Vol. 8. New York: New Directions, 1992. 1–116. Print.

Wilson, Ann. "Lying and Dying: Theatricality in *Here Lies Henry*." *Canadian Theatre Review* 92 (1997): 39–41. Print.

Woods, Gregory. *A History of Gay Literature: The Male Tradition*. New Haven: Yale UP, 1999. Print.

Younge, Gary. *Who Are We—And Should It Matter in the 21st Century?* London: Viking, 2010. Print.

Zimmerman, Cynthia. "Drama 1999." *University of Toronto Quarterly* 70.1 (2000): 246–71. Print.

Zinoman, Jason. "The Means of a Dead End." *New York Times*. The New York Times Company, 10 Dec. 2004. Web.

---. "Somewhere Under the Radar, a Discovery Awaits." *The New York Times* 23 Aug. 2006: E1. Print.

NOTES ON CONTRIBUTORS

John S. Bak is *Professeur* at the Université de Lorraine in France, where he teaches courses in literary journalism and American drama and theatre. He holds degrees from the University of Illinois, Ball State University, and the Sorbonne in Paris. He was a Fulbright Scholar at the Univerzity Palackého in the Czech Republic in 1995 and Visiting Fellow at Harvard University (2011), Columbia University (2013), and the University of Texas at Austin (2014). He is currently a Visiting Senior Fellow at Wolfson College at the University of Oxford. His articles have appeared in such journals as *Theatre Journal*, *Mississippi Quarterly*, *Journal of American Drama and Theatre*, *The Tennessee Williams Literary Journal*, *American Drama*, *South Atlantic Review*, and *Studies in Musical Theatre*. His edited books include *New Selected Essays: Where I Live* (New Directions, 2009) and (with Bill Reynolds) *Literary Journalism Across the Globe: Journalistic Traditions and Transnational Influences* (University of Massachusetts Press, 2011), and *Tennessee Williams and Europe: Transnational Encounters, Transatlantic Exchanges* (Rodopi, 2014). He is the author of the monographs *Ernest Hemingway, Tennessee Williams, and Queer Masculinities* (Fairleigh Dickinson University Press, 2009) and *Tennessee Williams: A Literary Life* (Palgrave, 2013).

Susan Bennett is University Professor in the Department of English at the University of Calgary. She is widely published across a variety of topics and periods in theatre and performance studies. In 2006 she edited *Feminist Theatre and Performance* for the Critical Perspectives on Canadian Theatre in English series. Her most recent work looks at the development of cultural infrastructure and circuits of international performance and includes the co-edited volume (with Christie Carson) *Shakespeare Beyond English*, about the Globe2Globe Festival in 2012 held at the Globe Theatre as part of the London Cultural Olympiad. The book was published in 2013 by Cambridge University Press.

Daniel Brooks is one of Canada's most accomplished theatre makers. As a writer, director, and performer he has collaborated with some of the country's finest talents in producing a body of daring and original work. He has created shows with Don McKellar, Tracy Wright, Daniel MacIvor, Guillermo Verdecchia, Leah Cherniak, John Mighton, Rick Miller, Diego Matamoros, and Michael Ondaatje, amongst others. His many achievements include a series of monologues created with Daniel MacIvor, direction of work by John Mighton, Samuel Beckett, David Mamet, and Goethe, the musical *Drowsy Chaperone*, and many creations including *Insomnia*, *The Eco Show*, *The Good Life*, *Bigger Than Jesus*, *Pokey Jones*, *Divisadero*, and a series of plays created with Don McKellar and Tracy Wright (the Augusta Company). He was co-Artistic Director of the Augusta Company, Artistic Director of Necessary Angel Theatre Companyfrom 2003–2012, and is currently an Associate Artist at Soulpepper, where he teaches. His many awards include the Siminovitch Prize. His work has toured across Canada and around the world.

Caroline Gillis has been an actor in Toronto for the past twenty-seven years. She has had a long-term working relationship with Daniel MacIvor since originating the role of Bob in his play *See Bob Run* in 1987. She has continued to appear regularly in his plays, including *Was Spring*, *Communion*, *A Beautiful View*, *How It Works*, *Marion Bridge*, *You Are Here*, and *Never Swim Alone*. In addition she's worked with companies across Canada, including the Tarragon Theatre, Factory Theatre, Buddies in Bad Times Theatre, the Belfry, GCTC, the National Arts Centre, the Blyth Festival, Neptune Theatre, Mulgrave Road, and the Stratford Festival. She has participated in several collective creations over the years including *The Lorca Play* and *White Trash Blue Eyes*. She is also the author of the one-woman play *Caveman Rainbow*.

In 2013 Caroline returned to school at the University of Guelph and received her M.A. in Theatre Studies in the fall of 2014.

Christopher Grignard has published articles on Marie Clements, Sky Gilbert, and Tomson Highway. He currently teaches a range of courses at the University of Lethbridge and Lethbridge College. Some of these courses are Canadian Theatre, Theatre History, Native American Literature, and Aboriginal Drama. Chris received his Ph.D. at the University of Alberta; his dissertation focused on Canadian gay theatre. He produced and directed his own gay hometown play in 2005, *The Orchard Drive* (set in Kelowna, BC). He is a co-founding member of the Edmonton Aboriginal theatre collective Old Earth Productions (est. 2006). In 2011, he moved to southern Alberta to work with the Blackfoot community.

Peter Kuling is a sessional lecturer of Communication Studies at Wilfrid Laurier University where he teaches courses on visual culture, media history, and performance studies. He received his Ph.D. in English from the University of New Brunswick for new research on queer adaptations of Shakespearean drama in Canada. He investigates invisible aspects of identity performance like nationality and sexuality in contemporary theatre, media, and digital environments. His current research explores evolving performances of identity politics in popular video games as well as new adaptations and appropriations of Shakespearean drama throughout Canada. He recently co-edited a special issue of *Canadian Theatre Review* on digital performance. He also works as the membership coordinator for the Canadian Association for Theatre Research and has been a past organizational chair for several of their annual conferences.

Daniel MacIvor was born in Cape Breton, Nova Scotia, in 1962. He is a stalwart of the Canadian theatre scene, having written and directed numerous award-winning productions, including *See Bob Run, Wild Abandon, 2-2-Tango, This Is A Play, The Soldier Dreams, You Are Here, How It Works, A Beautiful View, Communion,* and *Bingo!,* and his work has been translated into French, Portuguese, Spanish, Czech, German, and Japanese. From 1987 to 2007 with Sherrie Johnson he ran da da kamera, a respected international touring company that brought his work to Australia, the UK, and extensively throughout the US and Canada. With long-time collaborator Daniel Brooks, he created the solo performances *House*, *Here Lies Henry*, *Monster*, *Cul-de-Sac*, and *This Is What Happens Next*. Daniel won a GLAAD Award and a Village Voice Obie Award in 2002 for his play *In On It*, which was presented at Performance Space 122 in New York. His play *Marion Bridge* received its off-Broadway premiere in New York in October of 2005. In 2006, Daniel received the Governor General's Literary Award for Drama for his collection of plays *I Still Love You*. In 2007, his play *His Greatness* won the Jessie Richardson Award for Best New Play in Vancouver. In 2008, he was awarded the prestigious Siminovitch Prize in Theatre. Also a filmmaker, Daniel has written and directed the feature films *Past Perfect* and *Wilby Wonderful*, the short films *Permission* and *Until I Hear From You*, and is the writer of the feature films *Trigger*, *Marion Bridge*, and co-writer (with Amnon Buchbinder) of *Whole New Thing*.

Thom Bryce McQuinn is a writer and critic. His dissertation explores the semiotics of queerness and alcoholism on the American stage between 1940 and 1970. His main research interests are modern and contemporary theatre, queer theory, cultural studies, camp, psychoanalysis, and addiction studies. Past topics for his speaking engagements include the work of Tennessee Williams and Edward Albee, performance artist Nina Arsenault, and contemporary LGBT culture. He served as Research Intern for the thirty-fifth annual Rhubarb Festival, and continues to blog for Buddies in Bad Times Theatre. Thom currently lives in Toronto.

Ray Miller is a professor in Dance Studies and Theatre Arts in the Department of Theatre and Dance at Appalachian State University. He has served as President for the Congress on Research in Dance and has published in the areas of musical theatre, dance, and pedagogy. Most recently, Dr. Miller served on the editorial board and was a contributor to *Broadway: An Encyclopedia of*

Theater and American Culture and also contributed a chapter on the history of tap dance to the recently published anthology *Jazz Dance: A History of the Roots and Branches*. He has directed and choreographed over two hundred plays, musicals, and dance concerts, including *The Fantasticks, The Exonerated, Metamorphoses, Stop Kiss,* and *The Trojan Women*. He is completing a book on the history of dance on the American musical theatre stage and collaborating with folk singer Doris Bazzini, who is contributing music to *Tragedy at Kent State*, a play on the killing of students on the Kent State campus in 1970.

Wes D. Pearce is Professor of Theatre and currently Associate Dean (Undergraduate) in the Faculty of Fine Arts at the University of Regina. He co-edited *Out Spoken: Perspectives on Queer Identity* (2013), which was nominated for a Saskatchewan Book Award and has chapters published in a diverse number of anthologies exploring a variety of topics and interests. He is also an accomplished scenographer. Over the past twenty years he has designed elements for nearly a hundred productions across Western Canada and his work has been honoured with two Betty Mitchell and three Saskatoon and Area Theatre Award nominations for Outstanding Costume Design.

Jenn Stephenson is Associate Professor of Drama at Queen's University, where she teaches courses on dramatic literature, history, and theory. Her book *Performing Autobiography: Contemporary Canadian Drama* (U of Toronto P, 2013) received the Ann Saddlemyer Award from the Canadian Association for Theatre Research for Outstanding Book. Recent articles have appeared in *Theatre Research in Canada, New Theatre Quarterly,* and *English Studies in Canada*. Jenn is the editor of *Solo Performance*, volume twenty in the Critical Perspective on Canadian Theatre in English series from Playwrights Canada Press. She is co-editor with Natalie Alvarez of the Views and Reviews section of *Canadian Theatre Review*.

Richie Wilcox is a theatre director and scholar. He is currently an instructor at the University of Lethbridge in the drama department. Richie holds an M.A. in Directing from Texas State University and is currently a Ph.D. candidate at

York University. Richie has presented numerous papers on Daniel MacIvor's work at several conferences and received the Heather McCallum Scholarship for his research on MacIvor. Wilcox directed the world premiere of MacIvor's *I, Animal* in 2012 at the SuperNova Festival in Halifax and the SummerWorks Performance Festival in Toronto. He was also the assistant director to Daniel MacIvor for the world premiere of *Bingo!*

Ann Wilson is Associate Dean, Academic, in the College of Arts at the University of Guelph, where she has been a member of faculty since 1987. For many years, she was an editor of *Canadian Theatre Review*. Her research circulates around identity, particularly in relation to nation, gender, and sexuality. She has published widely on contemporary Canadian and British drama, including essays in the past three years on English-language drama for *University of Toronto Quarterly*'s annual review of letters in Canada. Her other area of research is Edwardian drama. Recent publications include "Shutting Out Mother: Vivie Warren as the New Woman" in *Shaw and Feminisms: On Stage and Off* (2013) and "Drama" in *University of Toronto Quarterly* (2013).

INDEX

2-2-Tango   3, 12, 69, 119, 120, 126–31, 147, 163

A

absence   11, 16, 61, 67, 180
abuse   70, 74–75, 99, 130, 198, 200–03
Adams, James   157
addictions   15, 115, 172
affinity   10, 43, 46, 47, 51, 52
afterlife conduits   4, 5, 6–7
Ahmed, Sara   98–99
AIDS   5, 7–8, 68, 69, 71, 72, 79, 87, 110, 115, 120, 188
AIDS crisis   7, 17, 68, 85, 186, 208
AIDS plays   11, 68, 185, 188, 197
Alberta Playwrights' Network PlayWorks Ink   15
alcoholism   113, 196, 198
Allman, Daniel   215, 216
Antigonish, Nova Scotia   33, 38
anxiety   45, 114, 133
Appiah, Kwame Anthony   105
Arigato, Tokyo   3, 13, 119, 136, 138, 145, 156–61
Artaud, Antonin   46
artifice   15, 17, 21, 25–27, 36, 39, 101, 122, 149, 171

Augusta Company   28, 30
Austin, J.L.   94
Austin, Texas   69
authenticity   15, 17–18, 21, 22, 25–27, 120, 127, 145, 167
autobiographical pact   96, 97
autobiographical self-rewriting   11, 70, 74, 77, 78

B

Baltimore, Maryland   39, 40
Banff, Alberta   152, 159, 163
Barnard, Elissa   51, 154
Barthes, Roland   211–12
A Beautiful View   2, 3, 5, 6, 10, 11, 12, 37, 39, 70, 109, 113, 115, 117
Beckett, Samuel   132
BeMe Theatre   12, 89, 104
Berkeley Street Theatre Downstairs   45, 49
The Best Brothers   2, 161, 169
Bingo!   2, 3, 13, 36, 119, 147, 152–58
biodrama   205, 210, 217, 220
biofiction   210–13, 217
biographemes   211–13, 215, 217, 220, 228
blah-de-blah   100–01, 104, 106
Bolt, Carol   139
Boni, Franco   141

Borges, Jorge Luis 126
Boutillier, Fabin 139
Brooks, Daniel 2, 10, 26, 45–48, 50, 68, 112, 136, 164
Buddhist art 177
Buddhist practice 92
Buddies in Bad Times Theatre 2, 11, 12, 13, 34, 48, 110, 111, 139, 148, 156, 157, 161, 162–63, 166, 167, 168, 170, 171–73, 175, 177, 178, 188, 190, 191, 195
Buisine, Alain 210
By the Way Café 110, 111

C

Calvino, Italo 132
Cameron House 116
Canadian Stage Company 49, 68, 69
Canadian Theatre Review 31
cancer 112, 113, 115, 117
Cape Breton Island 1–2, 8, 9, 14, 54, 117, 193, 194, 197–98, 202, 203, 204
Cape North 61, 62
Vieux Carré (Williams) 218, 220, 228
Chevalier, Albert 111
choreography 110, 114, 124–25, 132
communion 18, 20, 21, 23–24, 25, 37
Communion 10, 12, 109, 112, 114
Communion and Transformation, theatre of 10, 19, 22, 23, 24
confession 11, 60, 70, 71, 73, 79–80, 82, 83, 85, 88, 95
costume 97, 112, 116, 117, 144, 164
Crew, Robert 29, 190, 197, 199
Croc, Arlene 124
CrossCurrents Festival 152
cuckoldry 150, 156
Cul-de-Sac 4, 7, 10, 26, 28, 31, 34, 39, 70, 73, 78, 136, 163, 200

cultural identities 13, 138, 162, 176
cultural palimpsests 162, 165, 166, 169, 170, 178
cultural representation 164, 166, 167, 168

D

da da kamera 1, 10, 28, 35, 40, 45, 48, 51, 68, 91, 111, 112, 113, 145
Dalhousie University 16, 109, 110, 139
dance 110, 144, 146
dance-drama 118
darkness 21, 35, 66, 197
Leaving Home (French) 191
death 4–9, 12, 18, 39, 70, 71–72, 78, 79, 88, 106, 111, 113, 115, 117, 122, 123–24, 125, 146, 180, 186, 196, 197, 199, 200, 202
death and violence 184, 196–97, 200, 202, 204
de Jongh, Nicholas 196
D'Emilio, John 188
Denton, Martin 122
Derrida, Jacques 94, 100
Deschamps, Yvon 46
desire 13, 30, 76, 78, 93, 95, 99, 100, 101, 102–03, 105, 131, 132, 137, 138, 141, 145, 146–47, 149, 151, 152, 154, 156, 158, 160, 161, 176, 177, 180, 182, 188, 203, 209, 225
DesRochers, Clémence 46
Different Kinds of Dancing 110
disbelief, suspension of 17
Dora Mavor Moore Awards 68
drag 13, 138, 143, 158, 162, 166, 170–72
dramaturgy 118, 119, 132, 186
drinking 57, 61, 64, 152
drowning 59, 64, 65, 114, 131, 147
Dufays, Michael 160, 163, 167, 168

E

Eakin, Paul John 165
Edmundson, Wayne 225
Ejaculations from the Charm Factory
 (Gilbert) 190, 216
Epicurus 92
existentialism 8, 12, 115, 158

F

Factory Theatre 89, 152
failure 35, 44, 96, 97, 100, 101, 162, 172,
 219, 230
faith 53, 58, 60, 183
family 8, 16, 53, 54, 59, 62, 64, 72, 73, 82,
 85, 86–88, 121–23, 126, 187, 188, 191,
 193–95, 200–203, 209
fantasy 74, 139, 143, 150, 190
fear 3, 17, 24, 85, 91, 101, 102, 103, 105,
 111, 114, 115, 145, 148, 188, 209
Feren, Richard 39, 40
flash-back memory plays 73
flashbacks 193, 201
Foster, Norm 22, 152, 153
Frayn, Michael 142
free-association 213
Freeman, David 193
French, David 29, 142, 191–92, 193
Fringe Festival 28, 30, 111, 151

G

The Gateless Gate (Huikai) 92, 103, 106
gay communities 183, 186, 206, 207, 208,
 213, 229
gay hometown 14, 183, 184, 187, 189–90
gay theatre 181–84, 188, 189, 190, 196
gay writers 187, 188, 212

Gee, Cara 163, 167, 175
gender 93, 94, 126, 138
Genette, Gérard 164
George Brown College 110, 139
Gilbert, Sky 13, 14, 139, 182, 183, 188, 190,
 191, 193, 195, 206, 213, 215, 216, 220
Gillis, Caroline 11, 12, 28, 109, 145
Gindt, Dirk 13, 14, 71, 80, 82, 86, 87, 206–
 10, 213, 220
Girl Guides 80
Glace Bay, Nova Scotia 33
The Glass Menagerie (Williams) 127, 218,
 220, 228
God 22, 27, 58, 60, 66, 84, 100, 123, 157
gossip 207–09, 213, 220, 229
Grace, André 181
Gray, Spalding 9, 31, 46
guilt 79, 80, 82

H

Halifax, Nova Scotia 3, 8, 11, 46, 51, 69,
 109, 110, 111, 139, 152, 184, 185
Hamlet (Shakespeare) 121, 176
Hawkins, Erick 120
Healy, Brendan 145, 157, 161, 162, 167,
 170, 172, 173
Henry V (Shakespeare) 217
Here Lies Henry 2, 4, 5, 7, 10, 11, 28, 31,
 33, 36, 37, 38, 42, 44, 48, 70, 77, 136, 163
heteronormativity 13, 135, 136, 137, 155
heterosexuality 13, 136–37, 147, 148
 compulsory 136, 137
His Greatness 14, 70, 205, 206–10, 214, 217,
 218, 219, 220, 221–30
historiography 204, 220
HIV 68, 69, 71
Hodgman, Roger 221, 223, 224, 227
Hoffman, William M. 68

hometown 14, 180, 182, 184, 185, 187, 190, 191, 194, 199–200, 202–3

homophobia 129, 154

homosexuality 2, 3, 7, 77, 145, 185, 186, 191, 196, 212, 229

House 2, 4, 10, 28, 30, 32, 35–36, 42, 46, 48, 69, 70, 76–77, 116, 124, 136, 163, 200

Huikai, Wumen 92

humour 2, 55, 114, 115, 122, 128

Hwang, David Henry 118

I

I, Animal 3, 13, 135, 136, 138, 161

identity 11, 12, 53, 54, 60, 63, 67, 70, 74, 81, 87, 90, 93, 94, 97, 98–100, 105, 106, 107, 108, 120, 126, 131, 135, 138, 164, 165, 177, 185, 195

ideology 136, 137

illusion 85, 179, 218

innocence 8, 114

loss of 76

In On It 2, 3, 4–6, 11, 12, 39, 70, 90–91, 119, 120, 131, 132, 200

intimacy 19, 37, 43, 50, 51, 53, 129, 147, 156, 161

isolation 44, 60, 64, 212

J

James, Tyson 158, 163, 167, 170, 171

Japan 13, 156, 158–59, 162, 163, 165, 166, 168, 169, 172, 173, 175–77

Johnson, Sherrie 28

Jump 12, 109, 112, 132

K

Kareda, Urjo 192–95

King, David Allan 181

Knowles, Mark 129, 130

L

Lepage, Robert 46, 47, 69

lesbianism 91, 98, 99, 115, 138, 143, 153, 154, 182

Liitoja, Hillar 3, 71

Little Pickled Theatre Company 69

M

MacDonald, Bryden 185, 197

Magnetic North Theatre Festival 51

Marion Bridge 2, 3, 10–11, 70, 109, 114, 198, 199

Marion Bridge, Nova Scotia 53

Martha Cohen Theatre 50

McDougall, Ken 3, 12, 79, 110, 111, 112, 148

McIntosh, Yanna 19

memory 29, 46, 53–54, 55, 63, 66, 70–71, 73, 76, 78, 82, 83, 86, 87–88, 121, 123, 126, 201, 203, 204

memory and dislocation 73, 76

memory plays 11, 73, 124, 193

metatheatrical 4, 69, 77, 90, 96, 141, 162, 173, 217

Miller, Susan 180

mimesis 106

misreading 97, 98, 101

modern theatre 224, 226–27

Monluçon, Anne-Marie 211, 217

Monster 2, 4, 8, 10, 28, 33, 39, 42, 48, 49, 73, 78, 136, 163

Montreal, Quebec 11, 26, 34, 111

Morrow, Martin 42, 48, 69, 156, 157, 169, 207

mortality 4, 125
MU 93, 97, 99, 101, 103
Mulgrave Road Theatre 2, 13, 154
Munich, Germany 12, 89

N

Necessary Angel Theatre Company 49
Neptune Theatre 11, 152
The Never Broken Heart 110
Never Swim Alone 2, 12, 13, 39, 69, 109,
    111–12, 114, 119, 120, 131–32, 138, 145–
    51, 156, 159, 161
The New York Times 45, 124, 147
Noh theatre 158, 166
nostalgia 21, 70, 87, 147, 152, 179, 219
The Notebook of Trigorin (Williams) 229
Nova Scotia 8, 33, 48, 117

O

observation and appreciation 9, 18, 19, 22
Oedipus complex 11, 56, 65
One Yellow Rabbit Theatre Company 20,
    46, 50
otherness 163, 166–68, 177
Ottawa, Ontario 71, 83, 87, 122
Our Town (Wilder) 3–7, 179–80
Ouzounian, Richard 42, 43, 48, 51,
    152, 157

P

palimpsestic architextuality 163, 164, 166,
    170–74, 176
perfect pretend 75, 76, 84–85, 87
performance
  autobiographical 51, 93
  cultural 13, 167

drag 166, 171
  racial 167
performative
  discourse 100, 101
  miswriting 97
  naming 104, 107
  power 90, 102
  speech 94, 105
  utterance 94, 107
performativity 51, 90, 93, 107, 108
philosophy of theatre 22
Pitman, Teresa 67
Platform 9 Theatre 111
Playhouse Theatre 224
play-within 90, 93, 106
Tarragon Theatre Playwrights Unit
    111, 191
polysexuality 3, 13, 159, 170
Poor Alex Theatre 111, 145
power 38, 94, 102, 104–5, 108, 114,
    145, 177
Prairie Theatre Exchange 13, 152
Preston, John 185, 186, 187
Prism International 206, 224–28

Q

queer
  community 163, 168, 176
  desire 138, 141, 145, 149, 151, 156
  representations 151, 160, 161
  sexuality 3, 161, 170
  theatre 2, 3, 13, 148, 161
  theory 136

R

race 13, 93, 98, 99, 146, 149, 164, 166, 167
Rayside, David 208

realism 69, 127, 133, 166, 169

The Red Devil Battery Sign (Williams) 205, 207, 216, 222–25, 228

religion 18, 115

reperformance 89, 90

representations, cultural 164, 167, 168

rewriting 70, 73, 75, 76, 81, 85, 87

Rhubarb Festival 3, 139, 141, 191

Roy, Ed 112, 141

Royal Shakespeare Company 119

Rumi, Sufi 126

S

Salha, Agathe 211, 217

See Bob Run 10, 11, 12, 70, 74, 77, 84, 110, 111, 114, 145

selective editing 71

self, explosion of 31, 36

self-rewriting 70, 72, 73, 78, 79, 81

sentimentality 2, 25, 81, 188

sexual identity 169, 170

sexuality 3, 7, 13, 93, 99, 126, 136–38, 156, 162, 163, 182, 185

Shakespeare 119, 121, 217

silence 21, 23, 35, 100–102, 104–05, 106

Small Things 10

The Soldier Dreams 5, 11, 28, 109, 115, 119, 120, 121, 122–26

solo performance plays 2, 4, 7, 9, 10, 26, 28, 31, 32–38, 40, 44, 48, 49, 70, 163

Somewhere I Have Never Travelled 4, 13, 29, 30, 39, 111

Soyinka, Wole 118

space and time 21–22

spoken drama 118

Stephenson, Jenn 10, 11–12, 42–43, 45, 51, 89, 165

stereotype 142, 172

Still/Here (Bill T. Jones) 124, 125

Storch, David 159, 160, 163, 168, 173, 175

Stratford Festival 2, 12, 19, 116, 158

A Streetcar Named Desire (Williams) 143, 157

Sydney, Cape Breton 2, 8, 14, 109–10, 152, 184, 185, 194, 195, 197, 199–200, 204

syllogism 103

T

Tale of Genji 166, 177

Tarragon Theatre 11, 13, 29, 111, 112, 113, 188, 190, 191–93, 195, 198, 199

teleology 102

theatre
community 69, 179, 198
ego-based 18, 21, 22–24, 25, 92

Theatre Centre 34, 111

Theatre du Monde Festival 47

Théâtre du Soleil 118

Theatre Omaha's Production of The Sound of Music 141–45, 146, 147, 153, 161

Theatre Passe Muraille 32, 112, 145

theatrical language 118, 119, 126, 128, 132

This Is What Happens Next 2, 3, 4, 10, 28, 31, 34, 38, 136

Thompson, Robert Farris 128

Toronto, Ontario 2, 8, 11, 12, 14, 17, 19, 25, 33–35, 47, 48, 53, 60, 89, 99, 105, 110, 111, 116, 139, 141, 152, 156, 162, 163, 164, 166, 172, 173, 176–78, 199, 202, 204, 208

transformation 18, 20, 24, 25, 82, 189

translation 162, 166, 174

trauma 61, 70, 76, 79, 110, 146

Tremblay, Michel 191

truth 10, 20, 21, 23, 51, 97, 162, 209, 210–15, 217, 218, 220, 221, 228

U

underwear scenes 210, 214, 216, 220
University of British Columbia (UBC) 205,
    221, 222, 224
University of Guelph 13, 67, 105, 106, 109
Usine C 11, 34, 44, 47

V

Vancouver, British Columbia 11, 14, 69,
    70, 111, 163, 166, 175–76, 178, 205–10,
    215, 216, 219, 220–21, 223, 224, 225, 228,
    229–30
Vaughan, R.M. 198, 199, 204
Vertigo Theatre 46
Vidal, Gore 212
violence 3, 126, 130–31, 137, 184, 196, 198,
    200, 201
Volcano Theatre 89

W

waltz 120, 127, 129
Welles, Orson 31
White, Edmund 186
Who Killed Spalding Gray? 2, 28, 31, 32,
    46, 51, 119
Wilder, Thornton 3, 5, 179
Williams, Tennessee 14, 70, 127, 143, 157
Wood, Audrey 213
Wright, Tracy 12, 95, 113, 115

Z

Zen 101, 103
*Zen and the Art of Motorcycle Mainte-
    nance* 101